Victorian Times
QUARTERLY

Vol. 18
October-December 2018

edited by
Moira Allen

A Publication of
Victorian
Voices.net

Welcome to *Victorian Times Quarterly!*

Every three months, we bring together the last three issues of our e-magazine, *Victorian Times,* in a lovely print collection. Our colorful covers are drawn from a variety of sources, including Victorian magazine prints, trade cards and scrapbooks. *Victorian Times Quarterly* is available from Amazon, Amazon.co.uk and Amazon.ca. To obtain back issues, find out what's in each volume, and learn more about upcoming issues, please visit:

http://www.VictorianVoices.net/VT/index.shtml

Don't want to wait for print? Sign up for our free newsletter to be notified when the latest issue of *Victorian Times* is ready for download. Plus, newsletter subscribers have the option of accessing the most recent edition via Dropbox. Find out what's coming up in our latest edition, download back issues, and take a peek at what we're planning for future issues.

Want more Victoriana? Then pay a visit to **VictorianVoices.net** - the largest topical collection of primary-source Victorian articles on the web! **VictorianVoices.net** is home to literally thousands of articles from Victorian-era periodicals, including *The Strand, Harper's Monthly, Demorest, Peterson's, The Girl's Own Paper, Cassell's Family Magazine,* and many others. Find what you're looking for quickly and easily - or explore the site to discover new aspects of the Victorian world.

VictorianVoices.net covers a wide range of topics, including:
Victorian royalty • Recipes and cooking tips • Crafts and embroidery designs • Ideas for tea • Life in the Victorian home • Servants and servant life • Childcare and education • Women's issues, including work and education • Health and medicine • Science, technology, discoveries and inventions • History and archaeology • "Curiosities" - eccentric people and performers, collections, and oddities from around the world • Travel, exploration and world cultures • Holidays • Folklore and country traditions • Country life • ... and much, much more!

Visit us today at http://www.VictorianVoices.net

VICTORIAN TIMES QUARTERLY

Volume #18: October-December 2018

For more information, to sign up for our free monthly electronic edition of *Victorian Times*, download back issues and see what's coming up, visit: **VictorianVoices.net/VT/index.shtml**

Victorian Times Quarterly
Volume #18: October-December 2018

October 2018

November 2018

December 2018

Victorian Times

Vol. V, No. 10   October 2018

The Victorian Cat

When I began collecting Victorian ephemera, I was confidently looking forward to gathering lots of lovely illustrations of Victorian cats. I soon found that "lovely" pictures of Victorian cats were few, far between—and consequently hideously expensive. It seems that cats, like so many other things in the Victorian era, went through quite a period of "transition" in the 19th century.

It's hard to imagine a day when cats weren't popular or beloved as pets. Yet in the early Victorian period, cats were regarded as barely more than wild animals, suitable for catching mice but hardly pets to be pampered or even allowed in the better parts of one's home. One's mouser might find a place in the kitchen, but certainly not in the parlor. I've come across several articles in Victorian magazines written by cat lovers who have found that they need to "defend" their preference—including the article in this issue, which dates to 1890. For much of the Victorian era, dogs ruled supreme as the household pet, and cats skulked in the stable-yard.

This attitude toward cats shows up strongly in Victorian artwork. Most depictions of cats before the 1880's tend to be unflattering, to say the least. Most commonly, cats are depicted as feral and vicious, often with a snarl on the face, and not in the least cuddly or attractive. Even the wonderful animal artist Harrison Weir, who actually founded the very first cat club in Britain, never could quite capture the cat in his artwork. Weir could draw wonderful, expressive dogs and a host of other creatures, but his cats rarely resemble the real thing—and rarely look like something you'd want to pick up and cuddle or allow near your children.

Fortunately for our feline friends, things began to change as the century drew to a close. (I suppose "drew" could be a pun here, given that one can see the change in attitude toward cats, literally, in how they were drawn!) Artists like Henriette Ronner began to portray cats in a positive light; her cats are cute, cuddly, and utterly natural. A bit later, Helena Maguire began the trend toward anthropomorphizing cats, depicting cats engaged in a variety of human activities such as mixing Christmas puddings or ice-skating. Her cats often wore ribbons and bows, but no clothing—but fully dressed cats were soon to follow. (Actually, they had already appeared, though rarely; the 1875 book *Mrs. Mouser's Tea Party* is a delightful collection of very, very dressy cats!)

One of the biggest names in Victorian cat art was, of course, Louis Wain (who illustrated, with remarkable restraint, the article in this issue). Wain certainly qualifies as a "Victorian" artist, but his better-known comical cats began to appear around the turn of the century. (Watch for more of Wain's cats in our December issue!) Wain's cats were often fully clothed, and engaged in a variety of human behaviors. Yet, comical as they may have been, they remained still quite clearly *cats*—with expressions that cat lovers everywhere will recognize.

Wain coined the phrase "Catland" to describe the new, turn-of-the-century fascination with cats, and the growing trend to depict cats as fully clothed and just about fully human. (To find out more about "Catland," I recommend the book *The Catland Companion*, by John Silvester and Anne Mobbs; it is packed with wonderful illustrations.) More artists began jumping onto the cat bandwagon, including Arthur Thiele, whose marvelous postcards depicted kittens in school, cats cooking up a meal of fried mice in the kitchen, cats playing tennis, and a lovely series of cats wearing elegant hats.

It's tempting to attempt to draw some connections between the evolution of cats in Victorian society and concurrent changes in the roles of women. Such connections may not be totally fanciful (though I doubt anyone has ever done a study of the matter.) Cats are often associated with the feminine branch of society; even today, cats are more often viewed as a woman's pet rather than a man's. Cats are regarded as independent and non-obedient (compared to, say, dogs)—qualities that were certainly not highly regarded in the early Victorian woman (or, really, the early Victorian of either gender). As the independence and individuality of women became not only more common but more socially acceptable, one sees a similar acceptance of these characteristics in the cat. As the Victorian woman begins to be able to "walk by herself," so, then, does the Victorian cat. The cat, like the woman, is no longer a mere servant to the household, its role being to catch mice and nothing more.

Again, perhaps this is merely a fanciful conjecture—but it's an interesting coincidence. Perhaps, one day, some college will offer a course not only in Victorian women's studies, but in a study of Victorian women and their cats. In the meantime, thank goodness we have the wonderful artwork of Wain and Thiele and others to show us a side of cats we've always suspected, but never seen!

—Moira Allen, Editor
editors@victorianvoices.net

The Sea - Serpent.

BY ALFRED T. STORY.

HERE is a general disposition to regard the sea-serpent and all the tales of him as an everlasting joke. He only turns up, say the jokers, when Parliament is out of Session and the silly season arrives with its prize gooseberries and showers of frogs; and he usually turns up in America, in a local paper. Nevertheless, there is reason to believe that the sea-serpent is a living fact; or, perhaps, it is safer to say that there is evidence that great living creatures of a kind or kinds as yet unclassified by science inhabit the sea; probably in small numbers, and quite possibly not serpents in the usual sense of the word.

Every circumstance tends to deny a fair hearing to evidence as to the sea-serpent. A man reporting having seen it is laughed at, and a sailor doesn't like being laughed at by a landsman. Of course, a long trail of seaweed rocking upon the sea surface may, at one time and another, have been mistaken for a living thing, or a procession of porpoises may have been thought to be one great organism. But a sailor, as a rule, knows seaweed or a porpoise when he sees it, and is more likely to know actually what he does see on the water than a landsman who wasn't there; and it is unlikely that every sailor who reports a sea-serpent must be drunk, blind, or a fool. It has, however, become customary to assume that he is, and, as a result, a sailor is disposed to keep quiet about anything out of the ordinary which he may see, since he has nothing to gain by making announcement of it.

It may be remembered that tales of gigantic cuttle-fishes were regarded, until comparatively recently, with as much incredulity as those of the sea-serpent, yet the existence of such cuttle-fish is now as much a recognised scientific fact as that of the whale. Let us, then, examine such small part as we may of the large body of evidence on the subject.

The Norwegian fishermen regard the existence of the sea-serpent as a thing beyond all dispute, and can tell any number of stories of his appearance in their fiords; and a Norwegian book of travel published in the sixteenth century describes its appearance in the year 1522.

Olaus Magnus, who is careful to say that his description is from hearsay and not from personal observation, describes the sea-serpent as being 200ft. long and 20ft. in circumference, having fiery eyes and a short mane. He also gives a very surprising picture wherein the sea-serpent is represented curling about

SEA-SERPENT ATTACKING A VESSEL. FROM OLAUS MAGNUS.

entirely out of the water, and reaching over to snap a man from the deck of a ship.

Hans Egede, who afterwards became a bishop, travelled to Greenland in the year 1734 as a missionary. In his account of the voyage, he describes a sea-monster which appeared near the ship on the 6th of July. "Its head," he says, "when raised, was on a level with our main-top. Its snout was long and sharp, and it blew water almost like a whale; it had large, broad paws or paddles; its body was covered with scales; its skin was rough and uneven; in other respects it was as a serpent; and when it dived, the end of its tail, which was raised in the air, seemed to be a full ship's length from its body." A companion of Egede's, also a missionary, made a sketch of the monster, which is here reproduced.

Erik Pontoppidan (Bishop of Bergen), the

SEA-SERPENT SEEN BY HANS EGEDE IN 1734.

officers and crew of H.M.S. *Dædalus* in 1848. We reproduce, entire, the official report of Captain M'Quhae to Admiral Sir W. H. Gage on the subject:—

"H.M.S. *Dædalus*,
"Hamoaze,
Oct. 11th.

"SIR,—In reply to your letter of this day's date, requiring informa-

famous Norwegian naturalist, at first disbelieved in the sea-serpent, but confesses his conversion in his book (published in 1755) since he had received "full and sufficient evidence from creditable and experienced fishermen and sailors in Norway, of whom hundreds testify that they have seen them annually." Pontoppidan tells us that it is the habit of the sea-serpent (which he identifies with the Leviathan of Scripture) to keep at the bottom of the sea except in their spawning time, in July and August, when they rise to the surface occasionally, if the weather be calm, but make their way below immediately should the least disturbance take place. He discriminates between the Greenland and the Norwegian sea-snakes, the former being scaly as to the outer skin, but the latter perfectly smooth, and with a mane about the neck, hanging like a bunch of seaweed. From the various accounts he estimates the length of the serpent at about 600ft., this length lying on the surface in many folds in calm weather. The forehead in all varieties is high and broad, though some have a sharp and others a flat snout. The eyes are large and bluish, looking like bright pewter plates. The colour is dark brown, variegated in places. Thus Erik Pontoppidan.

tion as to the truth of a statement, published in the *Times* newspaper, of a sea-serpent of extraordinary dimensions having been seen from Her Majesty's ship *Dædalus*, under my command, in her passage from the East Indies, I have the honour to acquaint you, for the information of my Lords Commissioners of the Admiralty, that at 5 o'clock p.m., on the 6th of August last, in latitude 24° 44' S and longitude 9° 22' E., the weather dark and cloudy, wind fresh from the N.W., with a long ocean swell from the S.W., the ship on the port tack, heading N.E. by N., something very unusual was seen by Mr. Sartoris, midshipman, rapidly approaching the ship from before the beam. The circumstance was immediately reported by him to the officer of the watch, Lieutenant Edgar Drummond, with whom, and Mr. William Barrett, the master, I was at the time walking the quarter-deck. The ship's company were at supper.

"On our attention being called to the object, it was discovered to be an enormous serpent, with head and shoulders kept about 4ft.

THE SEA-SERPENT ACCORDING TO PONTOPPIDAN.

The *Zoologist* for the year 1847, too, contained many accounts of the appearance, during that year, of sea-serpents in the Norwegian fiords.

One of the most famous and best authenticated appearances of the monster is that recorded to have been observed by the

constantly above the surface of the sea; and, as nearly as we could approximate by comparing it with the length of what our maintopsail yard would show in the water, there was at the very least 60ft. of the animal *à fleur d'eau*, no portion of which was, in our perception, used in propelling it

THE SEA-SERPENT SEEN FROM H.M.S. "DŒDALUS."

servation of several educated men used to the sea, and set down in a sober, official report. A letter was printed shortly after in the *Globe* newspaper, giving an account of the appearance of a similar (very possibly the same) monster to the American brig *Daphne*, 20deg. further south, soon after it was seen from the *Dædalus*. The publication of the *Dædalus* adventure led to many stories of similar encounters being brought forward in the Press of the time.

Captain W. H. Nelson, of the American ship *Sacramento*, reported catching a glimpse of a strange sea-monster on July 30th, 1877, in latitude 31° 59′ N., and longitude 37° W. The man at the wheel (his name was John Hart) had a better view than Captain Nelson, since he first caught sight of it, and the captain did not arrive upon deck until it had proceeded some distance on its way. Some 40ft. of the creature, the helmsman estimated, was seen above the surface, and its girth appeared to be about that of a flour barrel. He afterwards made a pencil sketch, from which it would appear to be a different animal altogether from those usually reported, and somewhat resembling the ancient ichthyosaurus.

through the water, either by vertical or horizontal undulation. It passed rapidly, but so close under our lee quarter that, had it been a man of my acquaintance, I should have easily recognised his features with the naked eye ; and it did not, either in approaching the ship or after it had passed our wake, deviate in the slightest degree from its course to the S.W., which it held on at the pace of from twelve to fifteen miles per hour, apparently on some determined purpose. The diameter of the serpent was about fifteen or sixteen inches behind the head, which was, without any doubt, that of a snake ; and it was never, during the twenty minutes that it continued in sight of our glasses, once below the surface of the water ; its colour, a dark brown with yellowish white about the throat. It had no fins, but something like the mane of a horse, or rather a bunch of seaweed, washed about its back. It was seen by the quartermaster, the boatswain's mate, and the man at the wheel in addition to myself and officers above mentioned.

"I am having a drawing of the serpent made from a sketch taken immediately after it was seen, which I hope to have ready for transmission to my Lords Commissioners of the Admiralty by to-morrow's post.

"I have the honour to be, sir,
    "Your obedient servant,
        "PETER M'QUHAE, Capt.
"To Admiral Sir W. H. Gage,
    G.C.B., Devonport."

This is unassailable evidence from the best source possible—the ob-

SEA-SERPENT SEEN FROM THE SHIP "SACRAMENTO."

The next account I shall quote is that of an officer of H.M.S. *Plumper*, whose description is as follows :—

"On the morning of the 31st of December, 1848, lat. 41° 13′ N., and long. 12° 31′ W., being nearly due west of Oporto, I saw a

SEA-SERPENT SEEN FROM H.M.S. "PLUMPER."

long, black creature with a sharp head, moving slowly, I should think about two knots, through the water, in a north-westerly direction, there being a fresh breeze at the time and some sea on. I could not ascertain its exact length, but its back was 20ft., if not more, above the water, and its head, as near as I could judge, from 6ft. to 8ft. I had not the time to make a closer observation, as the ship was going six knots through the water, her head E. half S., and S.S.E. The creature moved across our wake, towards a merchant barque on our lee-quarter and on the port tack. I was in hopes she would have seen it also. The officers and men saw it, and (those) who have served in parts of the world adjacent to whale and seal fisheries, and have seen them in the water, declare they have never seen or heard of any creature bearing the slightest resemblance to the one we saw. There was something on its back that appeared like a mane, and, as

it moved through the water, kept washing about ; but before I could examine it closely it was too far astern." The illustration is from a sketch by the officer.

The following account of a sea-serpent was communicated to the *Illustrated London News* :—

"Colonial Agency,
"4, Cullum St.,
"London,
"Sept. 25th, 1853.
"We hand you the following extract from the log-book of our ship *Princess*, Captain A. K. N. Tremaine, in London Docks, 15th instant, from China, viz. : 'Tuesday, July 8th, 1853 ; latitude (accurate) 34·56° S. ; longitude (accurate) 18·14° E. At 1 p.m. saw a very large fish, with a head like a walrus, and twelve fins similar to those of the blackfish, but turned the contrary way. The back was from 20ft. to 30ft. long ; also a great length of tail. It is not improbable that this monster has been taken for the great sea-serpent. Fired and hit it near the head with rifle ball. At eight, fresh wind and fine.' The monster was seen by the entire ship's crew, as also by Captain Morgan, a passenger by the *Princess*."

Another well-authenticated sea-serpent is that seen by Dr. Biccard, of Cape Town, in February, 1857, a month later seen by Mr. Fairbridge and others. Dr. Biccard was at the lighthouse at Green Point in the afternoon of the day in question, about 5 p.m., when the lighthouse-keeper asked him to "come and see a sea-monster." "I proceeded to the lighthouse," wrote Dr. Biccard, "and from thence I saw on the water, about 150yds. from the shore, a serpent, of which some details have already appeared in print. (This refers to the account by

SEA-SERPENT SEEN FROM THE "PRINCESS."

Mr. Fairbridge.) It was lying in the position shown in the accompanying sketch, No. 1. I borrowed a rifle from Mr. Hall (the father-in-law of the lighthouse-keeper), and fired at the animal. The ball fell short in front of it by about four yards, as shown in the sketch. The animal did not move, and I then fired a second shot, the ball striking about 1ft. or 1½ft. from it. The serpent then, apparently startled, moved from its position, and straightened himself out, and went under water, evidently getting out of the way. He was invisible about

calm. Besides Dr. Biccard, the animal was seen by seven other persons.

One of our illustrations is of the great American sea-serpent, a young one of which was actually caught and dissected by members of the Linnæan Society of Boston (some of the parts being here shown). In consequence of the reports of a great sea-serpent having been frequently seen during the month of August, 1817, in the harbour of Gloucester, Mass., and at a short distance at sea, the Linnæan Society appointed a committee to collect evidence with regard to the

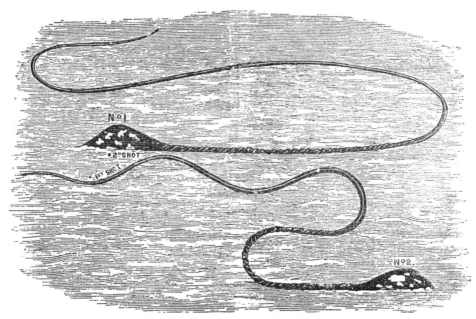

SEA-SERPENT SEEN BY DR. BICCARD, OF CAPE TOWN.

ten minutes, at the expiration of which interval he reappeared at about 200yds. distance, and, I should say, about 40yds. farther off. He then came right on towards the place where I first saw him ; but before arriving there, my son, who had joined me, fired at the animal. Unluckily the discharge broke the nipple of the rifle, and I was thus prevented from further firing. Upon reaching the place which he first occupied, the serpent formed himself into the position delineated in sketch No. 2, and then stood right into the bay, and soon afterwards we lost sight of him altogether."

Dr. Biccard goes on to say that the animal was about 200ft. in length, but its thickness he could not tell, only the upper part of its body being visible ; the head could be seen but indistinctly. He considered the protuberance to be the upper part of the head, but he could not discover the eyes. The body was of a dull, dark colour, except the head, which was maculated with white spots. The water at the time was very

existence and appearance of such an animal. In due course a report appeared, and if that alone was not convincing, the receipt by the Society a month later of an actual sea-serpent left the matter beyond dispute. It was of remarkable appearance, was decided by the Society to be the young of the great sea-serpent, and was named *Scolioplus Atlanticus*. It was killed on the sea-shore at no great distance from Cape Ann. The next cut is from an engraving of it in a pamphlet relating to the sea-serpent published by the Society.

In its issue of April 19th, 1879, the *Graphic* gave an illustration of a sea-serpent seen by its correspondent, Major H. W. J. Senior, of the Bengal Staff Corps, from a sketch by that gentleman, together with a description of the monster, as it appeared to him from the poop deck of the steamship *City of Baltimore*, in latitude 12° 28′ N., longitude 43° 52′ E. Major Senior first saw the creature about three-quarters of a mile distant, "darting rapidly out of the water and splashing in

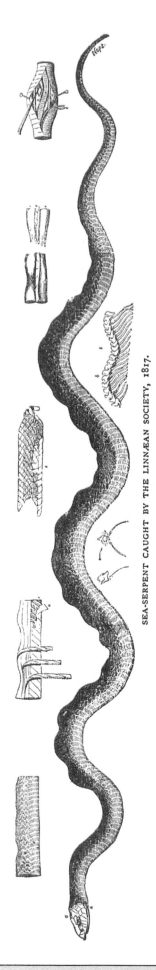

SEA-SERPENT CAUGHT BY THE LINNÆAN SOCIETY, 1817.

again, with a noise distinctly audible," and rapidly approaching the ship. It arrived within 500 yards before turning its course and finally disappearing. It moved so rapidly that it was impossible to fix it with the telescope, so that Major Senior is doubtful whether it had scales or not, but as well as could be ascertained by the unaided eye it had none. "The head and neck," says Major Senior, "about two feet in diameter, rose out of the water to a height of about twenty or thirty feet, and the monster opened its jaws wide as it rose, and closed them again as it lowered its head and darted forward for a dive, reappearing almost immediately some hundred yards ahead. The body was not visible at all, and must have been some depth under water, as the disturbance on the surface was too slight to attract notice, although occasionally a splash was seen at some distance behind the head. The shape of the head was not unlike pictures of the dragon I have often seen, with a bulldog appearance of the forehead and eyebrow. When the

monster had drawn its head sufficiently out of the water, it let itself drop, as it were, like a huge log of wood, prior to darting forward under the water." Major Senior's statement was countersigned by Dr. Hall, the ship's surgeon, and Miss Greenfield, a passenger, both of whom saw the creature.

SEA-SERPENT SEEN FROM THE SS. "CITY OF BALTIMORE."

One of the most extraordinary accounts of the sea-serpent was that given by Captain Drevar, of the barque *Pauline*, and declared before a magistrate by himself and his crew. Much ridicule was cast upon the story by certain journalists, who felt it necessary to be funny on the occasion, and Captain Drevar bitterly resented the doubts cast upon his veracity and capabilities for observation. It is difficult to dismiss the story as not proven, except upon the assumption that Captain Drevar and his crew agreed to tell a great lie for no earthly reason, and without the slightest inducement. This is the narrative, shortened in places, for considerations of space :—

"Barque *Pauline*.—July 8th, 1875; lat. 5° 13′ S., long. 35° W. ; Cape Roque, northeast corner of Brazil, distant twenty miles at 11 a.m.

"The weather fine and clear, the wind and sea moderate. Observed some black spots on the water and a whitish pillar, about 35ft. high, above them. At first I took it all to be breakers, as the sea was splashing up fountain-like about them, and the pillar, a pinnacle rock bleached with the sun; but the pillar fell with a splash and a similar one rose. They rose and fell alternately in quick succession, and good glasses showed me it was a monster sea-serpent coiled twice round a large sperm whale. The head and tail parts, each about 30ft. long, were acting as levers, twisting itself and victim around with great velocity. They sank out of sight about every two minutes, coming to the surface still revolving, and the struggles of the whale and two other

SEA-SERPENT ATTACKING WHALE. SEEN BY CAPTAIN DREVAR IN 1875.

whales that were near, frantic with excitement, made the sea in this vicinity like a boiling caldron, and a loud and confused noise was distinctly heard. This strange occurrence lasted some fifteen minutes, and finished with the tail portion of the whale being elevated straight in the air, then waving backwards and forwards and lashing the water furiously in the last death struggle, when the whole body disappeared from our view, going down head foremost towards the bottom, where, no doubt, it was gorged at the serpent's leisure . . . . . Then two of the largest sperm whales that I have ever seen moved slowly thence towards the vessel, their bodies more than usually elevated out of the water, and not spouting or making the least noise, but seeming quite paralyzed with fear; indeed, a cold shiver went through my own frame on beholding the last agonizing struggle of the poor whale that had seemed as helpless in the coils of the vicious monster as a small bird in the talons of a hawk. Allowing for two coils round the whale, I

SEA-SERPENT ATTACKING WHALE—THE END OF THE STRUGGLE.

think the serpent was about 160ft. or 170ft. long and 7ft. or 8ft. in girth. It was in colour much like a conger eel, and the head, from the mouth being always open, appeared the largest part of the body. . . . . I wrote thus far, little thinking I should ever see the serpent again. But at 7 a.m., July 13th, in the same latitude, and some eighty miles east of San Roque, I was astonished to see the same or a similar monster. It was throwing its head and about 40ft. of its body in a horizontal position out of the water, as it passed onwards by the stern of our vessel. . . . . I was startled by the cry of 'There it is again,' and, a short distance to leeward, elevated some 60ft. in the air, was the

great leviathan, grimly looking towards the vessel. . . . . This statement is strictly true, and the occurrence was witnessed by my officers, half the crew, and myself, and we are ready at any time to testify on oath that it is so, and that we are not in the least mistaken. . . . . A vessel, about three years ago, was dragged over by some sea-monster in the Indian Ocean.

"GEORGE DREVAR,
"Master of the *Pauline*."

Upon seeing doubts cast upon his account in certain newspapers, Captain Drevar appeared before Mr. Raffles, stipendiary magistrate at the Dale Street Police Court, Liverpool, accompanied by some of his officers and crew, and made the following declaration :—

"We, the undersigned, captain, officers, and crew of the barque *Pauline*, of London, do solemnly and sincerely declare that on July 8th, 1875, in latitude 5° 13′ S., longitude 35° W., we observed three large sperm whales, and one of them was gripped round the body with two turns of what appeared to be a large serpent. The head and tail appeared to have a length beyond the coils of about 30ft., and its girth 8ft. or 9ft. The serpent whirled its victim round and round for about fifteen minutes, and then suddenly dragged the whole to the bottom, head first.

"GEORGE DREVAR,
Master.
"HORATIO THOMPSON.
"HENDERSON LANDELLO.
"OWEN BAKER.
"WILLIAM LEWAN."

There were also two other declarations, relating to the subsequent appearance, and the declaration was again made at a Liverpool police-court.

Captain Hassel, of the barque *St. Olaf*, from Newport to Galveston, Texas, testifies to having seen, two days before arrival at the latter port, on May 13th, 1872, a large sea-serpent lying upon the surface of the water. Such part of the creature as was visible seemed about 70ft. long, and had four fins along the back. It was about 6ft. in diameter, and it was of a greenish-yellow colour, with brownish spots over the upper part. One of the mates made a sketch of the animal.

In June, 1877, the officers and crew of the Royal yacht *Osborne* encountered a sea-monster off the coast of Sicily. Lieutenant

SEA-SERPENT SEEN BY CAPTAIN HASSEL.

Haynes describes it thus : " My attention was first called by seeing a long row of fins appearing above the surface of the water at a distance of about 200yds. from the ship, and away on our beam. They were of irregular heights and extending about 30ft. or 40ft. in line (the former number is the length I gave, the latter the other officers). In a few seconds they disappeared, giving place to the forepart of the monster. By this time it had passed astern, swimming in an opposite direction to that we were steering, and as we were passing through the water at ten and a half knots I could only get a view of it 'end on,' as shown in the sketch. The head was bullet-shaped, and quite 6ft. thick, the neck narrow, and its head was occasionally thrown back out of the water, remaining there for a few seconds at a time. It was very broad across the back or shoulders, about 15ft. or 20ft., and the flappers appeared to have a semi-revolving motion, which seemed to paddle the monster along. They were about 15ft. in length. From the top of the head to the part of the body where it became immersed, I should consider 50ft., and that seemed about one-third of the whole length. All this part was smooth, resembling a seal. I cannot account for the fins, unless they were on the back below where it was immersed."

But we have still more recent witnesses to the fact of the existence of a sea-monster than the above. Captain R. J. Cringle, of the steamship *Umfuli*, one of the ten vessels of the Natal Line, belonging to Messrs. Bullard, King, and Company, less than two years ago commanded the following to be written in his ship's log :—

"Ss. *Umfuli*, Monday, Dec. 4th, 1893, 5.30 p.m., lat. 23deg. N., long. 18deg. W. —Sighted and passed, about 500yds. from ship, a monster fish of serpentine shape, about 80ft. long, with shining skin, and short fins, about 20ft. apart, on the back ; in

1. ROW OF FINS AS FIRST SEEN.   2. HEAD AND FLAPPERS.

SEA-SERPENT SEEN FROM H.M.Y. "OSBORNE."

circumference, about the dimensions of a full-sized whale."

The position indicated, as will be seen by reference to a map, is off the coast of Africa, a little south of the Canary Islands, and, broadly speaking, between Cape Bojador and Cape Blanco. When questioned more narrowly about the monster he had seen, Captain Cringle said he had never set eyes upon anything of the kind before, nor had any of the sailors on board the *Umfuli*. People had laughed at him for what they called his credulity, and said that both he and his crew and the passengers on board had been deceived; but he was quite certain his eyes did not deceive him. The sea was like a mirror at the time, with not a cat's - paw nor a ruffle upon it;

CAPTAIN R. J. CRINGLE.
From a Photograph by W. F. Greene.

"and this thing," he added, "whatever it was, was in sight for over half an hour. In fact, we did not lose sight of it until darkness came on."

Questioned as to how far the creature was away when they first saw it, Captain Cringle said, "When we first saw it I estimated that it would be about 400yds. away. It was rushing through the water at great speed, and was throwing water from its breast as a vessel throws water from her bows. I saw full 15ft. of its head and neck on three several occasions. They appeared and disappeared three times. The body was all the time visible."

Asked what the body looked like, Captain Cringle said he could liken it to nothing so well as to a hundred-ton gun partly submerged. It showed three distinct humps or swellings above the waves. Taking a pencil, he made a rough sketch of what he saw. (This was afterwards filled out by our artist, and is given in our illustration.) "The base,

or body," said he, "from which the neck sprang was much thicker than the neck itself, and I should not, therefore, call it a serpent. Had it been breezy enough to ruffle the water, or hazy, I should have had some doubt about the creature; but the sea being so perfectly smooth, I had not the slightest doubt in my mind as to its being a sea-monster. I turned the ship round to get closer to it, and got much nearer than we were at first; but the sun was then setting and the light gone, so that to have run the ship nearer to the coast would have been folly."

In reply to a question as to whether the creature seemed scaled, Captain Cringle said that so far as he could judge it was not. It appeared to have a smooth skin, and to be of a dark brown colour. They were at one time so near to it that one of the passengers, a Mr. Kennealy, a gentleman of some scientific attainments, said he could hear the creature hiss, but the first officer said, "No, that is the rushing of the water from his bows." The scientific gentleman had a camera on board, but he was so excited that he never thought of it. A little less excitement, and Mr. Kennealy might have immortalized himself.

It will be seen from the photograph of the *Umfuli's* log that the chief officer, who has the keeping of it, had a look at the monster through his glass, and describes it as having an enormous mouth, with great rows of teeth.

SEA-SERPENT SEEN BY CAPTAIN CRINGLE.

Log of the S S Umfuli from London towards Natal

H.	K.	F.	COURSES.	WINDS.	LEE-WAY.	Devia-tion.	REMARKS.
							Monday Dec 4th 1893 A.M.
1	10	5	S by W½W	S S W			
2	10	5	"	"			2. Light wind & overcast.
3	10	5	"	"			
4	10	5	"	"			4. do ― do
5	10	5	"	"			
6	10	5	"	"			Hands employed cleaning paint work
7	10	5	"	"			varnishing grain work & painting Forec'sl
8	10	5	"	"			Carpenter filling Engine Room Store
9	10	5	"	"			
10	10	5	"	"			12. Calm & clear.
11	10	5	"	"			
12	10	5	"	"			Pumps, wells carefully attended

Course	Dist.	Dif. Lat.	Dep.	Lat. by Acct.	Lat. by Obs.	Dif. Long	Long. by Acct.	Long. by Obs.
South	255	32			22 38 54 N	nil		17.26.00 W
				Barometer. 30 20	Sympiesometer.	Thermometer. 78°	Aneroid.	

H.	K.	F.		WINDS.			REMARKS.
1	10	5	"	Calm			P.M.
2	10	5	"	"			2. Calm & smooth sea
3	10	5	"	"			
4	10	5	"	"			4. Same weather Th 43
5	10	5	"	"			
6	10	5	"	"			5.30 Sighted and passed about 500 yards
7	10	5	"	"			from ship a Monster Fish of the Serpent
8	10	5	"	"			shape, about 80ft long with slimy skin and short fins at about 20 feet apart on
9	10	5	"	"			the back and in cir. about the same as a
10	10	5	"	"			full sized Whale, & distinctly saw the fishs
11	10	5	"	"			mouth open & shut with my glasses. The
12	10	5	"	"			jaws appeared to me about 7 feet long with large teeth In shape it was

Just like a Conger Eel, there were two of them

Master _____   C. C. J. Powell _____ Mate

REDUCED FACSIMILE OF PAGE OF CAPTAIN CRINGLE'S LOG, WITH ENTRY REGARDING SEA-SERPENT.

Captain Cringle, however, who does not appear to have seen the creature's mouth open, said nothing about it.

In concluding his account of what he saw on that notable 4th of December, Captain Cringle said, "I have been so ridiculed about the thing that I have many times wished that anybody else had seen that sea-monster rather than me. I have been told that it was a string of porpoises, that it was an island of seaweed, and I do not know what besides. But if an island of seaweed can travel at the rate of fourteen knots an hour, or if a string of porpoises can stand 15ft. out of the water, then I give in, and confess myself deceived. Such, however, could not be."

Three months before Captain Cringle turned the *Umfuli* round in order to get a nearer sight of his sea-monster, Dr. Farquhar Matheson, of London, had a still closer view of a similar creature. Dr. Matheson is a trained observer, and one of the men least likely to be the subject of an illusion. What he saw he described shortly afterwards to several gentlemen. They laughed at him at first, because it is so usual to laugh at sea-serpent stories; but they afterwards confessed that they thought there must be something in what he described, as he was not a person likely to be deceived. The ridicule to which he was subjected, however, made him decide to say very little about the matter. He gave the writer a succinct account of the monster he saw, which was made a note of at the time; but, as he declined to have his name go forth in connection with it, no use was made of the narrative. Having now, however, given his consent for his name to be mentioned, his interesting experience is here for the first time put on record.

The occurrence took place in September,

1893, while Dr. Matheson was spending some time at his home in the north-west of Scotland. He was at the time enjoying a sail with his wife on Loch Alsh, which separates the Island of Skye from the mainland. "It was a beautiful day," said Dr. Matheson, "clear as possible, the sun shining brightly, and without clouds. The time was between one and two. Our sail was up and we were going gaily along, when suddenly I saw something rise out of the Loch in front of us—a long, straight, neck-like thing as tall as my mast. I could not think what it was at first. I fancied it might be something on land, and directed my wife's attention to it. I said, 'Do you see that?' She said she did, and asked what it could be, and was rather scared. It was then 200yds. away and was moving towards us. Then it began to draw its neck down, and I saw clearly that it was a large sea-monster—of the saurian type, I should think. It was brown in colour, shining, and with a sort of ruffle at the junction of the head and neck. I can think of nothing to which to compare it so well as the head and neck of the giraffe, only the neck was much longer, and the head was not set upon the neck like that of a giraffe; that is, it was not so much at right-angles to it as a continuation of it in the same line. It moved its head from side to side, and I saw the reflection of the light from its wet skin."

Asked if the creature appeared to have scales, Dr. Matheson said he should judge not. It showed a perfectly smooth surface. He went on to say that it was in sight about two minutes and then disappeared. Then it rose again three different times, at intervals of two or three minutes. It stood perpendicularly out of the water, and

seemed to look round. "When it appeared the second time," said Dr. Matheson, "it was going from us, and was travelling at a great rate. It was going in the direction of the northern outlet of the Loch, and we were sailing in its wake; I was interested, and followed it. From its first to its last appearance we travelled a mile, and the last time we saw it it was about a mile away."

As to the body of the monster, Dr. Matheson said, "I saw no body—only a ripple of the water where the line of the body should be. I should judge, however, that there must have been a large base of body to support such a neck. It was not a sea-serpent, but a much larger and more substantial beast—something of the nature of a gigantic lizard, I should think. An eel could not lift up its body like that, nor could a snake."

As to the possibility of his being the subject of an optical illusion, Dr. Matheson said, "'That is a common theory. But what I saw precludes all possibility of such an explanation. In the case of an optical illusion, what the eye sees becomes attenuated, and thus gradually disappears. But in the case of the creature I saw, it slowly descended into the water; it reappeared the same way, gradually ascending. I saw it move its head from side to side, and I noticed the glistening of the light on its smooth, wet skin." The doctor added, "In the evening at dinner I described to some gentlemen who were present, Sir James Farrar amongst the number, what I had seen. As I said, they laughed at the story at first, and suggested various ways in which I might have been deceived; but when I showed them that none of their theories would fit the case, they admitted that the sea-serpent, or sea monster, could not be altogether a myth."

SEA-SERPENT SEEN BY DR. MATHESON.

RECIPES FOR OCTOBER.

OCTOBER brings us apples; we hardly wish for anything better than an apple in October. But it also brings us pears of many kinds; nuts too—cobnuts, walnuts, and chestnuts galore. Some young people fancy that all these good things are in readiness for Hallow e'en frolics, but older heads know that October's wealth must be stored in preparation for wintry days that will surely follow soon.

French people grow more pears in their gardens than we English think of doing, partly because it is their habit to eat more fruit in its natural state, while we prefer ours to be cooked. I remember our old French garden of years ago; there were more pears than apples there, and pears of such varied shapes and flavours, as made it quite a marvel to our English friends. I remember that it was our custom to bake all the pears that would submit to being cooked; we had a deep glazed earthenware pan with a lid; this we filled twice a week and it was sent to the baker to be put in his oven when bread-baking was finished, there to stay until he fired his oven for the next day's bread. He brought that pan back with him on his round the next day, and the contents of it were invariably done to perfection. We could never bake our pears half as well in our own oven at home. Doubtless the charcoal firing had something to do with it.

Baked pears and cream! What a delight. Try it, you who know not how good all those hard, unripe things can become by proper slow cooking.

We sometimes added a stick of cinnamon or one or two cloves to our jar of pears, but no sugar is ever needed, only water enough to well cover them.

By way of a variation, when "company" was expected, we used to make a more elegant dish of our pears, by removing the rind and the cores, slicing them rather thickly and adding a few lumps of sugar, then pouring on enough common claret to cover them, and stewing them in our own oven for quite two hours. This was a toothsome dish when eaten with small moulds of custard, turned out and smothered in cream. Or the same dish of pears might appear at dinner with a mould of blancmange or ground rice.

Our time for making *Apple Jelly* comes when the apples have attained a rich red colour, but while they are still young and full of juice. It is not possible to make jelly from old or kept apples. After wiping each apple place it in a deep gallon jar, but do not peel, cut or quarter it. Pour in enough water to half fill the jar and replace the lid tightly. Let the jar stand in the corner of a slow oven for some five or six hours, then strain, first through a coarse sieve, when a light pressure may be put on the fruit, then strain a second time through a suspended jelly bag. Measure the juice thus obtained, and to every pint allow a pound of the best cane sugar. Put the juice on to boil and lay the sugar out on trays that it may heat in the oven.

When the juice boils fast throw in the sugar, and at the same time one or two pieces of rase ginger. When the sugar has dissolved begin to stir the liquid and continue stirring for twenty minutes exactly. Lift out the ginger and pour the liquid at once into small glass jars that have been made thoroughly hot so that they shall not crack.

If carefully made in this fashion, the jelly will be found to be solid after twenty-four hours. Keep in a dry but even temperature.

Blackberry Jelly would be made very similarly to the above, giving plenty of time for the juice to "run" from the fruit in the first instance.

Quince Jelly the same, only more water must be allowed to quinces, as they are naturally a dry fruit. A few tart apples are a great addition to quince marmalade or jelly. The colour of quince jelly is so good that it becomes valuable for decorative purposes, if not as a dessert. Many people do not care for the peculiar flavour of the fruit, but its brilliant colour is universally admired.

An Apple Salad is delicious with roast pork or goose, only for this purpose the apples must be very ripe and rather juicy. Pare them, remove the cores and pips, and slice them very thinly into a salad bowl. Sprinkle with a little salt, a spoonful of castor sugar, a pinch of cayenne pepper, then pour on one dessertspoonful of chili vinegar, and two or three of finest Lucca oil. Toss very lightly, and do not let it have to wait long before serving, as the colour spoils readily.

Apple Beignets; the genuinely true fritter. Choose large firm apples; remove the cores without breaking them, then pare the rind off. Make a batter with the whisked whites of two eggs, a teaspoonful of castor sugar, two large tablespoonfuls of flour and enough salad oil to make a batter of the consistency of thick cream. Dip each round of apple into this, then drop at once into a saucepan containing boiling lard; let them boil until crisp and brown: drain and sprinkle liberally with sugar.

Apples en Croustades.—Pare, core and slice a couple of pounds of good cooking apples, stew them until they can be beaten to a froth with a fork. Do this, then sweeten sufficiently with sugar, add a pinch of spice and a little butter.

Cut some rounds from a stale roll about an inch thick. Scoop out a part of the middle but leave a thin bottom. Fry these croustades in lard until they are a pale brown; fill them with the frothed apple and pile on the top the whisked whites of one or two eggs, with sugar to sweeten. Allow one croustade to each person.

Apple Fool.—Pare, core and stew (without water) several tart apples. Sweeten well and beat the pulp until perfectly light. When cold whisk it with an equal quantity of thick custard or sweetened cream, and pour into a glass dish. Serve with sponge rusks.

Friar's Omelette.—Make a pulp of several cooked apples, sweeten it with sugar, and when cold add to it two well-beaten eggs. Butter a shallow tart-dish, strew it thickly with bread-crumbs, pour in the apple pulp and cover with more crumbs to the depth of an inch. Pour a little dissolved butter over the top, and bake in the oven for upwards of an hour. When cool turn it out on to a dish and sift sugar over.

Here is a hint that is worth noting with regard to apples, and that is, when baking apples in the oven, after scooping out a little at the top, to make an incision with a sharp knife all round, through the skin. Place a morsel of butter in the hollow at the top of each apple and a clove, if the flavour is liked. When baked the apples will have risen up, appearing twice as large as at first, while the cutting of the skin prevents the inside from boiling out.

Cheese is prime in October; witness the old custom of holding cheese fairs; it is excellent food too.

One of our American contemporaries has it that if we would be healthy we ought to eat cheese at least once a day. Many people hold to the idea that cheese will digest everything but itself, but that, it is hardly needful to say, is a fallacy. Ripe cheese is about one of the most nutritive and easily digested of all our foods. Where it is thought to be indigestible, however, a corrective would be found in adding as much bicarbonate of potash as would lie on a sixpence to a fair-sized cheese pudding, or sprinkle the potash between bread and butter and eating this with the cheese. The insufficiency of potash salt is the reason why some cheeses are difficult of digestion.

Grated Cheese is much liked by many who are prejudiced against eating it in the ordinary way. All dry pieces should be kept for grating.

Grated cheese should accompany potato soup, then it becomes true Potage Parmentier.

Roast Goose with its time-honoured accompaniment of apple sauce is a favourite dish at this time. Geese are indeed more wholesome faring now than later in the year; they have not had time to grow so fat and oily. A goose requires to be very thoroughly cooked, and as it browns quickly it should be well protected with stout papers until within half-an-hour of serving it, when these may be removed and the skin allowed to brown.

A stuffing of cooked and finely minced onions with sage is greatly improved by having half its bulk of mashed potatoes added; let it be highly seasoned also.

The apple sauce should be very little sweetened, not at all unless the apples are very tart.

At one of our well-known military schools for boys, where roast pork and apple sauce is the regular Sunday dish in winter, the sauce—ostensibly an accompaniment—is thought to be far too great a delicacy to be relegated to such a secondary place. Instead, the sauce tureens are left untouched until the meat has been consumed, then it is passed round as a separate course to the great delight of the appreciative diners.

Ginger Bread Nuts.—Rub half-a-pound of fresh butter into a pound and a half of flour, add nearly an ounce of ground ginger and sprinkle a very little cayenne pepper in. Warm a pound of treacle and half a pound of brown sugar together, then work in with the flour. Roll out to a thin paste and cut into biscuits with a sharp tin cutter. Bake on a buttered tin in a moderately quick oven for about twenty-five minutes.

Cocoanut Drops.—Rub four ounces of butter with an equal quantity of desiccated cocoanut, then add the whisked whites of four eggs. Beat all well together, then sift in sufficient cornflour to make a light paste, and work in half a teaspoonful of carbonate of soda dissolved in lemon juice. Drop by teaspoonfuls on to a buttered tin and bake very quickly.

Sugar Cakes.—Rub with the fingers half a pound of fresh butter into a pound of flour, with the grated rind of half a lemon, also half-a-pound of castor sugar. Mix with yolks of three eggs only, no other moisture. Roll out very thinly, using castor sugar with which to sprinkle the board instead of flour. Cut with a sharp cutter and bake in a moderate oven to a very pale brown.

These are delicious for afternoon tea.

The Champion Orange-Peeler.

Photos. specially taken by George Newnes, Ltd.

By A. B. Henn.

MR. BIRCH is a ship's cook by profession, but, let it be said, he is rather more than that: he is to all intents and purposes an accomplished *chef*, as his numerous medals and diplomas will show. More than that, again, he is an inventor. Mr. Birch is one of those extraordinary all-round men it is one's ill-luck to meet with but seldom. He is the one man we would wish to have as a companion on a desert island of the Pacific. He has the wonderful gift of making something out of what might well be called nothing at all, or the very next door to it.

He has manufactured with his own hands a set of kitchen utensils out of an ordinary hundredweight of cocoanuts. From an egg-separator to the most useful of soup-ladles, the shells were speedily transformed into useful and business-like utensils. Now, for a man who can make an up-to-date egg-separator out of the most common of cocoa-nut shells in less than ten minutes, it is not too much to expect something still more wonderful and startling.

It so happens that at times the most careful and industrious of ships' cooks will find time *lie heavy* on his hands; whenever such has been the case Mr. Birch contrived to fill in his odd moments in his endeavour to

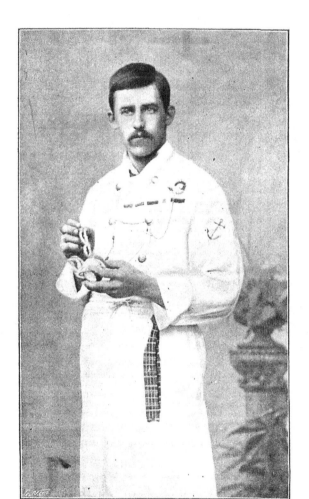

MR. BIRCH, THE CHAMPION ORANGE-PEELER.
From a Photo.

perfect himself in one of the various hobbies which he has made his own.

When a man happens to travel in the company of some thousands of cases of oranges his mind will naturally dwell for a considerable part of the journey upon the luscious fruit and its possibilities. Our champion happened to travel once in such companionship, and he then and there decided to form a closer acquaintance with his fellow-travellers, and the photographs which illustrate this article will serve to show the fruits (no pun intended) of his endeavour.

No Christmas dinner is considered complete without its *addenda* of oranges. It may therefore not prove uninteresting to show how the peel of this popular dainty may be used as a means of ornament and, let us add, amusement.

Though much time and patience are required to attain the perfection of our champion, it is nevertheless possible to acquire the art of ornamental orange-peeling in a few self-taught lessons. The photos. here reproduced of oranges peeled by Mr. Birch in our presence will give sufficient aid to a beginner should he care to devote his attention to the art for a few hours only. The well-sharpened blade of a penknife is all that is required. The oranges, of course, are a *sine quâ non.*

FIG. 1.

FIG. 4.

Look at Fig. 1, which illustrates the first cut. We see that the initial stage consists in making four slits at right angles from the top, but not quite to the bottom, of the peel. The nail of the thumb is then inserted

goodly strip of peel such as is shown in Fig. 3 —in the second stage on the right, and in the third stage on the left of the fruit. Figs. 4 and 5 show different ways of cutting or carving; but Fig. 6 will show how to use

FIG. 2.

FIG. 5.

beneath the peel in order to separate it from the body of the fruit.

Fig. 2 shows how thin slices or strips are cut from the sides of the four main sections, or leaves. These four leaves must then be cut again from top to bottom, and from bottom to top alternately, but never quite to the end, so as to form one continuous strip of smaller leaves, that with gentle pulling will lengthen into a

the original cutting of Fig. 3 in the ornamental building up of Figs. 7 and 8.

Here we shall have to give away "a trick of the trade," if we may call it so.

In order to mount the orange-peel artistically, small bits of wood the size of large Swedish matches, pointed at each end, will be found useful. Also longer bits of wood, such as are shown in the centre of Fig. 6, with tiny bits of wire upon

FIG. 3.

FIG. 6.

owing, of course, to the loss of colour; but our picture will show sufficiently well what can be made of carved oranges with a little skill and a handful of greens and flowers,

which the ends of the peel strips may be firmly fixed, will come in with advantage. Fig. 7 shows how an orange suitably peeled, carved, and trussed can be placed on an ordinary wine-glass, which glass has been

FIG. 8.

FIG. 7.

such as are easily found in every well-appointed household.

Fig. 9 is what must be called a piece of fancy carving. We call it carving, for it can hardly be called peeling, though, perhaps, the difference is insignificant. It is intended to represent a Japanese house-boat, with folding doors, and very pretty do these

FIG. 9.

previously ornamented with a small square of white or coloured paper cut in any suitable design. In Fig. 8 we find an orange also carved and trussed, but ornamented in a more elaborate shape.

It is difficult to show in a photograph the charming effect of such table decoration,

doors look, for they can be opened and closed at will, and give room for considerable amusement.

Fig. 10 is one that represents a great deal of skill, coupled with no little amount of patriotism. Mr. Birch's enthusiasm for the Crown is exemplified here in a striking manner. He has endeavoured to represent in orange-peel the symbol of our power and greatness.

FIG. 10.

fashioned. There is no limit to these designs. A favourite form of amusement suggests itself. There are, for instance, endless possibilities in trying to carve your partner's features in the peel of an orange. Try it.

In the course of conversation Mr. Birch suggested the erection of an elaborate table-centre decoration by means of one hundred carved oranges.

FIG. 11.

FIG. 12.

Considering the frailty of the material, we venture to suggest that he has met with no small amount of success.

There is a comic side to orange-peeling, and, though Mr. Birch mostly inclines to the artistic, there is nothing to prevent our digressing a little from his methods, and to suggest a somewhat novel kind of entertainment for after-dinner amusement.

Fig. 11 is an illustration in point. In less than two minutes this clever representation of Mr. What-you-may-call-him has been

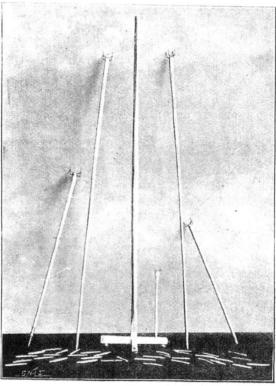

FIG. 13.

We challenged him to perform the feat, and forthwith ordered one hundred of the finest fruit extant.

Upon the receipt of these Mr. Birch set to work on the extraordinary structure which is illustrated in its various stages by the pictures that follow. In the construction of such an elaborate "set piece," as we may be permitted to call it, several accessories are of course necessary.

Those shown in Fig. 13 are of the simplest. They are the accessories that were used in the construction of the centre-piece

FIG. 14.

close inspection of subsequent stages you will find that they have been put right, and this is part of the careful finishing touches that must be given as reasonable advance is made.

Look at Fig. 15. Here we have a number of rows added to the first, and our pyramid is already assuming respectable proportions. The centre support has been firmly fixed into its base, and forms, as it were, the main-mast of the whole concern.

It must not be forgotten that, as the process of piling up goes on, the various supports must be tied together by means of tape, wire, or even strong thread, whichever, in fact, is most handy, in order to give the whole struc-

under notice. They consist in the first place of a base made of wood in the shape of a cross, with one long piece of wood fixed in the centre thereof and projecting vertically upwards.

Four pieces of wood, similarly shaped, are fixed into the ends of the arms of the cross in such a manner as to remain rigid in an upright position. The shorter pieces are fixed at suitable intervals, according to the form of design that is intended.

It must be understood, of course, that this staging is but an elementary one. If wire were used there is no end to the designs that might be produced. These may be left to the ingenuity of our readers.

In Fig. 14 we find what we will call the table-centre orange pyramid in its first stage. The oranges have all been carved in one and the same design. In the first row they are placed side by side in an oval, and form the base of the pyramid. It is not necessary to place the "foundation" or "staging" in the middle of the structure until at a later stage.

In some places you will see that bits of refractory peel have fallen back as though neglected, but on

FIG. 15.

FIG. 16.

elaborately carved and "trussed." It is necessary that it should be firm in its setting, for should it vacillate there is danger of the whole structure collapsing owing to top-heaviness. Additional oranges, carved, trussed, and decorated, may with advantage be placed at the four corners or around the pyramid, such, in fact, as are shown placed upright on the wine-glasses in the picture.

In Fig. 17 we have a pretty view of the table-centre complete. About one hundred artistically peeled oranges are here shown, forming as pretty a centre-piece as has ever been devised. Streams of smilax trail down its sides, and maidenhair ferns peep out here and there; as also do little bunches of flowers to add the necessary colour. In fact, the whole structure reflects much credit on its originator, and suggests endless scope for the ingenuity of our readers.

ture its required stability. If a wire frame were first constructed in much the same manner as those used for ornamental lamp-shades, the result would be more secure and, no doubt, more artistic also; but failing that, a wooden structure, such as the one indicated, will meet any ordinary case, and has on its side the advantage of simplicity, not to speak of economy.

Fig. 16 shows the pyramid practically completed, without, of course, its additional ornaments of ferns and flowers. The orange which forms the "masthead," so to speak, must be carefully and

FIG. 17.

AUNT MEHITABLE'S WINTER IN WASHINGTON.

BY MRS. HARRIET HAZELTON.

TENTH PAPER.

WELL, girls, I'm a'most through with my last winter and spring's visit to the Capitol. If I go there next winter I reckon I'll write an' tell you all about the fashionable doin's. An' it runs in my mind pretty strong that our Nat'll be a-gittin' married some time next season. I couldn't help seein' how much he thought o' *her*, an' I reckon the best of 'em all would take Nat for the askin'. Leastways, I think they might be glad to git him; and I know Miss Rankin likes him very much, though she ain't like some widders I've seen, a-flirtin' an' tryin' to act like a young girl all the time. If she was, I know Nat wouldn't like her. He never could bear a flirt sence he was a very young man, an' that Arethuse Simpkins down to Petersburg jilted him. Poor boy! he thought then that he never would be happy ag'in. But, laws a massy! gracious me! if he'd a married her, where do you think he'd a been now? Don't know? Well, I can tell you. Just out in the field a-hoin' an' a-plowin', in his unbleached shirtsleeves, an' coarse butternut pants, an' stogy shoes, all covered with mud. Then at home would 'a been a coarse, slattern of a woman, an' four or five dirty tow-headed children, with no books or flowers or any nice, tasteful things around. When a man marries so young he don't know his own mind, and then, if his wife ain't what he expected she was, he gives up a tryin' to be anything. Why, it just wouldn't 'a been our Nat at all as he is now. No, after that trouble (as he thought it was then, and for which he thanks the Lord now), he drooped a little while, an' then after a good talk with me one day, he straightened up an' went to work, an' after a while went to college with what he'd made an' what 'Siah could do to help him; for we wasn't as rich then as we are now. An' so he graduated, an' see where he is now! An' when de *does* marry, you may be sure he won't lower himself, after all the experience he's had! An' that's a great comfort to me. I always knowed that Nat was as smart as anybody's son, no matter whose. But—*if he'd 'a married that Arethuse, nobody'd ever 'a heard of him!*

Well, we only had a few more days to stay, an' so we was out in the carriage every day. Our next drive was to Soldiers' Home, the loveliest place, all full o' fine drives, miles on miles; an' the cunnin'est little lakes, with willer trees growin' around 'em; an' patches o' woods, with little branches and bridges; an' clumps an' old roots, turned up, an' the honeysuckles a-runnin' all over 'em; an' the finest trees, in the Corcoran part o' the grounds, brought from foreign countries, an' costin'

mints o' money. In one wild nook o' woods there's a thicket of underbrush, an' a spring o' cold water, with a great chestnut tree nigh it, where Nat and his friends went for a picnic last year; an' up on the hill in another grove o' trees is a pretty little church. Then there's summer-houses, an' all kinds o' pretty seats in out-o'-the-way lookin' places; an' there's the old soldiers—here, there, an' everywhere, a lookin' as happy an' bright as possible—all dressed in the old army blue. Some was at work about the flowers, an' some o' the weakest an' oldest settin' around in the nice seats a-sunnin' themselves, an' enjoyin' the trees an' flowers. An', speakin' o' flowers, you never seen such lovely ones. An' so many o' 'em, too, while every walk is kept just as clean as our kitchen floor of a Saturday night; an' every border's trimmed an' kept in apple-pie order.

Nat says I just ought to see Soldiers' Home in October, when the woods is a-changin' color; that it's perfectly grand. He knows how I love the autumn woods. We looked through the houses at the Home: one's where Mr. an' Miss Lincoln used to pass their summers—when everybody that *was* anybody wasn't obleeged to go to a fashionable waterin'-place. Then we went up into the tower, where I seen the finest view in the world, a'most; leastways, it appeared so to me. On the north was the beautiful hills an' valleys, all rich in farms an' fine old houses; on the east was the same, with a part o' the city an' Kendall Green, with the Deaf and Dumb Asylum near it; southeast was the grand old Capitol, the Eastern Branch an' the Anacosty hills; an' away off, miles and miles, south and southwest was Alexandry, an' Fort Washin'ton, an' Arlington, an' the wide river shinin' like a smooth sea, with the great city between, an' the lovely grounds at our feet. Oh, it's wonderful! an' I do hope you'll all git to see it some day. It minded me o' the Arcady that Nat read to me about once; or the Beulah land; or the new heaven an' new earth in the Revelations; for it seemed to take in the heavens an' the earth both, an' everything was perfect. The sun was a-gittin' low in the west, an' the whole sky was one blaze o' light, with clouds o' purple, an' red an' gold; an' there was a kind o' haze in the air that made the distant town look like the enchanted city in little Arthur's fairy book. Oh, I think if Paradise is any brighter or lovelier than that scene was that day I don't know how we'll ever be able to bear the sight! The western part o' the city, and the heights o' Georgetown was very beautiful too; so there was no end to the beauty o' the view.

We stopped an' talked to several o' the old soldiers, and found they was all proud o' their home, as they have a good right to be. Gineral Scott's the one that set it a-goin', an' each soldier in the reg'lar army has to give a little mite every year, an' that keeps it up. One o' the old fellers we talked to was in the war of 1812. He's very old, of course. Several was wounded in Mexico in 1848—an' one poor man that wasn't old at all, an' looked in pretty good health, went around in a little wagon that he worked with his hands, and when we asked him what was the matter, said he had his feet both froze off when he was a-soldierin' in the Northwest. He was in the reg'lar army, of course, an' was stationed at one of our forts. How sorry I was for him, an' yet how glad that he had such a nice place provided for him. A-plenty of everything comfortable, with a beautiful home to live in; an' plenty o' books, with the sunniest or shadiest places to wheel himself into to read. It might be worse, though it's bad enough, dear knows, when a man's lost both his feet.

It was late when we got home to dinner. Next day we drove out the same road to the old Rock Creek Church. It's a fine old place, all the trees bein' left a-growin' as God made 'em; an' grand trees they are, too. All through the graveyard they let 'em stand; an' it's pleasant to think o' the dead a-lyin' there, with the birds singin' above 'em all the spring and summer, an' the leaves a-fallin' over 'em in the autumn like a coverlet—leaves of red an' gold an' brown, all mingled together above their sleepin' forms, as they did once above the lost Babes in the Wood. One o' the trees just in front o' the church is the finest old oak I ever seen. There ain't one like it in our whole valley, from one end to the other. An' if there's one thing in the world that minds me of a strong, brave man, it's a great oak tree; an' this one looks as old as Methusalem, with its gnarly old arms a-reachin' out, like they growed there on purpose to protect the church. Under the tree an' all over the front yard it's one great bed o' myrtle a foot deep, with its blossoms a-peepin' up from the glossy green bed, like a thousand bright blue eyes.

The church is built o' bricks brought from England, some dark an' some light, an' it's a hundred year old. It's always been attended by the old families in the country around; an' considerin' the war an' all its changes, it's wonderful how many o' these have kept their old homes.

In the church-yard here there's a good show o' fine old family tombstones; but we noticed partic'larly a small, square stone, ready to put up, an' marked with the name o' Gineral Ketcham, the man that was supposed to be pizoned by Miss Wharton in Baltimore. Nat had sent me all the papers at the time o' the trial, an I'd read the whole thing through, so I felt very strange a-standin' over his grave. An' I thought that, very likely, the whole truth of this thing would never be found out till the great day that will open out the se-crets of all hearts. The gineral's wife died first, an' is buried by his side.

From there we drove out to Fort Stevens, where there was busy times durin' the war. Now it's levelled down on the top, an' a handsome little 'Piscopal church, of rough gray stone, built there. It shows for miles around. Away off, in every direction from this fort, the old country houses may be seen, many of 'em very grand old places. "Bleak House," Mr. Shepherd's country place, stands on a hill, an' is seen for miles around, lookin' bleak enough in the distance, but very nice when you reach it. It's named after the house in one o' Dickens's books; maybe you remember. It's the one with Lady Dedlock, an' Jarndice an' Jarndice, an' little Miss Flite, in it. Then we come home across Rock Creek, a lovely little stream, as pretty as our own river, only it lacks the mountains; an' then through the pretty little village o' Mount Pleasant, an' back to the hotel. I'd like to tell you more about Rock Creek, an' Pierce's Mill, an' Mount Pleasant, an' other places we drove to next day. But I reckon I won't have time. I'll only say about this creek that it runs on, dashin' over rocks, an' through wild woods, around by Georgetown, an' then into the Potomac; an' that some o' the lovellest places may be found everywhere along the stream. Painters go out every summer to make pictures from these little spots, an' some of 'em's very fine.

I'd been so long at the hotel that I'd got to feelin' pretty much at home there; an' when I went to bid my friends good-by, I really hated to go. But I knowed the folks at home was a-gittin' tired o' doin' without me, an' the spring was come, an' I began to pine for my dear old home, an' for 'Siah, an' I longed to see the young chickens an' ducks, an' the lambs an' calves, an' the old mountains, as well as the children an' neighbors.

So one mornin' early we started for home, Nat an' me. The last sight o' the Capitol from the Long Bridge made me choke a'most, thinkin' I might never see it agin. But that, an' Arlington, an' the dear old river, was soon gone, an' on I went home, clickity-clack, clickity-clack, thumpity-bump, thumpity-bump, an' the nearer home I got, the more nervous I growed, for fear 'Siah might be dead, or Annie, or the baby, or somebody else. But at last we reached the station, an' there, sure enough, was our own old rusty carriage (an' how rusty it did look, to be sure!), an' 'Siah himself a-waitin' for me. I was powerful glad to see him, but couldn't help a-noticin' how rough he looked, and how careless he was dressed. I asked him why he didn't fix up more, an' he says, "Highty-tighty, Hitty! ain't I good enough for you an' Nat in my work-a-day clothes? I reckon you'd better go back to Washin'ton, hadn't you?" But his eyes twinkled when he said it, for he seen plain enough how glad I was to see him. An' when we got to the old house again, an' Pete an' Annie run out with the baby, an' Mose an' Kitty, an' you, girls, an' even old Towser, you'd better believe I was glad! But, my! how squatty the house looked! an' how low our rooms was! an' how rough the walls seemed! an' how coarse my new rag carpet, that I was so proud of before I went away! But all this come right in a few days, an' I felt as if I never could git tired o' lookin' at the mountains. They never had seemed so grand-like to me before. An', though I knowed it was a long an' rough road to git out from among 'em, I appeared, somehow, to have more room, more breathin' space, than I'd had all winter. I never rested till I'd been to the sugar tree grove by the river, an' to the big iron spring an' the little sulphur one, an' all the nice places I'd been used to all my life. I never knowed how much I cared for 'em before. An' right here I'll say that I do think it's a good thing for everybody to go away from home once in a while. They'll never know how dear it is till they do. Here I'd been more 'n thirty year on this farm, an' never away more 'n three days at a time in my life. An' when I did go, it took two days out of the three to go over the mountain an' back, so it was only one day's visit after all, an' me a great sight too tired to enjoy that a mite. This time I'd been gone—let me see—December, Jenooary, Febooary, March, April, an' a good part o' May—almost six months! Well, nobody but Nat ever could a-kept me that long from home. Still, I enjoyed it all; but I enjoyed comin' home as much as any of it. Annie had kept the house in prime order (so much for teachin' her right when she was a girl), an' I didn't have any worry at all, like most women do that's been away so long. An' I declare that the second afternoon, as I was a-settin' all alone in my room (for Nat was gone to see some o' the neighbor boys, an' all the others was at work), when a great pile o' clouds riz over the mountain, an' then rolled up an' spread out above us, with the sun a-gleamin' through the rifts; an' when the rain come down, soft-like, and thin, at the first, makin' the mountain look like it wore a gauze veil over its dear old face, but fairly pourin' down after a while, hidin' it altogether; an' when it broke away, an' all was lit up agin in the evenin' sunlight, an' the fogs rose up from the clefts of the mountains, an' chased each other like huge flyin' swans up the river, *then* I felt a'most like shoutin' with joy that I was once more in my mountain home! Oh, girls! it don't make no difference about bein' old, if the good God leaves us our eyes. We can always find somethin' to make us happy in this world, providin' we have a cheerful spirit an' a hopeful disposition, which I thank Him for to-day. An' I never knowed how much I really had to enjoy in this quiet valley in the mountains till I'd been away from it so long. An' there's no danger in life of me ever spendin' the *summers* away from my dear old home.

MAN is a sort of tree which we are too apt to judge of by the bark.

SUPPOSED CHARMS AGAINST EVIL. — Amongst other charms against evil may be named that of our ancestors, who, when eating eggs, were careful to break the shells, lest the witches should use them to their disadvantage. We do the same for a similar reason; it is accounted unlucky to leave them whole. They avoided cutting their nails on Friday, because bad luck would follow; but we have improved upon their practice, and lay down the whole theory as follows:—

"Cut your nails on Monday, cut them for news;
Cut them on Tuesday, a new pair of shoes;
Cut them on Wednesday, cut them for health;
Cut them on Thursday, cut them for wealth;
Cut them on Friday, cut them for woe;
Cut them on Saturday, a journey you'll go;
Cut them on Sunday, you'll cut them for evil,
For all the next week you'll be ruled by the devil."

Most grandmothers will exclaim "God bless you!" when they hear a child sneeze, and they sum up the philosophy of the subject with the following lines, which used to delight the writer in days of his childhood:—

"Sneeze on a Monday, you sneeze for danger;
Sneeze on a Tuesday, you kiss a stranger;
Sneeze on a Wednesday, you sneeze for a letter;
Sneeze on a Thursday, for something better;
Sneeze on a Friday, you sneeze for sorrow;
Sneeze on a Saturday, your sweetheart to-morrow;
Sneeze on a Sunday, your safety seek,
The devil will have you the whole of the week;"

These lines may be taken either as charms or spells to produce the effect predicted, or as omens of warnings of the results to follow. In most parts of Lancashire it is customary for children to repeat the following invocation every evening on going to bed, after saying the Lord's Prayer and the Apostles' Creed:—

"Matthew, Mark, Luke, and John,
Bless the bed that I lie on;
There are four corners to my bed,
And four angels overspread,
Two at the feet, two at the head.

If any ill thing me betide,
Beneath your wings my body hide,
Matthew, Mark, Luke, and John,
Bless the bed that I lie on. Amen."

Godey's, 1873

A RURAL SCENE IN AUTUMN.

THE WHITE LADY OF THE BERLIN CASTLE.

BY KARL BLIND.

THREE days before the German Emperor recently fell sick, a sentinel declared that he had seen, exactly at midnight, the "White Lady," or Ancestress, pass down the corridors of the Royal Palace. Hence a great deal of awe among superstitious people; for the *Weisse Frau*, or *Ahn-Frau*, of the House of Hohenzollern is reckoned to be a harbinger of death whenever she thus walks through the Castle at the ghostly hour.

Few people have, probably, very clear ideas about the mythic connection of this spectral apparition. Yet the gruesome tale has its root in a creed once common to the forefathers of Englishmen, Germans, and Scandinavians—a creed whose divine figures have, in course of time, been changed into hobgoblins and spukes. This is a fact well known to, and well worked out by, specialists in matters of mythology and folk-lore. All the greater is the pity that among the masses the results of these researches are utterly ignored. And so it now and then happens that some soldier, fresh from the country, and rather green, suddenly mistakes, in his frightened fancy at night, a belated cook in his or her white apron for the terrible Ancestress. Even among some better-educated people, especially among women, the strange superstition is difficult to eradicate. So great is the hold that these ancient forms of faith have on the public mind, until the light is spread by a scientific explanation.

To put the Berlin story at once into its proper connection, it may first be mentioned that the White Lady is by no means peculiar to the Prussian House, but that similar wraiths are from olden times reported to haunt various princely palaces, as well as noblemen's castles, all over Germany. Only a few years since, the *Weisse Frau* was said to have appeared in the Hofburg at Vienna. There was much excitement, lest some sudden case of death, or some terrible event, should happen in the Imperial and Royal House of Habsburg. Inquiries were diligently set on foot; but nothing came of them.

From early youth I remember that in south-western Germany the White Lady was spoken of, in words of affright, as playing a similar part in the ruling house of the Grand-Duchy of Baden. Any one conversant with the pedigree of that royal family will easily understand why there should be a White Lady also in the case of the House of Zähringen. The fact is, in its pedigree there figures a semi-mythic ancestor (Berchtold), whose name at once suggests that of the heathen goddess (Berchta) of whom I shall presently have to speak as the prototype of all the ghostly and castle-haunting Ancestresses. From boyhood I furthermore recollect some amusing stories as to the doings of this White Lady. Once she was personated by a wily schemer at Court, for the purpose of attaining certain political objects, through working upon the poorly cultivated minds of some "exalted personages." Upon this notable occasion, the Woman in White was bodily "collared" at Karlsruhe, when it was found that she was a *man!* This made the ghostly survival look extremely ridiculous, and even punishable at law.

Turning away from such meaner aspects of the legend, the question arises as to how a supernatural lady, clad in white, comes to be a herald of death in so many royal and noble families of Germany. The answer is not far to seek. It is clearly contained in the pre-Christian faith of our forefathers, of which there are even now the most remarkable remnants in the folk-lore, the popular beliefs, and the castle traditions of our country, as well as of other Teutonic nations.

Almost in every case, very few excepted, in which a White Lady is mentioned, she is called Bertha. This noteworthy fact at once points to the great German goddess, Perahta, Perchta, or Berchta (in modern German, Bertha), whose very name means Shining Light, as typified by the white colour. She is the same as the northern Goddess of Love, Freyja (in German Freia, Freia-Holda, or simply Holda), who was equally represented in *white* garments. In a great many tales still current in German folk-lore, she appears, not only as clad in white, her white headgear and robe being moreover covered with a white veil which falls from her golden hair; but also as of snow-white body—a perfect Woman in White.

Now this Bertha or Freia-Holda, besides being a Teutonic Venus, was also a Goddess of Domestic Virtue, and at the same time a Mother of Life, in whose beautiful gardens the Unborn dwell. As usual with Mothers of Life in mythology, she is, moreover, a Mistress of Death. In the heathen Norse creed we find one-half of the departed assigned to Freyr, for her palace Folkwang, whilst the remnant of the dead went up to Walhall, to be with Odin; or to Thrudheim, where the God of Thunder resided; or to

Alfheim, which was the heavenly palace of Freyr, the God of Peace, Love, and Fertility, and brother of Freyja; or to Gefion, who received those that died unmarried. Thus we see in Freyja a white-robed deity in her double quality of a progenitress or ancestress, and of a ruler of the dead. The transition to a similar phantom, haunting castles, is easy.

Actually, Bertha, or Freia, being a Mother of Life, was fabled, in heathen German antiquity, to be the supernatural ancestress of noble and royal families. In Norse myth she bears, of course, as such, the name of Frigg; the original deity in question having, in Scandinavia, branched off into two figures: Freyja (the Love-Goddess and consort of Odur), and Frigg (the consort of Odin); whilst in Germany, Freia-Fricka has remained one and the same. Kingly races, it need not be said, have grown out of aristocratic ones. For the sake of better impressing and governing the crowd, they always appear, in the dawn of history, as being of heavenly descent. Anglo-Saxon, Norwegian, Danish, German princely families trace their origin to " Woden, whom we call Oden." So the Norse Royal Genealogy (Langfedgatal) has it. This Woden or Oden, it is true, if we look closely at the Icelandic " Heims-Kringla " record, is a semi-historical army leader who, from his kingdom near the Black Sea where he was said to have had a fortress called Asgard, went forth through Gardariki (Russia) and Saxony (Germany) for the conquest of Scandinavia. But the image of this semi-mythic, semi-historical Odin is somewhat confused in the northern tale with the god of the same name.

Be that as it may, there can be no doubt of a great many " Berthas " occurring in the ancestral legends of Teutonic ruling families. Almost invariably these progenitresses are of a mythic character. Bertha was said to have been the name of the mother of " Charlemagne," as the French call him, though the Frankish emperor, Karl the Great, was a full-blooded Teuton, careful of his German speech, and usually dressed in his national Frankish garb. The Bertha who is alleged to have been his mother, belongs not, however, to history, but to the circle of myths of pre-Christian times.

A stag (so the tale runs) led Pipin, the father of Karl the Great, to a forest glade where Bertha had found an asylum, after her would-be murderers had regarded her as dead. In an old French record she is curtly and most ungallantly described as *Berthe as grand piès*—that is, Bertha the large-footed. The expression corresponds with the old German *Berhte mit dem fuoze—i.e.*, " Bertha with the foot." This large foot of the legendary eldermother of the House of the Carolingians, or Kerlings, was represented in sculptures of old French (Frankish) and Burgundian churches as a swan's foot —or rather as a goose-foot! The queen in question is therefore called *Reine aux pieds d'oison*; clearly not a human being, but a fairy-form belonging to mythology.

But why a goose-foot, or a swan's foot? Here, again, the explanation is to be found in the " grand and weird creed," as Southey calls it, of our Teutonic forebears. In her earliest form, Freia-Holda-Bertha was figured as a Storm-Goddess, the wife of the Ruler of the Winds and the Clouds, by whom she is chased —even as the cloud is by the wind. Minor cloud-goddesses, or cloud-women, surround her; in some myths they are conceived as swans or mares. They are the swift-running, fast-sailing cloudlets, of sombrer or more silvery hue. Freia-Bertha herself was in this way at first regarded as a Walkyrian Swan-Virgin, or even as a downright Swan.

Later on, when the nature-myth changed into a more human-like representation of deities, nothing remained of the characteristics of the Swan-Virgin, or of the Swan, but the foot. Under a new deterioration of the tale, a goose-foot is substituted for the swan's foot. The goose-foot, again, is afterwards changed into a flat-foot, a large foot—nay, into a club-foot. And so, out of a white-robed Goddess, Freia-Bertha —an Elder-mother of All Life and a Mistress of Death, who originally was a Swan-Virgin—we get Berthas, ancestresses of kings, who are represented as swan-footed, goose-footed, flat-footed, ay, club-footed; as well as White Ladies who are harbingers of death in royal palaces.

It is a peculiarity of the tales referring to the divine circle among all nations, that certain heavenly figures show double qualities apparently opposed to each other. Apollo is a dispenser of bliss and fertility, as well as a far-hitting bringer of death. Under a southern sky, this twofold conception of a Sun-God can be easily understood. Hel,* the Norse Mistress of the Underworld, who hides the dead, is at the same time a secretly-working Mother of Life. This, again, explains itself from the fertilising character of the lower regions of the Earth or Underworld. In the Edda, Hel is half black and half of the colour of human flesh. Death and Life are combined in her. This, so to say, Darwinian, but also old Greek and old Hindoo, notion of the incessant changes wrought in all things, was thus symbolised by a divine figure among the Germanic nations. So also we meet with, in Frankonian and Swabian tales, a Hilda-Bertha, in whose name Darkness and Light, Death and Life, are united. The same quality pertains to Bertha, the Ancestress and the Messenger of Death.

In the legends of German castles, the White Woman, or Ancestress, sometimes carries a heavy, tapping walking-stick. Her ghostly approach is thus heard from afar. This characteristic, too, is explainable from an attribute of the goddess on whose type the spectral apparition in question had been moulded. As a representative, not only of amorousness but also of housewifely accomplishments, Perchta, or Bertha, was figured with a distaff. She is in this, as well as in some other respects, like the Trojan Athene, of whom we hear a great deal that is new and highly interesting, in the works of that indefatigable explorer, Dr. Schliemann, who, in addition to his previous matchless labours, has a few months ago made a fresh

* In English dialectic speech, " to *hele* " means, even now, to conceal, or to hide.

wonderful discovery of a vast pre-historic palace at Tiryns, in the Peloponnese.

The distaff of the former German goddess Perchta still plays its part in current folk-tales. About Twelfth-night—it was once believed, and it is believed even now in some dark nooks and corners where superstition lingers—a fairy, called Freia or Berchta, visits the households, looking after the industry of the maidens at the spinning-wheel. No wonder, "Bertha with the Distaff" is the name of that mythic mother of Karl the Great ; her image having been evolved out of the ancient Teutonic creed rather than out of historical fact. In the usual course of the deterioration of tales, the distaff of Freia-Bertha, the White Goddess, has degenerated into a heavy staff carried by a spectral white woman.

It will thus be seen that the phantom whose apparition, in German castles, is said to portend the death of some member of the family, or some other tragic occurrence, is none else than the fabulous Ancestress of the heathen faith, who either calls back her descendants to the region she herself inhabits, or wishes to give them important warning. As usual in such legends, they become, after awhile, loaded with all kinds of extraneous historical matter. For instance, in the story of the lordly family of Neuhaus and Rosenberg, the Ancestress—whose name, of course, is Bertha—is said to have built the Castle of Neuhaus in the fifteenth century ; promising the workmen, if they got things all right, a festive treat, which is even now annually given to the poor, in her remembrance, on Maundy Thursday. This festive treat, however, consists exactly of the viands which once were sacred to the goddess Berchta, and which are still eaten, in some parts of Germany, at Twelfth-night, or Twelfth-day—which is there called *Berchtentag*, or Berchta's Day !

In the same way we find at Oxford University, even now, a Boar's Head Dinner, the origin of which is explained from an alleged adventure a student had with a wild boar in the forest of Shotover ; whereas the Boar's Head Dinner was in reality once a religious ceremonial feast among all Teutonic races—Anglo-Saxon, German, and Norse—in honour of Freyr (the brother of this very Freyja-Berchta), whose sacred animal was the golden-bristled, swift-running boar, representing the sun in his career over the sky.

If the scientific treatment of these tales—which under a cover of ghastliness have sometimes traits of considerable charm—were popularised and brought home to the understanding of the masses, superstitions would soon vanish and nocturnal scares become impossible. Nothing would then remain of them but the poetic enjoyment of their contents ; and White Ladies at Berlin, Vienna, or in noblemen's ancestral mansions, would cease to trouble a frightened fancy.

HOME MANAGEMENT MONTH BY MONTH.

OCTOBER.

" Then came the autumn, all in yellow clad
As though he joyed in his plenteous store."

———

YES, the summer has gone once more and autumn is with us, and it behoves us to, in some measure, prepare for the winter which is almost at our doors, and preserve some of autumn's "plenteous store." So in this letter I will give you some hints on preserving autumn fruits in their raw state, and also some recipes for jams and jellies.

STORING APPLES, PEARS AND ONIONS.

In setting aside fruit or vegetables for storing, it is best to make two selections, first choosing all the perfectly sound and not over-ripe fruit, and discarding (for storing purposes) any which may be the least damaged, and then, from these choosing the larger fruits and putting them by themselves, and reserving the smaller fruits for earlier consumption.

Of course, in the case of apples and pears the fruit for eating should be kept separate from the fruit for cooking.

In storing apples, it is better if possible to put them in a dry loft or outhouse, they make a house smell very strongly if kept in one of the rooms.

The loft should be dry, and should have a good current of air through it.

Some rough shelves may be made, a few feet from the floor along the wall, composed of pieces of lath one or two inches apart. This allows a free passage of air. Over the laths put a thin covering of straw, being careful that the straw is quite dry and fresh, otherwise it will give a musty taste to the fruit.

Many people store their fruit in hay, but I much prefer straw, as, being coarser, it allows a freer circulation of air, and also hay is liable to impart a slight taste to delicately flavoured fruit.

The apples should be laid on the straw, not touching one another, and they should be looked over from time to time, in order that any fruit which is over-ripe or rotten, may be removed.

Pears and quinces may be treated in exactly the same way, and I recommend that quinces should be kept quite separate from other fruit on account of their strong smell and flavour.

Onions should be tied by the stalks into long strings and hung in a dry place, or they may be hung up in nets (a piece of old garden netting answers the purpose very well).

Onions should not be placed on the floor, or in a dark place, the least moisture or lying in a damp dark place, where the air cannot penetrate, will either make them begin to sprout, or they will become soft and unfit for use.

They should be looked over occasionally, and those which show signs of sprouting or decay should be used first.

Onions are one of our most useful vegetables, and there are so many ways of utilising them that they repay any small amount of trouble we may take in storing them for use during the winter.

As October is a time when any apples, except those

which will keep through the winter, should be used up, and also as many fall to the ground and become bruised and unfit to store during the process of pickling them, I will give you a good recipe for apple chutney, and one also for apple jelly and apple jam.

Apples contain a large percentage of malic acid, and they are considered to be both purifying to the blood, and beneficial in many ways, therefore, preserves composed of apples are useful for those who are unable to take the fruit in its raw state. Here is a simple recipe for

APPLE JAM.

Three pounds of apples, two pounds and a quarter of sugar, a few cloves or a small piece of lemon rind to flavour according to taste.

This is the method: Wipe the apples clean (but do not peel them), and cut them into quarters. Put the apples, the sugar and the flavouring of lemon or cloves into an earthenware jar and cover the jar down closely. Then place the jar containing the apples into a saucepan of hot water over the fire. The water in the saucepan must only come three parts up the jar, and must be replenished with boiling water as it evaporates. When the apples are quite tender (which they should be in about three-quarters of an hour), rub them through a wire sieve to get rid of the peel and core, and also to render the pulp smooth. Then turn the apple pulp into a preserving-pan and boil it quickly for twenty minutes, stirring well during the cooking to prevent it from burning. Put the jam into dry warm jars, and cover down in the usual way.

N.B.—The reason I cook the apples without peeling them in making the jam, is that most of the mineral salts, both in fruit and vegetables, lie close to the skin and are lost if the fruit is peeled. Also by cooking the skin of the apples the jam attains a richer colour.

APPLE JELLY.

For this recipe it is necessary to select the most juicy fruit you can obtain. The close, dry, crisp apples which keep well into the winter are not suitable for converting into jelly. For the jelly, take ten pounds of juicy sweet apples, half a pint of cold water, loaf sugar, and six cloves.

This is the way to make it: Wipe the apples clean and cut them into slices. Place the sliced apples into an earthenware jar, pour the water over them, and cover the jar closely down. Now put the jar into a very moderate oven, and allow the apples to cook gently until they are reduced to a pulp. When the apples are quite tender, pour the pulp into a clean jelly bag, and strain the juice into a basin. To every pint of juice thus obtained, allow three quarters of a pound of loaf sugar, which must be broken up but not powdered. Place the juice, the sugar, and the cloves in a preserving-pan and boil all together quickly, until it will jelly in a few moments if a spoonful is put on to a cold plate. A quarter of an hour to twenty minutes should be long enough. The jelly must be kept well skimmed the whole time, and it should be stirred occasionally to prevent it from burning. Remove the cloves and put the jelly into dry, warm glass jars. Allow the jelly to get cold and then cover the jars down.

N.B.—This jelly may be put into moulds and stored, and makes a most delicious dinner sweet, served with custard or whipped cream.

APPLE CHUTNEY (a good home-made pickle).

Five pounds of apples, one pound and a half of moist sugar, one pound of salt, half a pound of mustard seed, two quarts of vinegar, a quarter of a pound of ground ginger, half a teaspoonful of cayenne pepper, one pound and a half of onions, one pound of raisins.

These are the ingredients we shall require for eight or nine pounds of chutney, and as with care it will keep for years, it may not be too large a quantity to make at a time, but if a smaller quantity is required, all the ingredients may be divided except the vinegar, but of that I should take rather more than half, on account of the quicker evaporation of liquid in cooking small quantities.

This is how we will proceed to make it:—Peel, core, and cut up the apples; place the vinegar in an earthenware-lined saucepan; add the apples to the vinegar, and boil both together till the apples are quite tender. Bruise the mustard seed and put it in a small basin; pour sufficient cold vinegar over it to just cover it, and allow it to soak for half an hour. Chop the onions finely; stone and chop the raisins. When the apples are quite tender, add to them all the other ingredients and boil the whole for one hour. The mixture must be stirred frequently to prevent it from burning, which it is liable to do when the moisture has evaporated. Put the chutney away in glass jars or wide-mouthed bottles. Tie the jars down securely, and store the chutney in a dry place.

I was surprised last summer to learn how few people know anything about quinces, and how to preserve them. And fewer still seem to have any idea what a delicious preserve they make. So I determined to bring this rather neglected fruit before the notice of my readers in my letter for October, and am giving two recipes for preserving them which will be found most satisfactory. But before I give the recipes, I must give my readers one or two hints about quinces.

Never pick quinces either for storing or preserving when they are wet. Be careful that the fruit is not over-ripe. And lastly, in making any kind of preserve of quinces always cook the fruit first without any sugar, if you add sugar to the fruit when it is raw, the fruit will harden, and no amount of cooking afterwards will render it tender.

And with this preface on the best manner of picking and cooking the fruit, I will proceed to give you an excellent recipe for

QUINCE MARMALADE.

Take equal quantities of fruit and sugar; peel and core the quinces and cut them into thin slices across the fruit, thus forming rings. Place the fruit in an earthenware jar and allow to each three pounds of fruit three-quarters of a pint of cold water; pour the water over the fruit in the jar; cover the jar tightly over and place it in a moderate oven. Cook the contents in this manner until the fruit is quite tender, but not broken. Now make a syrup to the proportion of one quart of water to four pounds of sugar; add six cloves to the syrup, and boil it for a quarter of an hour, keeping it well skimmed as it boils. Now add the cooked quince to the syrup, and allow all to boil together for twenty minutes. Allow the marmalade thus made to cool a little, then place it in warm dry pots. The next day cover the pots down in the usual way and store in a dry place.

A friend of mine had some pears which were so hard and tasteless that every year they were left to rot on the tree as being worthless. It seemed a pity that they should be wasted, so I made some marmalade of them by this recipe, but as the pears were wanting in flavour, I added half an ounce of root ginger bruised, and the juice and rind of one lemon to every three pounds of fruit, and the result was most delicious, and now my friend uses up all her hard pears in this way.

Medlars make a most delicious preserve, but I think they are often wasted because people do not know how to preserve them, so I will close my letter by giving an old and well-tried recipe for

MEDLAR JELLY.

Wash the medlars till they are quite clean, then put them into a preserving pan and cover them with cold spring water. Place the preserving pan on the fire and allow the contents to cook until the medlars are reduced to a pulp; now place the pulp into a jelly bag and strain the juice into a clean basin. The jelly bag may be slightly squeezed if the juice takes long to drip. To every pint of juice thus obtained allow three-quarters of a pound of preserving sugar. Place the juice and sugar together into a preserving pan and allow the contents to boil quickly for about twenty minutes. The jelly must be kept well skimmed while it is being boiled. Try a teaspoonful of jelly on a cold plate at the end of twenty minutes' boiling, and if it becomes firm in a minute or two it is sufficiently cooked. Put the jelly into dry warm pots and cover down.

MARY SKENE.

ARTISTIC BEAD-THREADING.

THE fashion that has arisen for bead-stringing has given girls possessed of taste an opportunity of obtaining, at a very small cost, one of the most beautiful objects of personal adornment within their reach—a necklace. Beads are (or may be) among the most fascinating of human productions, and, so far as æsthetic worth goes, run gems very close indeed. Beads are, in fact, artificial gems, and the love of beads may be looked upon as a primeval instinct, for the manufacture of beads takes us back a very long way in the world's history. A young fellow of my acquaintance, who volunteered for the

in the best Venetian beads gives the most brilliant and striking effects, the translucent glass enclosing the metal yielding lovely iridescent colours.

The sketches accompanying these notes will give the reader some idea of the makes and shapes of beads, but alas, the colour, which is their greatest charm, cannot even be hinted at. I have, however written in the colours, so that readers can gain an idea of the various colour-schemes, for it is here, in the combining of colours, that successful bead-stringing is shown. It is by no means easy out of a box of

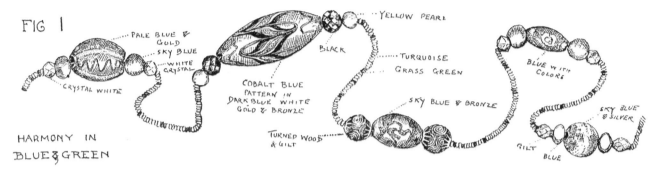

FIG 1

PALE BLUE & GOLD
SKY BLUE
WHITE CRYSTAL
CRYSTAL WHITE
COBALT BLUE PATTERN IN DARK BLUE WHITE GOLD & BRONZE
TURNED WOOD & GILT
YELLOW PEARL
BLACK
TURQUOISE
GRASS GREEN
SKY BLUE & BRONZE
BLUE WITH COLORS
SKY BLUE & SILVER
GILT
BLUE

HARMONY IN BLUE & GREEN

war in South Africa, brought back with him some articles made of beads strung by the Basuto women from whom he purchased them. He tells me that bead-threading is one of the chief amusements of their leisure hours; that they use no needle, yet produce most ornate and complicated effects, showing great executive skill and considerable taste in combining and arranging the various colours. As it may interest my readers to get an idea of these Basuto bead ornaments, I have sketched portions of three necklets. The beads used are the ordinary common glass ones, mostly opaque, which children are fond of threading. Had these

miscellaneous beads to arrange an effective and harmonious necklace. Of course, a girl about to thread a necklace, and who had to buy the beads expressly for the purpose, would naturally select her beads on some well-considered plan, i.e., she would have some colour-scheme in her mind and choose her beads accordingly. I shall direct the reader's attention to the question of colour-schemes in the notes accompanying each illustration, but I may say as a generalisation that a certain tone of colour should predominate in strung beads. We can have a blue, white, yellow, golden brown or other scheme, and yet introduce contrasting colours sparingly so

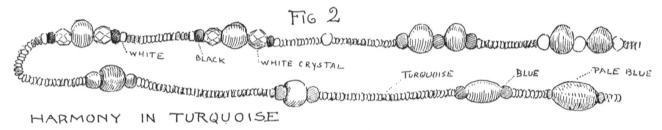

FIG 2

WHITE
BLACK
WHITE CRYSTAL
TURQUOISE
BLUE
PALE BLUE

HARMONY IN TURQUOISE

Basuto women the very beautiful Venetian beads to use, which are obtainable in London, they would doubtless produce some striking and original effects.

Their bead-work, as may be estimated from the sketches, are often elaborate arrangements and show considerable ingenuity in the way they link them together.

In obtaining the best results with beads two things are indispensable—pretty beads and a pretty taste. As regards the beads, there is an enormous selection to choose from at any shop where beads are a speciality. The colours are most varied and gem-like, and the use of gold and silver foil

as not to upset the harmony; but the general effect of the necklace must produce a oneness, i.e., golden brown, blue, etc., and not a mere jumble of opposing colours.

An important point to be observed in bead-threading is the spacing of the principle beads, for the best effects, it seems to me, produced are those in which large beads, or at all events more important beads, occur at regular intervals. It is customary to produce the effect by repetition, i.e., beads of the same shape, size and colour recurring at regular intervals, as in Fig. 5, but a very good effect can be secured by stringing beads of various shapes, provided the spaces

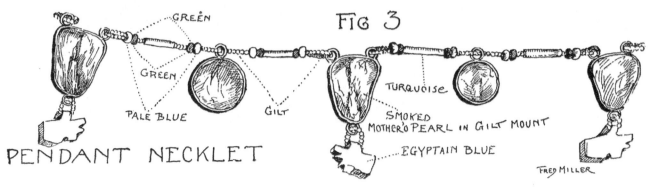

FIG 3

GREEN
GREEN
PALE BLUE
GILT
TURQUOISE
SMOKED MOTHER'O PEARL IN GILT MOUNT
EGYPTAIN BLUE

PENDANT NECKLET

FRED MILLER

between are, to a great extent, repetitions of each other, and that the important beads are arranged so as to balance one another. Such an arrangement is seen in Fig. 4, which is part of a necklace composed of various-shaped beads which I obtained as samples of the various makes that are to be purchased.

It is customary, as it certainly is effective, to have a pendant attached to the necklace to form a sort of centre. It may be a sort of tassel, as in Fig. 4; a large beautifully-coloured bead, as the large oval one in Fig. 1; a copy of an antique, as in Fig. 5; a piece of mother-of-pearl in an ormolu setting with a porcelain pendant, as in Fig. 3.

Beads are sold in strings and vary greatly in price according to size and make. The large Venetian beads vary from a penny to sixpence each. The small beads,

Fig. 1 is a portion of a chain composed of handsome Venetian beads with small turquoise ones, with an occasional green bead forming the intervals. Thus a harmony in blues is secured, and yet yellow and black beads are used as *blocks* to the large centre bead, with white crystal ones in other cases in conjunction with sky blue ones. The box-wood turned beads were some old ones that the threader had by her, and, being of a golden brown colour with gilt shields harmonised very well with the prevailing tone of blue. Gold, except in some of the large beads, is kept out of this scheme.

Fig. 2 was strung for a little girl and was kept entirely in blues—turquoise, sky blue and sparrow-egg blue. The black and crystal beads were introduced as a centre, but could be left out if desirable.

Fig. 3 is based upon the ancient Greek method of

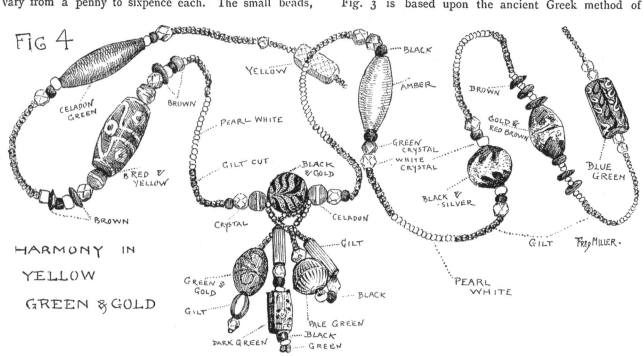

FIG 4

CELADON GREEN — BROWN — YELLOW — BLACK — AMBER — BROWN

PEARL WHITE — GREEN CRYSTAL WHITE CRYSTAL — GOLD & RED BROWN

B RED & YELLOW — GILT CUT — BLACK & GOLD — BLUE GREEN

BROWN — CRYSTAL — CELADON — BLACK & SILVER

GILT — GILT — FRED MILLER.

HARMONY IN YELLOW GREEN & GOLD

GREEN & GOLD — GILT — BLACK — PEARL WHITE

DARK GREEN — PALE GREEN — BLACK — GREEN

even the gilt ones, are quite cheap, so that the beads for a really nice necklace could be purchased for five shillings, including dentist's silk for threading them with. This silk should be employed double and well waxed before it is used.

The holes through the large beads are large enough to allow of the small beads passing through them, so that the threader must be careful to have a *block* bead against the large ones to prevent this happening. Some bead threaders use gut. This is strong and does very well.

Double, triple and quadruple necklets are very effective. They can be produced by simply winding a long chain so many times round the neck, but there is this disadvantage, that the hoops tighten round the neck after a little time of wearing. By having a watch catch and a ring (see Fig. 7) each necklet keeps its place.

forming a necklet by having a series of pendants strung on a chain. Mother-of-pearl is by its iridescence very beautiful and harmonises in a blue scheme. These pendants of various shapes set in ormolu can be purchased where beads are obtainable.

Fig. 4 was made practically out of a number of sample beads, and the difficulty here was to give a sense of harmony and unity to the whole. My chief object in sketching this is to let the reader see the many shapes and makes of beads which are obtainable. The brown flat beads are really seeds taken off a Basuto necklace. These dark brown beads gave a certain "barbaric" quality to the scheme which was helpful. Black beads were also introduced to the same end. The general tone of colour of this necklace is a rich golden brown.

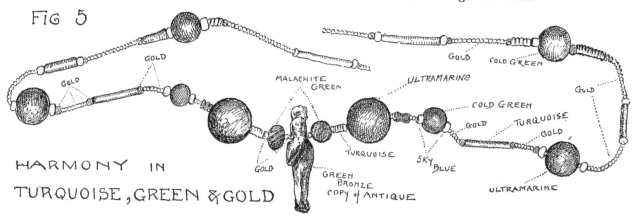

FIG 5

GOLD — GOLD — COLD GREEN

GOLD — MALACHITE GREEN — ULTRAMARINE — COLD GREEN — GOLD

GOLD — TURQUOISE — GOLD

SKY BLUE — GOLD

HARMONY IN TURQUOISE, GREEN & GOLD

GOLD — TURQUOISE — GREEN BRONZE COPY OF ANTIQUE — ULTRAMARINE

Fig. 5 was strung by Miss Pocock, who has gained some distinction for this work. The blues, turquoise and green, with the small gilt beads as a filling, yield a most harmonious result, and evince a very nice taste and discrimination on the part of the threader. Personally I am particularly fond of all shades of blue and turquoise in beads, and the latter in this necklet are imitations of ancient Egyptian beads. The green beads are between *terre verte* and cobalt green. The beads varied very much in tint and gave the chain a very beautiful appearance.

This variation in the tint of beads yields a far more beautiful result than if the beads were uniform in tint. In this scheme every tone of blue could be seen, and yet, viewed as a whole, one only saw a beautiful harmony in blues.

Fig. 6 shows how a triple necklace could be arranged. The inner chain might be composed of round beads, the middle of oval, with small round ones at intervals, and the outside of square and oblong ones, but the chains should be in harmony as to colour, *i.e.*, all of them should be affiliated in tone, and not one blue, one yellow, and one some other colour.

Many girls will find old beads lying by in drawers. Those boxwood beads in Fig. 1 are some very old ones, yet they come in well. Shells and pieces of coral can be introduced into a scheme with excellent effect.

FRED MILLER.

FIG 7

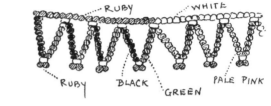

BASUTO WORK

RUBY — WHITE
RUBY — BLACK — GREEN — PALE PINK

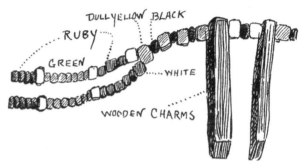

DULL YELLOW BLACK
RUBY
GREEN
WHITE
WOODEN CHARMS

FIG 6

F.M

TRIPLE NECKLACE

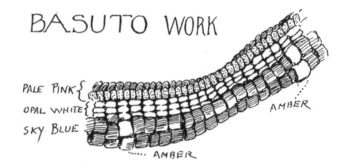

BASUTO WORK

PALE PINK
OPAL WHITE
SKY BLUE
AMBER
AMBER

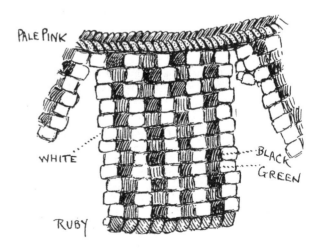

PALE PINK
WHITE
BLACK
GREEN
RUBY

And that his place for evermore,
  Undoubtedly and clear,
Was mainly back *behind* the door—
  Poor humble Brother Spear!

TRUE TO BROTHER SPEAR.

BY WILL CARLETON.

I.

I can't decide why Brother Spear
  Was never joined to me:
It wasn't because the good old Dear
  Hadn't every chance to be;
If Poetry remarked one time
  That Womanhood is true,
It's more than probable that I'm
  The one it had in view;
For, search the city low and high,
  And no one will you hear
To say or hint but what that I
  Was true to Brother Spear.

II.

I mothered all his daughters when
  Their mother's life cut short,
Although they didn't—now or then—
  So much as thank me for't;
I laughed—though scorched with inside rage—
  And said I didn't care,
When his young son, of spank'ble age,
  Removed my surplus hair;
I called and called and called there; why
  He ne'er was in seemed queer:
The house-maid even owned that I
  Was true to Brother Spear.

III.

I hired a sitting in the church
  Near him, but cornerwise,
So his emotions I could search
  With my devoted eyes;
And when the sermon used to play
  On love, divine and free,
I nodded him, as if to say,
  "He's hitting you and me!"
He went and took another pew—
  Of "thousand tongues" in fear;
But what sin was it to be true
  To good old Brother Spear?

IV.

Poor man! I recollect he spoke,
  One large prayer-meeting night,
And told how smallish we all look
  In Heaven's majestic sight:
He said, Not worthy he had been—
  By conscience e'er abhorred—
To be a door-keeper within
  The temple of the Lord;

V.

And then *I* rose, and made a speech,
  Brimful of soul-distress,
And told them how words could not reach
  My own unworthiness;
How orphanage I tried to soothe,
  And cheerless widowerhood;
But in the Lord's great house, in truth,
  I too felt far from good,
And that my trembling heart and mind
  Compelled it to appear
That my place henceforth was behind
  The door, with Brother Spear.

VI.

Poor man! he ne'er again, they say,
  Was heard to strongly speak;
He took down ill that very day,
  And died within a week.
But one prayer oft they heard him give—
  That when his days were o'er,
I still upon this earth might live
  A thousand years or more.
As his betrothed I figure now,
  And shed the frequent tear;
And all his relatives will vow
  I'm true to Brother Spear.

CATS AND KITTENS; OR, "IN DEFENCE OF THE CAT."

By J. E. PANTON.

Illustrated by LOUIS WAIN.

IT is impossible to believe that those who so ruthlessly condemn the "harmless, necessary cat," and as ruthlessly demand its extirpation, or at least its taxation, can have ever studied the fascinating animal, or have even attempted to treat her with the kindly respect and warm affection that are the sole means of developing those valuable characteristics which make a cat a real companion, and which are never formed at all in the unfortunate specimen of the race who all too often spends an uneventful life of catching uncongenial mice in an equally uncongenial London kitchen.

It has been stated over and over again that a cat is not for one moment to be compared to the more intelligent, affectionate, and reasoning dog; that she (it is always she—please to remember that) is a time-server, has no real love for anything save her own comfort; that she is utterly selfish, never answers to her name, and that above all she is most uninteresting and stupid; and that except for mousing purposes she had better be extinct at once, for she is entirely untrustworthy, and as useless to the world at large as she is disturbing and destructive to gardens; and to the nocturnal rest of any who may be unhappy enough to have to sleep near a colony of cats who meet beneath the light of the moon, and discuss—not always in the very sweetest voices possible—the matters of state in cat-land, and make love, fight, argue, and no doubt obstruct the course of business, in the present parliamentary fashion prevalent among beings of higher organization than poor Puss is supposed to possess.

But again we venture to state that all this long catalogue of *cons* can be replied to emphatically by as equally a long list of *pros*, and that those cats who are selfish, uninteresting, and unaffectionate, come of a long line of misunderstood ancestors, whose wrongs rankle in their hearts, and have caused their descendants to cease to cultivate virtues which were never comprehended, and which were allowed to languish and die out, under the cold breezes of unappreciation; while we can point triumphantly to a score of examples on the other side, which will, we trust, prove conclusively, that a cat who is properly treated, spoken to kindly, called by its own name, and has its senses cultivated by an appreciative owner, not only becomes in every whit as companionable as a dog, but in her turn bears progeny that are in advance of their parents, and bid fair in time to develop qualities that have been denied the race for generations.

In the first place, who ever expected a dog to come at call, if the mere word "dog"—even softened to "doggie"—represented its patronymic? Why, the veriest cur in the kingdom would resent the rudeness, and would refuse to follow any one who denied him his orthodox cognomen; and yet stately Angora, beautiful Chinchilla, aristocratic Persian, noble Siamese, common or garden tabby and tortoiseshell alike, are all expected to know immediately that she and she alone is required when any member of the family calls "Puss," and is called idiotic if she merely pricks her ears and stretches herself again to sleep, refusing to believe that she only can be meant by such a universal title. And on the other hand, who ever talks to the cat as the dog is invariably talked to by his master? Is he not consulted on the subject of his walks, taught to know his way about, to understand friends from foes, encouraged to show his feelings, and be, in fact, a happy, natural creature? while Puss is left curled up in her chair or on the rug, and though stroked and sometimes kissed is never really spoken to or consulted, or taught in any way to use her faculties, or to spend her life in anything save sleep, and an occasional stalk after a mouse, or a harmless bird; which she is as often as not punished for killing, regardless of the fact that she has only followed out entirely the instincts born in her, and which have been neither softened nor subdued by a course of education; such as teaching a setter or a pointer

PERSIAN AND LONG-HAIRED ENGLISH TABBY KITTENS.

to bring the game unharmed in his mouth to his master; and that causes him to subdue his inborn destructive faculties, and makes him simply obedient and quite trustworthy even during this most tempting opportunity of doing as he likes.

It is obvious that the present lowly state of the domestic cat is the outcome of the fact that the race has become so numerous as to be no longer valuable; for in the bygone ages not only were they appreciated properly in Egypt, where, as all the world knows, temples were erected to their honour and they were treated with reverence and affection, but in the time of one of the old Princes of Wales, who died in 948, says the nameless author of *Recreation in Natural History*, which is dedicated to "the ingenious YOUTH desirous of obtaining knowledge on the most important subjects," cats were of considerable value: the price of a kitten before it could see was fixed at a penny; till proof could be given of its having caught a mouse, at twopence; after which it was rated at fourpence—a very considerable sum in days when money was so scarce; while, as a farther proof of the estimation in which cats were then held, the author goes on to relate that a law was made by the same prince, who rejoiced in the name of Hoel Dha, or Howel the Good, which declared that if any one should steal or kill the cat which guarded the prince's granary the offender was to forfeit either a milch-ewe, her fleece, and lamb; or as much corn as, when poured on the cat, suspended by the tail, the head touching the floor, would form a heap high enough to cover the extreme tip of its tail: though whether this punishment was inflicted on the stealer of the prince's cat alone, the historian does not think it necessary to state.

The Mohammedans were equally attached to the cat; obviously because of their

Prophet's great love for the animal ; who, as is well known, preferred to cut off the sleeve of his robe to disturbing the sleep of his pet, which had curled herself up comfortably on that voluminous portion of his attire ; and in the time of the Prophet, cats were allowed to enter the mosques and were caressed there as Mohammed's favourite animal ; while the dog that should dare to appear there would pollute the place with his presence, and would be punished with instant death. But as time went on, and cats increased and multiplied, they appear to have gone out of favour, except in the minds of old maids and venerable bachelors, who have always been fond of them, and have, no doubt, had more time than the generality of folks, to study their amiable characteristics and learn what delightful companions they can be when properly treated and really understood ; and who thoroughly appreciate the soft, warm, purring creatures who are never dirty, never rough, and who are always willing to be stroked and petted in the soothing manner, that in some mysterious way is transmitted from the stroked to the stroker ;

SHORT-HAIRED BLACK AND WHITE KITTEN "PETER."

and which has often in my own case resulted in bringing rest to an over-worked brain, and sleep to eyelids that had resolutely refused to close before, when Sam, our large black Manx cat, jumped up on the bed, and began his usual process of pressing down the clothes into a comfortable space for himself—a reminiscence, by the way, of the days when his far-distant ancestor, the tiger, used to pad down the high-growing grass in the jungle in order to make himself a lair which should at once be secretive and comfortable—prior to placing himself near enough to be stroked in the even and regular manner which pleases him best, and which as invariably sends us both to sleep in an equally speedy manner.

But we began this article especially that we might write about kittens, and at present have not said one word about these darlings, blessed with whose presence no house can possibly be dull, no one can be without material for constant and hearty laughter, and the veriest cat-hater—the individual who from lack of training in his or her youth, declares he or she cannot live in the house with a cat, and who "shoos" them remorselessly the moment they appear on the scene—has been known to declare that, given a kitten which would always remain in the kitten-stage, the antipathy would no longer exist, and affection instead of detestation would be given to the delightful little creatures.

Who, for example, could resist the fascinations of the two charming aristocratic kittens in the first sketch before us ? The white Persian puss is looking half-asleep, and the long-haired English tabby (which species has the most perfect of all faces, surrounded by a soft fluffy gray ruff) is pretending not to see his companion ; but in a moment the soft paw will be extended, the white paw will stretch out to give an inquiring or tentative pat, and in a second the two kittens will be scampering hither and thither, up and down the curtains, in and out of the chairs ; one will hang on the seat, and tap the tail of the one on the floor, and finally they will both indulge in a regular game of hide-and-seek, copying the graceful movements, and often enough the absolute tactics, of a couple of children employed in the same game ; until the spectator, exhausted with laughter and anxious for peace, catches up the miscreants, and either soothes them to sleep, or turns them bodily out of the room to resume their antics on the stairs, where presently they may be heard tearing up and down, and making as much noise as a small regiment of soldiers.

The white Persian is rather a risky subject, as a rule, for one to give one's affections to. She is delicate, highly organized, and requires immense and constant care, and is not, in our opinion, capable of so much culture as the less aristocratic long-haired tabby. She is given to softer living and has few ambitions, and being quite content with a warm corner by a fire, does not discriminate as finely between old and new friends as does a kitten whose pedigree is shorter and whose intellect is quicker and more capable of being cultivated. Out of the several Persian kittens we have possessed none have ever really grown up, or lived more than a couple of years; we have kept them daintily and warmly, we have watched them carefully, and had what servants call "the best of advice" for them, but they have never rewarded our care by living to a respectable old age; and we have therefore come to the conclusion that we shall not attempt to keep them any more; for no sooner have we become attached to them than they develop some complaint, and either dwindle away to a small, miserable heap of

TORTOISESHELL, SIAMESE, AND RED TABBY KITTENS.

dingy fur, or die quite suddenly in the most heart-breaking manner. The long-haired English kittens are, in our opinion, quite as pretty, and certainly live much longer; their only faults being that they are virulent poachers and night disturbers—two faults which must be legislated for very young, for, if cats are properly brought up, they never wander about at night, but come home with a regularity, at exactly the same time, that is really astonishing: one old cat, for example, a regular short-haired tabby, which we possess, and which is the fourth of his generation we have brought up—his great-great-grandmother having been given to us by "Idstone" of the *Field*—always presenting himself at one of our windows just before ten o'clock every night, when he jumps in, makes his way to the kitchen, and at once curls himself up on his own chair, where he sleeps most comfortably until the maids open the down stairs windows, when out he jumps and takes his "constitutional" until he knows it is breakfast-time, when he comes in at once, and demands with a curious open mouth (for he is absolutely dumb, and has never mewed in his life) his ordinary saucer of milk. Now Max began by being a regular chicken-slayer and night-wanderer, but being punished severely and managed judiciously has overcome both faults; and no doubt all evilly-disposed cats can be managed in the same way if only trouble is taken with them in the matter in very early youth. Of course among cats there are not the numerous differences in breed and race that there are among dogs, and we have no such contrasts as, for example, exist between the St. Bernard and the toy-terrier. Yet that there are great differences no one can deny; the face of Peter, the short-haired, black and white kitten on page 35 , being entirely different from either of the fluffy pets in the first sketch. He is square, and sturdier, has far more character, even if he possesses less refinement and beauty, and could be taught far more than either of the lovely ladies whose fur seems to absorb so much of their time and intellect, and who would be likely to grow up far more selfish members of society than such as Peter, whose appearance is not so perfect, but whose qualities would be appreciated by any real cat-lover a thousand times more than the mere good looks of the couple of beauties, who would, we feel convinced, utterly refuse to have anything to say to him. And yet it was just such a sturdy cat as this of whom we must stop to tell an anecdote which is absolutely true, and which happened to one of our oldest friends. She was going home through the snow one wretched December night, when she discovered she was being followed by

CHINCHILLA LONG-HAIRED KITTEN.

the most miserable little mewing cat she had ever seen. She carried it home, fed it, made much of it by her fire, and was rewarded for her trouble by seeing him develop into a square-shouldered, broad-browed, black-and-white, short-haired kitten. She kept it for a fortnight, and one day was told the creature had disappeared. She was in despair, and was on the point of offering a reward, when her maid came rushing up to tell her that Frisk had returned in company with a very beautiful gray Chinchilla kitten, which was wearing proudly a broad riband with his name and address on it, worked in gold thread. With a sinking heart Miss S. looked at the two cats and read the address: the new cat looked too polished, too beautiful altogether, to steal, and yet the square where evidently she lived was a good four-mile drive away. Both cats seemed absolutely content, absolutely happy; Frisk purred as never before. Honesty had a severe struggle, but at last it conquered; and putting both cats into a large, soft basket, Miss S. drove off, and discovered that Frisk had absolutely fetched the Chinchilla cat all the way to Miss S.'s house. "The fact is," said the owner, "Frisk, as you call it, is the kitchen cat, and we never take any notice of him, and we never encourage Pearl to do so either. I think he must have been happier and made much more of with you than he was with us, and he must have returned to fetch Pearl. We don't care for him, and you may keep him if you like," and Miss S. departed, taking Frisk with her, who lived to a great age, highly appreciated by all who knew him, albeit he made one more attempt to fetch Pearl, and being discovered with her, was punished severely and kept in a dark closet for twenty-four hours, until Miss S. could send to fetch him. He never went after her again, though he seemed at first to pine for her. She forgot him almost as soon as his back was turned; in fact, her own mistress thought she never forgave him the long wet walk through the streets, finally landing her in a house in a far less aristocratic neighbourhood than her own, and in a far less comfortably-furnished abode than the one she had left. Frisk looked despairingly at her when Miss S. took him in her arms to carry him off, but Pearl was idly biting or smelling at a fuchsia, and bore his departure with great calm!

That cats are cruel is a fact we have perpetually dinned into our ears; they may be, but we maintain stoutly, not more cruel than the dog who chases a hare despite its screams, the hound which runs the fox to earth, or the tiger which slays its thousands. Nature herself is cruel, so is all connected with Nature; and a cat's cruelty is, after all, very mild, and is really caused more by her love of play than from her delight in pain. Sam, one of our cats, will chase bees, butterflies, and moths, the whole of the summer months, and we have never seen him destroy a single specimen of either insect. He will spring feet into the air after a bee, and will strike it with his paw and bring it down unfailingly among the grass; he will stand over it for a moment, give it a pat, and once more knock it down, should it respond to his gentle hint by flying up; but he will then leave it alone and pass on elsewhere, continuing the amusement untiringly for as long as there are any creatures to play with, the greatest amusement being found in the great cockchafers, whose buzzing seems to be taken for a challenge to him ; and it is most entertaining to watch the weird, tailless, Manx creature springing three or four feet into the air in the dusk after the cockchafers, never resting until he has caught one or more of them, releasing them unhurt once he has fairly captured them. But there is no cruelty here, Sam merely wishes to play, just as the three kittens in the sketch wish to play with the tortoise, who does not understand them, and is no doubt wretched—as wretched as a miserable toad the shrieks from which once roused us from our work, and we rushed out, thinking murder was being committed, to discover that Sam was playing in the conservatory with a toad, which did not enter into the spirit of the game at all, and which was yelling with fright ; for

WHITE SHORT-HAIRED KITTENS.

every time it hopped Sam put a black paw on its back, it would then scream, and Sam would remove his paw, only to repeat the same amusement at the next hop : there was no attempt to harm the toad, and evidently the cat's sole ambition was to see it hop, and he took the only steps he knew of to obtain the desired movement.

The Siamese cat is not often seen in an English household, as it too is remarkably delicate, and can hardly ever face a winter. It is of a particularly beautiful soft brown colour, and has black markings singularly like those of a pug. Its fur is shorter and less silky, but makes up in colour what it lacks in any other attraction. Its temper is not quite to be depended on, and though we have never ourselves had any specimens in our care, all our informants agree in confessing that almost any other cat is pleasanter and safer to live with. But we must own to hankering after a specimen, as we have been often and solemnly warned against Manx cats, while our own experience teaches us that it is by far the most affectionate and intelligent of all the cat tribe ; far more teachable and in every respect far more like the dog in its habits and in its capabilities of becoming a real companion. Sam came to us in a hamper by carrier, when he was only about six weeks old, and he certainly was the very funniest creature we had ever seen : his hind-quarters were and are considerably higher than the front legs, he was quite black, though, as in all young cats, the stripes of the tiger were visible in an intense light, and the soft black patch which did duty for a tail was so absurd that he was saluted with a chorus of laughter, which annoyed him intensely, and caused him to retire under a chair, where he remained until forced to emerge from his retreat by the pangs of hunger. He was never a rollicking, idle kitten like the majority of small cats, and has always taken life soberly ; he never ran after an empty reel—he *could* not run after his tail, poor dear!—and his only relaxation consisted in chasing bees, toads, and other creatures, as related before; but he is the only cat of whom we ever heard that nearly pined to death the only time he was ever left alone with the servants, when all the family were away together; the only cat who knows when you are ill, and spends his days on your bed trying his best to comfort you; who knows his name like a dog, and comes running when called, and who is capable of keeping three big dogs in such constant awe—an awe that custom never stales—that they slink away appalled before him, and no more dare eat before him, or share his milk, than they dare steal or poach or bite, or commit any of the ungentlemanly sins so often ascribed to the canine race. When we go away to stay, Sam and Max go too: they never attempt to stray, they never attempt to get lost, they walk solemnly all over the house, then over the garden, and finally each selects a permanent chair, and, to do them both justice, their selection generally speaks volumes for their love of comfort. They have had three complete moves in their time, and have never even in the most uncomfortable moments of those moves given us the least anxiety about their welfare; and we never boarded them out, save once, when Sam ruthlessly turned out the cat of the house, and refused to allow him to enter his own domicile all the time he was there—a course of conduct which resulted in our being obliged to keep him ourselves, in all and every muddle, for he really caused acute misery by his conduct to the small mistress of the banished cat, who could not understand a stranger being cherished and her own pet being relegated to the stable entirely.

Sometimes cats are decidedly cruel. We had one, Wrinkleface by name, who deliberately and actually and with her own paws beat her first kittens to death. She was very young, and she could not understand why she must remain in a basket away from her adored mistress. She kept leaving the squealing little creatures, and at last we shut her up with her family in the tool-house, where later on she was discovered by us with three dead kittens in the basket, and actually banging the head of number four against the wall until the poor little creature was quite dead. The others had been trampled on, and we shall never forget the fiendish way in which she looked first at the corpses and then at us, finally leaping out of the tool-house and coming indoors as if nothing had happened. For months we never petted her or spoke to her, and the lesson went home; she became an admirable mother, although she was not always lucky, for a white terrier, whose ears she had boxed more than once, watched her out into the garden (we saw him do this ourselves), and then, rushing hurriedly down stairs at the top of his speed, he went and killed every one of that litter while the mother was out in the garden; and yet people talk of the noble animal the dog, and have nothing but abuse for the cat. Still there never was, we maintain, a clearer case of a meaner revenge than this! Cats are constitutionally brave, yet are undoubtedly timid: they will keep great dogs at bay, but an unknown object will terrify them almost to death; their fur begins to rise, their backs are arched, their claws come out, they make an admirable show of defence, but at last terror is too much for them, and with a howl of despair they rush wildly up a tree should they be out of doors, or career madly to some place of safety indoors, should they be suddenly confronted with any animal with which they have never made acquaintance before; while perhaps their most curious trait is the utterly inhospitable manner in which they receive a strange member of their own race, for nothing will induce the cat denizens of a household to be even moderately civil to any new cat or kitten which may be introduced to them without a stand-up fight—a fight that only too often continues for weeks, and sometimes, indeed, it is months before the latest arrival becomes really a member of the family, free as are all the rest of its privileges and emoluments.

We were once the proud and happy possessor of thirteen cats, all of which had been born on the place, and were all progeny of a venerable Tom called Tim, and of Wrinkleface mentioned before, and it was a most curious study to see how Tim kept his numerous family in order. We had in those days a very large garden, and as the dogs roamed freely therein, Tim and his family had a habit of taking the air on the branches of a large fir we always used to call the "cat-tree," and a more strange sight surely was never seen in any other garden than the dark wide branches each forming a resting-place for a white, black, gray, or Chinchilla kitten, while Tim lay solemnly out on the top branch of all, and woe betide the son or daughter that aspired to share that elevated spot! a box on the ears soon reduced him or her to order, and never while Tim lived did he allow any other cat to climb above him or share his perch: he was head of the family indeed, and ruled the whole twelve, Wrinkleface included, with a paw of iron. A curious survival of some far-back ancestor used often to be found among these special cat-friends of ours, for, while both Wrinkleface and Tim had not the smallest evidence of blue blood in their appearance, one kitten in each family would be an almost perfect specimen of the long-haired English tabby, and once we had a quite beautiful French-gray, or Chinchilla-coloured cat—but only once. This cat used to beg like a dog, learned to open the door, first by jumping up at it and striking the handle until it turned, and then by standing on an adjacent table and stretching out its paw from that to the handle; he would ask to be taken for a walk, and would

THEIR MORNING MEAL.

solemnly pace up and down the long garden walk, following his mistress as steadily as possible, and stopping every now and then to scent the white pinks or violets of which the garden was full in spring and summer—and, in fact, was the cleverest animal we ever saw, and our one regret is that, overdone with our thirteen, we gave him away, and had no real opportunity either of developing or watching talents which were so far above the average; but he never forgot us, and the moment he heard our voices in his mistress's house, he used to come rushing up to us, and purr round us, talking to us in a manner that was as pathetic as it was undoubtedly clever, and out of the common.

A winter's absence from our home dispersed our family of thirteen, and although they were left on board wages, and amply fed by the usual hands, they resented our absence, found homes for themselves with our neighbours, and when we returned prior to giving up the old home for good, we found that Tim had fallen a victim to his fondness for ambitious heights, and had broken his neck among the machinery of a neighbouring brewery, and that only Wrinkleface and one kitten were left to us out of all that goodly tribe. It was a severe blow; still, as we were emigrating to a much smaller garden, perhaps it was as well that our family was diminished for us; we should never have had the heart to do this ourselves.

We have found quite common cats produce one or two beautiful kittens in a litter among four or five quite hideous brothers and sisters, and when we moved to our present abode we experienced a very curious example of this. We found in the stables one of the plainest and hungriest cats it has ever been our misfortune to see; we did not like or want her, but we cannot be unkind to any creature, and in consequence we fed and entertained her, and to our astonishment our own cats were quite civil to her. When she had been our property for some time, we were led to believe that she had taken advantage of our hospitality and had foisted a family upon us; but nowhere could the family be found, and we were beginning to think we had suspected her wrongfully, when one morning on the front door-step we found, apparently alone and unattended, the most beautiful red-and-white long-haired kitten, of quite six weeks old, that we had ever seen. We brought it in, fed it, made much of it, welcomed the beauty in every way, and wondered to whom it belonged; made all inquiries without any result, and after two days we named it, and introduced it properly to the rest of

ENGLISH SHORT-HAIRED TABBIES.

the family; and then on the third morning we were astonished to find a second kitten, equally beautiful, equally long-haired, but this time owned and obviously chaperoned by the stable cat, who as obviously had introduced number one tentatively, and to see what we should do, and then produced number two, believing, by the reception given to number one, that we should not resent her family as much as she feared we should do. But the matter did not end here, for although the stable cat now stayed indoors, and seemed quite happy with her beautiful children, we were attracted by the sound of mewing to an arbour covered thickly with twigs, and there among the twigs, and just like birds in a nest, we discovered two more kittens, but these were just as ugly as their mother, and had evidently been forgotten by her in her pride and joy at our reception of the beauties; or could she have subtly argued to herself that she would introduce the lovely sisters first, and then would have brought forward the others? However, her plot was frustrated, for we could not bear three editions of the stable cat, and reluctantly gave orders which resulted in the death of the plain members of the family.

If space allowed, we could tell endless anecdotes of Thomas, the white cat who lived to the honoured age of twenty-two, who went to bed every night of his life in a basket with a couple of blankets, and who would not sleep in them if they were the least soiled or dirty, who would literally scream with rage if his mistress went up stairs without first putting him to bed like a child, and who finally, when he found he was dying, dragged his poor old limbs quite a mile away to the stable of a friend to save his mistress the anguish of watching his last moments; of Peter, who plays games with her owners, and who can take a piece of bread in her paw from the centre of a napkin-ring without moving the ring, and who, despite her name, has constant families of kittens, at which nothing will induce her to look; of a family of four cats which have been taught by their little mistress each to wait their turn to be fed, as she sits at her table eating her bread and milk, and calling to them one after the other to claim their share; and, finally, of our much-beloved Sam, of whom we have spoken before, but of whom pages might be written did we dwell at length on his curious cunning, his patient insistence on having his own way and securing his own comfort, his really passionate attachment to his mistress and to one or two favoured friends to whom he goes without a demur, curling himself up on their laps as a matter of right, his as passionate dislike to other people, and his detestation of anything like "company"—in fact, his entire resemblance to a crusty old bachelor, who is civility itself when no one interferes with his special arrangements, and who adores one or two old cronies, but is miserable enough should he be upset or put out of his routine.

We could quote anecdotes of other cats, notably of one, who, like Schwartz, attempted to commit suicide by throwing itself repeatedly head foremost from a high shelf on a stone floor, and although it did not accomplish its end, bruised itself so much that it had to be killed; of another cat, who was put into a sack and thrown into the river to be drowned, and which, having found a hole in the sack, swam home, and presented itself a dripping ghost before the eyes of its outraged and frightfully alarmed master; of another cat at the Wareham Mills, which used to sit and fish for the eels which were always to be found there, and which brought them out and ate them in the cleverest way possible; but we fear we have already transgressed the space at our disposal; however, we trust we have said enough to prove our case, and to enlist sympathy in the cause of this most misunderstood creature: if we have not, a glance at the trio of fascinating tabbies gazing into the fire must surely do the rest, for who could resist the inquiring eyes of the middle darling, or the sweet, sleepy fat ball of gray fur which is already giving way to the attacks of slumber, and is falling against his next-door neighbour, in a manner that will result in a moment in an agonized squall of reproach, and the probable administration of a "good pat" from the small outstretched paw?.

THOUGHTS ON THE HIGHER EDUCATION OF WOMEN.

By A Man.

THERE are all sorts of legends in Cambridge about Girton and Newnham girls. The beautiful ideal girl-graduate depicted by Tennyson does not exist in the imagination of the ordinary under-graduate. If you ask him for a description of a Girtonite or Newnhamite, he will immediately picture a lady whose personal attractions are *nil*, a wearer of spectacles, a being whose thoughts soar above such small details as fashion or harmony of colour in dress. This is doubt-less a libel on lady students, and if they chose to retort upon us, they might just as well take their type of the average undergraduate from the ranks of the typical smug; the gentleman who dresses worse than his gyp, who has been known at rare intervals to brush his hair and indulge in a clean collar; the man whose life consists of chapels, lectures, reading, and bed, with an interval of one hour for the Trumpington walk, and a few odd moments for meals.

It would be just as fair to judge "'Varsity men" from such specimens as these, as it would be to judge Girton or Newnham by their exceptions.

I must say personally that my only ex-perience at Cambridge of a Girtonite was not altogether happy. I make no claim to be in any sense a learned man, only an ordinary specimen of the great majority, the οἱ πολλοί of Cambridge, those whose ambition is limited to obtaining in their three years an ordinary degree and as much social life as possible. One evening at an "At Home," or Perpen-dicular, I was introduced to a lady who hailed from Girton. The trivialities of ordinary con-versation were not sufficient for her mighty intellect, however, and in a moment I was appalled with the question, "Are you mathe-matical?" I replied as best I could, and shortly afterwards turned the tables by intro-ducing the subjects of music and art, of which I possess some slight smattering. Doubtless I met with one of the exceptions, and it would be wrong to form an opinion from such slight data, and so I willingly believe what others have told me—that just as our finest specimens of English manhood are to be met with at our universities, so there also are to be found our finest specimens of English girlhood.

My thoughts on woman's education, how-ever, have nothing whatever to do with Girton or Newnham. All women cannot avail them-selves of such a great privilege as a university course, and it is quite possible to fulfil the best ideals of womanhood and of education away from either Oxford or Cambridge. It is my purpose rather to send to the GIRL'S OWN PAPER what I believe are not my own thoughts and opinions alone, but the thoughts and opinions of many Englishmen upon a much-vexed question.

What is the ideal of an educated woman? Not a woman's ideal, but a man's ideal. Here I must confess myself to be old-fashioned, for the whole question depends upon what is woman's mission in this world.

I am old-fashioned because I believe that woman's true mission and man's true mission are one and the same. I am no believer in single blessedness; I believe there is no more miserable object in the world than a bachelor condemned for life to the tender mercies of a landlady; and just as in an old bachelor you see vestiges of good qualities which have withered, and perceive an incomplete man—one whose life has been to a great extent a failure, so do you see often in ladies who have never married many lovely and beautiful qualities—qualities which would have bright-ened and made happy any home; and seeing this, feel a sense of sadness that such lives should have been warped and arrested in their development by the force of circumstances. Yes, reproach me as you may, no argument will ever shake my conviction that the true ideal of life for man and woman alike is marriage; not society marriages of con-venience, not marriage for the sake of marriage, but marriage based upon a union of souls; the old-fashioned, much abused, love-match; when all the joy and happiness of life ceases to be centred in self, but is centred instead in another, apart from whom life ceases to be worth living.

Now what is the common complaint of educated men at this present day—I mean the educated man who is in a position to marry? Is it that he cannot find girls with money, or girls possessing beauty and refinement? Is it this? I know full well we men are called mercenary, and that we are believed to look for only one great charm in woman—money. I know full well that the world is becoming every day more mercenary and less romantic; that Cupid is fast losing his bow and arrow, and is arming himself instead with bags labelled £ s. d.; I know all this, but I still say the lament of all true, manly Englishmen is that the girl of the nineteenth century is shallow and insipid; and far from wishing to see women beautiful automatons, able to pre-side at our tables, and to do the honours of the house and credit to their dressmakers, we, as men, desire to see them thoroughly well edu-cated; not *bookish*—something more than that, *educated*—able to give opinions on varied subjects, well read, well travelled, well refined, our mental equals in every respect.

Do I then consider woman's intellect inferior to man's?—that is to say, the average woman inferior mentally to the average man? By no means. I do not believe that any sensible man holds that there is any real inferiority, but there is a considerable difference. As well compare the physical development of a woman with that of a man, as compare her intellect with the masculine mind. That which is masculine is essentially masculine, and that which is feminine, is feminine. We look for muscular strength, breadth of shoulder, length of limb, hardness of the facial lines, and general angularity in man; we look for that which is graceful in woman; no hard lines, no masculine biceps, but smooth undulating curves. A manly man is just as much an object of beauty in nature as a womanly woman; but it is beauty regarded from an entirely different standpoint, and that which is lovely in man is very unlovely in woman. And the same physical differences prevail in the composition of the mind—no inferiority, but an essential difference.

Now what are the characteristics of the feminine mind? This is a very difficult question for a man to answer. It requires considerable experience and knowledge of character; I must therefore ask pardon if I err in my conclusions.

It has always struck me that women are not strictly logical: they do not possess that power of advancing step by step to a conclu-sion which men possess; but at the same time they have a power which is in advance of logic, a power of forming a conclusion without proceeding through each stage; and the con-clusion is generally an accurate one, although not arrived at by strictly logical steps. Women will form opinions, and correct opinions too, at a glance, which it takes men a long time to arrive at. I should say, therefore, that quick-ness in reasoning is feminine, as opposed to solidity and depth of reasoning in man. I think the Greek compared to the Roman intellect in some respects resembles the com-parison between the female and male intellect. The Greek certainly was logical, and therefore I may appear to contradict myself; but his great qualities were quickness in reasoning, brilliancy rather than depth, versatility, adap-tability, and, above all things, love of the beautiful. The Roman intellect was, on the other hand, practical and prosaic. It was the essentially masculine qualities of the Roman which led to Rome being the mistress of the world. It is to Greece, however, we owe all the refinement of antiquity, and a large por-tion of the refinement of the present.

Personally, I much prefer the Greek tem-perament. Vague longings after the ideal, an eye for beauty of form, a mind for beauty of thought, an ear for beauty of sound, are far to be preferred to the power of solving deep and abstruse problems. The artist is in reality a far greater man than the mere scholar; he is born, the other is made. The artistic temperament is one of the greatest of God's gifts, and is, to my mind, more often found in women than in men. We find many men without one spark of imagination or romance, but very few women. Almost every woman has some romance in her composition. Versatility is essentially part of woman's nature; concentration a part of man's nature. And here arises a strange paradox. A man who concentrates himself upon one subject, while naturally less versatile than a woman, at the same time does not lose his versatility by his concentration. Let a woman, however, once concentrate herself upon one particular thing, and she loses all her natural versatility, and becomes a creature of only one idea.

A man may be reading law, medicine, theology, mathematics, or any other subject, making one special subject the study of his life; but he will still take an interest in general matters, and be able to converse upon a score of other subjects; and oftentimes the more learned he is, the more will he delight in the most sensational of all sensational novels by way of relaxation. A learned, or rather *bookish*, lady, on the other hand, is essentially a crea-ture who moves in a groove and is never able to get out of it. It does not matter what the subject is, the fact still remains. I have known even theological ladies, ladies whose greatest ambition would be to get up in a pulpit and preach, and my experience tells me they have only one topic, which they must literally drag in by the hair of the head on every occasion. I have one friend, for instance, whose great subject is the moral and social welfare of the London cabby. At first it is refreshing to know that the man who looks with disgust at anything less than double his legal fare is such a delightful character; but when you know him by heart he ceases to be refreshing, and when he is served up daily at every meal until your mental atmosphere reeks of him, and you begin to dream of him and to spend most of your nights in phantom growlers, he becomes, to put it mildly, a nuisance. It is the same with other subjects. The legal lady is always full of some interesting point of law, the medical lady of some interesting demonstration or operation; and if in a crowded room she can possibly button-hole you and discover you are really an M.B. Cantab., you may be sure of getting through the whole or greater part of "Quain's Anatomy" at express speed.

But I fancy I am wandering somewhat from my subject, and will, before proceeding further, sum up what I have said. Woman's ideal, I have said, is marriage; that is, the making the life of the man she loves as happy as it is possible to make it. I also hold the same ideal for a man, for all true love is unselfish and reciprocal. Woman's great natural gift is versatility; man's great complaint is that the women of the day are dull and insipid. What education, then, will serve to make women good wives and real companions for their husbands? It will be an education which develops the natural endowment, *versatility*; an education which aims rather at general culture than deep knowledge. The deeply-read specialist is not necessarily a cultured individual, for culture spreads itself over a very wide area. My ideal of an educated woman would not exclude classics, history, modern languages, music (if she be musical), art, some knowledge of mathematics, and even science. She should be, however, widely rather than deeply read.

The ladies of Girton and Newnham are only allowed to go in for an honours course, I believe. I cannot help thinking, however, that if the ordinary degree course were encouraged, and more ladies' colleges started, it would be better. The averagely well-educated English-woman should be at least educated up to that standard as a basis; and then, if there be any special subject which will cultivate the taste and increase the imagination, let it be studied. Harmony, counterpoint, all the higher branches of music for those who are musical; as much

classics and history as you please; anything which will develop a taste for the beautiful or re-people a world long since dead; anything which will make our ancient ivy-clad ruins and stately cathedrals once more alive with the forms of those who long since have mouldered into dust; anything which will call up for us the spirit of the past; for while "the old order changeth, yielding place to new," "God repeats himself in many ways."

The subjects to be avoided, save in an elementary manner, are mathematics, and possibly science—certainly, however, the former. The subjects most to be encouraged are classics and history. These two widen and refine, while the tendency of mathematics for women is to make them narrow, and creatures of only one idea.

But what of those women who have to earn their living in the world; those who wish to be independent; to marry if they have the opportunity; but to be certain, if necessary, of earning their living? How are they to be educated? I would venture here to point out that women educated on the lines laid down are best able to educate their sisters on the same lines. It often happens that the women who would, if properly educated, make the very best of wives, by persisting in pushing the higher education craze to its limits, become creatures to be avoided by the average man; avoided not because of their culture, but because of their lack of culture; because they have become the creatures of an idea. At the same time there are exceptions. Some women are naturally masculine in their ideas, just as some men are feminine. Let such as these by all means immerse themselves in mathematics, science, or medicine; but may the day be long distant when any numbers of England's fair

daughters follow in their footsteps. It does not follow that all mathematical, medical, or scientific women are to be avoided. The type is, indeed, as a type; but there are exceptions to every rule, and some very charming and delightful exceptions too. Personally, I cannot associate the tenderness of true womanhood with the torture of frogs, in order to see the action of galvanism upon the nerves, or with many other things inseparable from a deep scientific or medical education. And these are not my own thoughts alone, but the thoughts of men who have themselves been in for science. Depend upon it, ladies, the judgment of the Cambridge undergraduate represents fairly the judgment of English manhood upon your sex; and if there is anything he hates and ridicules, it is a masculine, unwomanly woman. His idea of womanhood is a lofty one. He wants to find sympathy in his pursuits—true womanly sympathy; a help-mate, not a lady who understands differential and integral calculus, who will discourse learnedly and drearily upon one everlasting subject. Nor, on the other hand, a lady who will endanger his life and spoil his sport when after the birds, by blazing away haphazard with the light gun specially made for her, and who loves to join in sports and occupations suited to men alone. No; he seeks and admires neither of these types, but those women who are still true to the best traditions of their sex; those whose mission in life is to make homes happy and cheerful with their presence; those whose influence is a holy and pure one; those who will make him what in his inmost nature he wishes to be, though perhaps far removed from that ideal now—a chivalrous, high-minded Englishman; a man who shall leave this world better than he found it.

OCTOBER.

Illustrated London Almanack, 1851

SOME AUSTRIAN SWEETS.

IT has been said by an authority, that throughout Austria the puddings have reached the summit of perfection; the same may be said of the sweets generally, many of which are of such a nature that they are as acceptable at one meal as another, and serve the purpose of a pudding or a cake. Cleanliness is a leading feature, and one reads again and again, in directions for the making of delicate dishes, that the hand should not be used where it can possibly be avoided. The use of porcelain utensils in the form of rolling-pins, pastry cutters and the like, has much to recommend it. Such articles are kept cleaner than when made of wood, while the material equals marble in its coolness.

Tyroler Zelten.—This is a dish that would be certain of a welcome, though very cheap, and there are many ways of sending it to table. It is first-rate with a simple sweet sauce, as a pudding; and, with butter, it may go in either hot or cold for tea. Those who bake at home would do well to try it, for any nice light yeast dough will form the foundation. Supposing a pound and a half of dough, take about half a pound of the following materials, mixed : raisins, currants, figs, and almonds, the latter in small quantity only ; then season well with cinnamon, or any spice to taste, and add some grated lemon peel. All the fruits should be finely divided, and the mixing should be very thorough. This is sometimes baked as a cake, or it may be rolled and baked as a pudding. When done, a shiny surface is secured by a sprinkling of sugar, and the use of the salamander, for appearances are by no means forgotten in Austria, and many simple dishes are raised from the commonplace to the high class by care in the finishing touches.

Lemon Chandeau. — This sauce is so good with almost every sort of sweet that it deserves to become a standing dish in any household, and we need scarcely say that it is delicious with the above dish. The materials are a couple of good lemons, water, four eggs, and four ounces of sugar, and it is to the method rather than the cost that the success is due. Watch an Austrian cook peel those lemons, and you might almost read through the rind ; certainly you will find it as yellow on the inner as the outer side, but only the rind of one will be put in the above sauce. The juice is carefully strained, for pips would spoil it ; it is then left to blend with water, to make half-a-pint, in a covered vessel for some time. The yolks of eggs go next, and the whole is whisked over the fire, and carefully watched that it does not boil. Those who know how to make chocolate by the process termed " milling " will have no difficulty in making this sauce. This is ready for serving in the hot state, but as a cold sauce there is a further treat in store. The sauce is beaten until cool, then the whites of the eggs are put

in, and what a mass of sauce these materials make ; but the eggs must be fresh, and let none cease beating the whites until they are stiff enough to bear the weight of a raw egg.

There seems, at first glance, nothing to warrant the excellence of a dish called *Dampfnudeln,* for the ingredients are homely enough for use in any kitchen ; but when one considers the perfection of the flour of the country, and the care taken in sieving it, combined with the energy that is thrown into the kneading of the dough, one begins to understand the delicious lightness of these dainties. A pint of flour will make a good number ; to it should be put a pinch of salt, and a dash of sugar, about an ounce ; the less sugar, the lighter the dough ; this fact is undeniable. An ounce of the freshest of dried yeast, if one may use such a term, is next added, with enough lukewarm milk to make a leaven ; then a couple of ounces of butter and two eggs must be added, with as much more milk as is needed, and the whole left to rise, when, after the final kneading, the dough is cut into lumps, which emerge from the oven not unlike the penny sponge cakes with which we are all familiar, but *so* puffed up and *so* brown ; and are not these perfections due mostly to the glowing heat of the oven, and the freedom from the *peeps* that a too-anxious English cook will often take during the baking process? We think so. When served with a sweet sauce, as they often are, and they are just as delicious with jam, the sugar may be left out altogether. The salamander, or its substitute, an old shovel, gives the last touch to these.

Here is a very peculiar pudding ; only a sort of roly-poly made from apples. Are you tired of apple puddings as usually met with ? If so, try this, and you will not shelve it afterwards. The foundation is a plain sheet of pastry, but mixed with lukewarm water instead of cold, and strewn with bread crumbs that have been fried in butter to a dainty crispness. The next layer is composed of apples in slices, raisins and currants, and the indispensable cinnamon—a spice much favoured by the Austrians. This is then rolled and baked, and served with dissolved butter poured over it generally, but we venture to recommend a nice sweet sauce, served apart, as the more enjoyable. Those who will take the trouble to fry a few more crumbs to sprinkle on the outside when the pudding is dished, will probably agree with us that the taste and appearance are improved ; but this is an English innovation.

Next on our list comes a pudding that, judging from the materials, is only a batter pudding of the ordinary sort, except that there is a good proportion of eggs in it ; but we will not pass it over, it is so good as to be more like a soufflé, but to eat it in perfection the flour of the country must be used for it, and a fire-proof china dish is required for the baking. A quarter of a pound of flour, half-a-pint of milk, an ounce of sugar, a saltspoonful of salt, and five eggs. These are the materials; it is the blending that does most to bring about perfection. After beating the flour and milk until as smooth as cream, the yolks of eggs are put in, with the sugar and salt, and the mixture left awhile. Then the whites are added in the same frothy condition above referred to, and there is art in the way in which they are mixed in; a few strokes of the whisk only, *no beating*, to make them fall again; and not a moment is lost in pouring this delicious batter into the dish, in which a couple of ounces of butter have been heated.

The sight of this makes one hungry, for it equals an omelette in appearance. It may be noted that no flavouring is mentioned in connection with this dish; there are, however, many suitable ones. Amongst the most delicious are vanilla sugar, orange flower water, rose water, or any essence of good quality; but it must be remembered that when a liquid of the nature of either of these waters is employed the milk should be proportionately reduced. We may be pardoned for reminding the reader that butter *is* butter in Austria; no concoction that would be considered unfit for table would find a place in such a pudding as this, and the eggs would be really fresh.

A dish that will commend itself to the juvenile members of the family is an *Auflauf*, made from jam. This is nothing more or less than a meringue mixture, mixed with jam, of which apricot is favourite. For the whites of four eggs, the same number of tablespoonfuls of white sugar, and about the same, or a trifle less, of jam would be used. The mixing takes some time, a little of each being put in the bowl and whisked well. When all are used up the mass is piled on a dish, and a goodly pile it makes; then baked, or we might say dried, in the oven, so slow is it, until a pale brown. It is eaten hot or cold; in the latter form it is a good dish for a children's party, eaten of course in moderation.

Speaking of the children reminds us of a dainty *Snow Cake*. Butter, sugar, and flour, in equal weights, are wanted for this, and for twelve ounces of the mixture the whites of four eggs; the best flavouring for it is grated lemon peel. The ordinary method of creaming the butter and sugar is followed, the flour is sifted in by slow degrees, and most carefully blended (you will not find an Austrian cook beating it), the eggs, beaten to a snowy pile, are put in with the same light touch, and when baked with care there are few more delicious cakes than this. Those who would like a novel pudding should try this hot, with the lemon sauce above; the combination is first-rate, and in this case we advise that the sauce be poured over the cake, to soak it a little. A cake similar to the above is composed of equal parts of corn flour and wheaten flour. Another owes its goodness to a mixture of potato flour and wheaten flour; by the latter we refer to the fine flour of Austria.

Here is an old friend, with a very new face, in the shape of *Potato Pudding*. In some cases there may not be much in a name, but those who may try this will own that there is a good deal in method. But the

mixing! We dare not venture to give this in the original, for who can give the hour demanded for the blending of the materials? Well, we have found it so excellent when made in less than half the time that we make no apology for the deviation. The materials are a quarter of a pound of mashed potatoes, the same weight of sugar, and four whole eggs, with the yolks of four more for a first-class pudding; but the four alone will bring about very good results if the potatoes be increased by an ounce, and a tablespoonful or two of milk be put in. The dryness of the potatoes is of primary importance, and if they are not sieved the pudding will be but a poor substitute for the original. The best way to make this is to whisk the ingredients until they resemble a thick custard, or thin batter. The flavouring is a matter for the individual, and so is the sauce; a very good one is made from thin melted butter, with a nice jam or fruit jelly mixed in, or some fruit syrup is just as good. The mould should be thickly buttered, and coated with bread crumbs; and the oven should be gentle.

A sweet famed through Austria is made from a mixture of chocolate, bread crumbs, sugar, eggs, almonds and spice. The peculiarity consists in the unpeeled condition of the almonds. We must say that, having tried this in both forms, we give the preference, both on the ground of flavour and digestion, to the peeled almonds of every-day life. A very nice sweet of this sort is to be had from four eggs, to two ounces each of the other materials; but many will increase the sugar to four ounces, and the varieties of spices that are used are many. Cinnamon with nutmeg is a favourite, but we prefer the old combination of vanilla and almonds, which perhaps many have never tried, for one would hardly think that the result would be good; but it is, in our opinion. This wants careful baking.

Cherry Cake must close our list, and it is an excellent illustration of a cake and pudding in one. About a pint of bread crumbs will form the basis of a good-sized one, and to them should be added half their weight of fine sugar, three eggs, the chopped peel of half a lemon, and a generous handful of ripe cherries, the darker and juicier the better. For this, half an hour's beating is demanded, and at the last the whites of two more eggs should go in. The custom of adding some of the eggs at the end, and with the whites separately whisked, is almost universal, and those who are inclined to begrudge the trouble, or think there is "nothing in it," a term we have often heard, should note the difference in size and lightness of a pudding so made, and one to which the eggs are added in the ordinary manner. This is baked in a buttered mould lined with bread crumbs, and served hot or cold, and with sauce or without. This principle, we may say in conclusion, may be carried out with other fruit as well as cherries. We have an idea that damsons would yield a delicious dish of this sort; and we are sure that any fruit juice, boiled to a syrup with sugar, and served as sauce, will recommend itself.

BUSINESS HOURS IN LONDON STREETS.

THE lower we descend in the scale of commerce and traffic, the harder and more oppressive becomes the labour of those by whom business is carried on. When the great Baron Rothschild used to take his station at that pillar in the Royal Exchange, and transact his momentous bargains more by nods and signs than by articulate speech, he was seldom there for more than an hour or an hour and a half in the day; yet in that brief space of time it was nothing unusual for him to gain from fifty to a hundred thousand pounds. Our merchant princes spend but little time, comparatively, in their offices and warehouses, and derive their magnificent incomes without undergoing anything like bodily labour, being able to delegate all that to others. It is much the same with the prosperous banker: his hours are fixed, to be sure, but they are few and limited, and followed by certainly-recurring leisure. So with the wealthier class of dealers and traders in the money-making callings; they can and do shut up their shops and places of business early in the evening, and betake themselves to the enjoyments they most affect. It is different with the average trader, who pleads that he must make the most of his day in order to keep his credit good; and it is still more different with the struggling one, who must rise early and go to bed late, and eat the bread of carefulness, that he may make both ends meet, and have bread to eat at all.

It is in the traffic of the streets that the limitations as to time are the widest, and the struggle for bread is the fiercest. There are peripatetic traders of one class or other pursuing their occupation in the highways and byways of London for more than twenty hours out of the twenty-four; they are the earliest and the latest of all the traffickers of the metropolis: so early and so late, indeed, are some of them, that to many people it is a mystery what business they find to do. Let us glance at one or two of them.

The early breakfast-houses in London, thousands in number, though they open long before sunrise, are anticipated in their labours by the early breakfast-stalls erected in the streets. We have come upon these stalls at their first appearance less than three hours after midnight. They are among the oldest of the street institutions in London, and are doubtless a boon to a large class of early workers, who, rising long before dawn, are enabled by their means to break their fast with something solid and something hot at the price of a penny or threehalfpence; and they are no less welcome to the poor night-wanderer, who, not having twopence to pay for a bed, camps out, and hoards his one penny to pay for a breakfast. The breakfast used to consist of a thick hunch of bread, with dripping or salt butter, and a cup of saloop, which was a decoction of sassafras

chips, in place of salep (the dried and pounded tuber of *orchis mascula*), sweetened with coarse sugar. Since the fall in the price of tea, saloop is gone much out of fashion, though there are still a few of the old stagers who supply it to customers to whom use has made it pleasant. The salopians pitch their stalls in all weathers at all seasons of the year, and for the most part in spots where in daytime the traffic is densest: we have seen them in the Strand, in Holborn, on the bridges, and in the most frequented parts of the City. They vanish before the business hours, and that of necessity, for the crowd would crush them out of the way did they attempt to remain. An exception seems to be made in their favour in Covent Garden, where they do business under the piazzas to a later hour.

The milkman is known for an early bird, but he is not generally known for such an early bird as he really is. He has to turn out often before four in the morning, to get his horse in the cart and load his empty cans, that he may drive off to the railway-station and exchange them for full ones—most of the London milk now coming daily from the country, and being sent up by the earliest trains. Almost as early, the watercress hawkers betake themselves to Farringdon Market to buy their stock, and to cleanse and bundle it in preparation for hawking. About the same time the straggling hosts of costermongers begin to invade Covent Garden and Billingsgate. Few people who have not witnessed their matutinal gatherings have any conception of the numbers of these gentry. They not only inundate the district, but literally overflow in all directions, blocking up the channels of approach from every quarter, and presenting in their motley assemblage a spectacle as startling as it is significant.

Of the mass of traders of all descriptions who throng the thoroughfares during the ordinary business hours, we can say but little here. Their numbers, which have always been great, are constantly on the increase. With the growth of wealth around us there is, and always must be, a corresponding growth of poverty—and numbers are being constantly thrust into the streets to earn a living, who in times past were able to maintain themselves at home. This is one reason—perhaps the principal reason—why within the memory of the existing generation the traffic of the streets has assumed so many and such various phases. Time was when little if anything besides comestibles was sold in the street. Pies, gingerbread, cakes, nuts, fruits of all kinds when they were in season, fish just arrived from the sea, vegetables for the table—such used to be the stock of the street trader, supplemented in summer by flowers "all a-growing and a-blowing" in pots, and flowers in bouquets and posies gathered from the garden. We have changed all that now, and indeed have been long familiar with the change. At the present moment you can buy almost anything in the streets of London without troubling the shopkeeper—anything, that is, which is at all portable. The travelling stationer hawks his writing paper and envelopes; the printseller sets out a gallery of art in the concavity of an upturned umbrella; the cabinet-maker decks the dead-walls with his writing-desks, work-boxes, and letter-racks; the cutler sidles up to you with his razors; the working optician claims attention to his eye-glasses and spectacles; the toy-maker displays his stock of toys on the kerb; walking-sticks, padlocks, dog-collars, carpenters' tools, microscopes, mirrors, musical instruments, flat-irons, roasting-jacks, pots, pans, brushes, mops, glass, china, tin-ware, jewellery, statuary, paintings in oil—all these things, and a thousand things besides, walk the streets of London on the backs of their producers and purveyors, all eagerly on the look-out for a market. The number of wandering commercials engaged in this multifarious traffic has never been even approximately ascertained, and probably is not ascertainable; they must amount to some tens of thousands, and seeing that the rents of shops are constantly growing dearer, while the flag-stones are free from both rent and taxes, there is little likelihood at present of their diminishing. We leave this heterogeneous cosmos of commerce to the reader's tender mercies, confessing, however, to a substratum of regard for them all, and commending them to his kindly consideration.

But now evening draws on, and the nomads whose business has special reference to the decline of day begin to make their appearance. Hark! that is the muffin-bell, followed by the voice of the muffin-man! Of all the "wandering voices" that charmed the ear of the poet, commend us to him. No *vox et preterea nihil* is his, but *vox* and muffins to boot, with other succulent dainties which muffins bring in their train. Listen to what he says—

> "Come buy my nice muffins, and crumpets, and pikelets,
>   Come buy them of me!
> You'll find them hot, and large, and good,
> And they're all fresh baked for tea!"

He composed that beautiful lyric himself, without assistance from the poet-laureate or any one else; and if you feel disposed to criticise the muffin-man's muse, recollect, if you please, that whatever you may think of his metre, his muffins are irreproachable, and be sparing of your strictures. For our part, we never find fault with the "good man's poortry," as he calls it, choosing rather to confine our remarks to the burden of the song—the muffins themselves. Still there is one thing mysterious about the muffin-man, which has perplexed us any time these forty years, and which we could never satisfactorily get over—and it is this: why muffin-*man*? or muffin-*boy*, which is the same thing in the future tense? What have the women and the girls done, that they are rigidly shut out from the commerce in muffins? Who ever heard of a muffin-woman, or a muffin-girl? And if not, why not? as argumentative people put it. Is there any salique law that forbids the succession of the softer sex to the sovereignty of the muffin-basket? If so, give us the authority for it and set our minds at rest. For more years than make up an average generation have we looked for the muffin-woman, and have never found her, or even a trace of her. Nay, more; amid all the stir that has been made of late for woman's rights—notwithstanding all the women's conventions that have been held—the muffins have been kept carefully in the background, and usurping man (and boy) left in undisputed possession.

It is summer-time, and the sun is setting, his level beams piercing the hazy atmosphere and garbing the London chimney-pots in red shirts, till they look like an irregular squad of Garibaldians. About this time there is a branch of street trade carried on for an hour or two which always has a claim on our sympathies. Of the growing flowers in pots which left Covent Garden in the morning, many yet remain unsold. They have drooped and languished under the fierce mid-day sun, and their owners have been obliged to carry them to some sheltering shade, and quench their raging thirst, in order to restore their failing blossoms; and now they have revived again, they are brought forth in the cool of the evening to be sold for what they will fetch. Buy a few of them, my friend, for your bow-window or parlour flower-stand, and don't allow your knowledge of the fact that their owners have no place wherein to stow them safely for the night lead you to drive too hard a bargain.

About the same time you may chance to fall in with the country lad who brings to London a dripping hamper of water-lilies in the bud. He never gathers them in flower, as, once blown, they will not long survive away from their native pools; but he plucks them by hundreds in the bud, and pulls them into full bloom as fast as they are wanted—converting the shiny, unsightly cone, into a glorious vision of beauty by a few touches of his fingers—or he will sell you a couple of the buds for a penny and leave you to open them yourself if you prefer it. You don't catch him in the full glare of sunshine, but either in some shady shelter or in the cool of the twilight hour.

At certain recurring seasons old ocean sends up her supplies of food to our shores, of the arrival of which the Londoner gets his first information from the cries that resound through the streets after dark. At one time it is sprats that are hoarsely vocal in the thoroughfare as the hour of supper draws near. It is a current notion that everybody sups off sprats once a year, though they might do worse; what may be nearer the truth is, that everybody has the opportunity of doing so when the sprat season comes round. At another time it is mackerel, and it is noteworthy that these fish are allowed to over-ride the fourth commandment, and the statute of Charles II enforcing its observance, and to be hawked and bawled for sale on the Sunday—a privilege, if it be a privilege, which our customs accord to no other fish that swims. Crabs and lobsters are often roving about the suburbs up to ten and eleven o'clock, but they only indulge in these rakish habits in hot weather; the truth being that they are in a hurry to be eaten while they are worth eating, which they assuredly will not be if they are relegated to the chances of the morrow.

One might suppose that when all the world had had their suppers, and the major half had gone to bed, there would at least be a cessation of the trade of hawking eatables in the street. By no means. It is not at all unusual for us to be roused out of our first sleep by a cry which may reach us while it is yet a quarter of a mile off, and is shot explosively from lungs of prodigious power, to the tune of "Hot! all hot! smoking hot!" As late as half an hour after midnight have we heard this cry in the far suburbs; it proceeds from the vendor of baked potatoes, who, carrying his wares on his head, and travelling at the quick march, literally hunts down his belated customers, sending forth his stentorian cry to herald his coming. Who and what are the unenviable class dependent upon him for a meal, we must leave to the conjectures of the reader.

Thus it is seen that the latest supper-time of the street nomad and his earliest breakfast-time are but a brief space apart: a little more, and we should have brought the serpent's tail round into his mouth, and made of the street traffic one complete circle. It is not so, however, we are thankful to say; there are two or three of the small hours still left in the morning when the busy spirit of traffic is lulled to quietness, and the echoes have rest in the interminable thoroughfares. We should like to extend the narrow margin of silence, and stretch it over a few more of the hours of darkness; and we cannot help longing at times, amidst the boastings of onward progress, for so much retrogression at least as shall give back to our homes the silence of the night, and to the labourer the hours of sleep for his needful refreshment and repose.

The Magic Shop.

By H. G. Wells.

I HAD seen the Magic Shop from afar several times, I had passed it once or twice, a shop window of alluring little objects, magic balls, magic hens, wonderful cones, ventriloquist dolls, the material of the basket trick, packs of cards that *looked* all right, and all that sort of thing, but never had I thought of going in until one day, almost without warning, Gip hauled me by my finger right up to the window, and so conducted himself that there was nothing for it but to take him in. I had not thought the place was there, to tell the truth—a modest-sized frontage in Regent Street, between the picture shop and the place where the chicks run about just out of patent incubators—but there it was sure enough. I had fancied it was down nearer the Circus, or round the corner in Oxford Street, or even in Holborn; always over the way and a little inaccessible it had been, with something of the mirage in its position; but here it was now quite indisputably, and the fat end of Gip's pointing finger made a noise upon the glass.

"If I was rich," said Gip, dabbing a finger at the Disappearing Egg, "I'd buy myself that. And that"—which was The Crying Baby, Very Human—"and that," which was a mystery and called, so a neat card asserted, "Buy One and Astonish Your Friends."

"Anything," said Gip, "will disappear under one of those cones. I have read about it in a book.

"And there, dadda, is the Vanishing Halfpenny—only they've put it this way up so's we can't see how it's done."

Gip, dear boy, inherits his mother's breeding, and he did not propose to enter the shop or worry in any way; only, you know, quite unconsciously he lugged my finger doorward, and he made his interest clear.

"That," he said, and pointed to the Magic Bottle.

"If you had that?" I said; at which promising inquiry he looked up with a sudden radiance.

"I could show it to Jessie," he said, thoughtful as ever of others.

"It's less than a hundred days to your birthday, Gibbles," I said, and laid my hand on the door-handle.

Gip made no answer, but his grip tightened on my finger, and so we came into the shop.

It was no common shop this; it was a magic shop, and all the prancing precedence Gip would have taken in the matter of mere toys was wanting. He left the burthen of the conversation to me.

It was a little, narrow shop, not very well lit, and the door-bell pinged again with a plaintive note as we closed it behind us. For a moment or so we were alone and could glance about us. There was a tiger in *papier-maché* on the glass case that covered the low counter—a grave, kind-eyed tiger that waggled his head in a methodical manner; there were several crystal spheres, a china hand holding magic cards, a stock of magic fish-bowls in various sizes, and an immodest magic hat that shamelessly displayed its springs. On the floor were magic mirrors: one to draw you out long and thin, one to swell your head and vanish your legs, and one to make you short and fat like a draught; and while we were laughing at these the shopman, as I suppose, came in.

At any rate, there he was behind the counter—a curious, sallow, dark man, with one ear larger than the other and a chin like the toe-cap of a boot.

"What can we have the pleasure?" he said, spreading his long, magic fingers on the glass case; and so with a start we were aware of him.

"I want," I said, "to buy my little boy a few simple tricks."

"Legerdemain?" he asked. "Mechanical? Domestic?"

"Anything amusing," said I.

"Um!" said the shopman, and scratched his head for a moment as if thinking. Then, quite distinctly, he drew from his head a glass ball. "Something in this way?" he said, and held it out.

"'WHAT CAN WE HAVE THE PLEASURE?' HE SAID."

The action was unexpected. I had seen the trick done at entertainments endless times before—it's part of the common stock of conjurers—but I had not expected it here. "That's good," I said, with a laugh.

"Isn't it?" said the shopman.

Gip stretched out his disengaged hand to take this object and found merely a blank palm.

"It's in your pocket," said the shopman, and there it was!

"How much will that be?" I asked.

"We make no charge for glass balls," said the shopman, politely. "We get them"—he picked one out of his elbow as he spoke —"free." He produced another from the back of his neck, and laid it beside its predecessor on the counter. Gip regarded his glass ball sagely, then directed a look of inquiry at the two on the counter, and finally brought his round-eyed scrutiny to the shopman, who smiled. "You may have those

too," said the shopman, "and, if you *don't* mind, one from my mouth. *So!*"

Gip counselled me mutely for a moment, and then in a profound silence put away the four balls, resumed my reassuring finger, and nerved himself for the next event.

"We get all our smaller tricks in that way," the shopman remarked.

I laughed in the manner of one who subscribes to a jest. "Instead of going to the wholesale shop," I said. "Of course, it's cheaper."

"In a way," the shopman said. "Though we pay in the end. But not so heavily — as people suppose. . . . Our larger tricks, and our daily provisions and all the other things we want, we get out of that hat. . . . And you know, sir, if you'll excuse my saying it, there *isn't* a wholesale shop, not for Genuine Magic goods, sir. I don't know if you noticed our inscription—the Genuine Magic shop." He drew a business-card from his cheek and handed it to me. "Genuine," he said, with his finger on the word, and added, "There is absolutely no deception, sir."

He seemed to be carrying out the joke pretty thoroughly, I thought.

He turned to Gip with a smile of remarkable affability. "You, you know, are the Right Sort of Boy."

I was surprised at his knowing that, because, in the interests of discipline, we keep it rather a secret even at home; but Gip received it in unflinching silence, keeping a steadfast eye on him.

"It's only the Right Sort of Boy gets through that doorway."

And, as if by way of illustration, there came a rattling at the door, and a squeaking little voice could be faintly heard. "Nyar! I *warn* 'a go in there, dadda, I WARN 'a go in there. Ny-a-a-ah!" and then the accents of a down-trodden parent, urging consolations and propitiations. "It's locked, Edward," he said.

"But it isn't," said I.

"It is, sir," said the shopman, "always— for that sort of child," and as he spoke we had a glimpse of the other youngster, a little, white face, pallid from sweet-eating and over-sapid food, and distorted by evil passions, a ruthless little egotist, pawing at the enchanted pane. "It's no good, sir," said the shopman, as I moved, with my natural helpfulness, doorward, and presently the spoilt child was carried off howling.

"How do you manage that?" I said, breathing a little more freely.

"Magic!" said the shopman, with a careless wave of the hand, and behold!

sparks of coloured fire flew out of his fingers and vanished into the shadows of the shop.

"You were saying," he said, addressing himself to Gip, "before you came in, that you would like one of our 'Buy One and Astonish your Friends' boxes?"

Gip after a gallant effort said "Yes."

"It's in your pocket."

And leaning over the counter—he really had an extraordinarily long body — this amazing person produced the article in the customary conjurer's manner. "Paper," he said, and took a sheet out of the empty hat with the springs; "string," and behold his mouth was a string-box, from which he drew an unending thread, which when he had tied his parcel he bit off—and, it seemed to me, swallowed the ball of string. And then he lit a candle at the nose of one of the ventriloquist's dummies, stuck one of his fingers (which had become sealing-wax red) into the flame, and so sealed the parcel. "Then there was the Disappearing Egg," he remarked, and produced one from within my coat-breast and packed it, and also The Crying Baby, Very Human. I handed each parcel to Gip as it was ready, and he clasped them to his chest.

He said very little, but his eyes were eloquent; the clutch of his arms was eloquent. He was the playground of unspeakable emotions. These, you know, were *real* Magics.

Then, with a start, I discovered something moving about in my hat—something soft and jumpy. I whipped it off, and a ruffled pigeon — no doubt a confederate — dropped out and ran on the counter, and went, I fancy, into a cardboard box behind the *papier-maché* tiger.

"Tut, tut!" said the shopman, dexterously relieving me of my headdress; "careless bird, and—as I live—nesting!"

He shook my hat, and shook out into his extended hand two or three eggs, a large marble, a watch, about half-a-dozen of the inevitable glass balls, and then crumpled, crinkled paper, more and more and more, talking all the time of the way in which people neglect to brush their hats *inside* as well as out, politely, of course, but with a certain personal application. "All sorts of things accumulate, sir. . . . Not *you*, of course, in particular. . . . Nearly every customer. . . . Astonishing what they carry about with them. . . ." The crumpled paper rose and billowed on the counter more and more and more, until he was nearly hidden from us, until he was altogether hidden, and still his voice went on and on. "We none of us know what the fair semblance of a human being may conceal. Are we all then no better than brushed exteriors, whited sepulchres——"

His voice stopped—exactly like when you hit a neighbour's gramophone with a well-aimed brick, that instant silence, and the rustle of the paper stopped, and everything was still. . . .

"Have you done with my hat?" I said, after an interval.

There was no answer.

I stared at Gip, and Gip stared at me, and there were our distortions in the magic mirrors, looking very rum, and grave, and quiet. . . .

"I think we'll go now," I said. "Will you tell me how much all this comes to?. . .

"I say," I said, on a rather louder note, "I want the bill; and my hat, please."

It might have been a sniff from behind the paper pile. . . .

"Let's look behind the counter, Gip," I said. "He's making fun of us."

I led Gip round the head-wagging tiger, and what do you think there was behind the counter? No one at all! Only my hat on the floor, and a common conjurer's lop-eared white rabbit lost in meditation, and looking as stupid and crumpled as only a conjurer's rabbit can do. I resumed my hat, and the rabbit lolloped a lollop or so out of my way.

"Dadda!" said Gip, in a guilty whisper.

"What is it, Gip?" said I.

"I *do* like this shop, dadda."

"So should I," I said to myself, "if the counter wouldn't

suddenly extend itself to shut one off from the door." But I didn't call Gip's attention to that. "Pussy!" he said, with a hand out to the rabbit as it came lolloping past us; "Pussy, do Gip a Magic!" and his eyes followed it as it squeezed through a door I had certainly not remarked a moment before. Then this door opened wider, and the man with one ear larger than the other appeared again. He was smiling still, but his eye met mine with something between amusement and defiance. "You'd like to see our show-room, sir," he said, with an innocent suavity. Gip tugged my finger forward. I glanced at the counter and met the shopman's eye again. I was beginning to think the magic just a little too genuine. "We haven't *very* much time," I said. But somehow we were inside the show-room before I could finish that.

"All goods of the same quality," said the shopman, rubbing his flexible hands together, "and that is the Best. Nothing in the place that isn't genuine Magic, and warranted thoroughly rum. Excuse me, sir!"

"HE HELD A LITTLE, WRIGGLING RED DEMON BY THE TAIL."

I felt him pull at something that clung to my coat-sleeve, and then I saw he held a little, wriggling red demon by the tail—the little creature bit and fought and tried to get at his hand—and in a moment he tossed it carelessly behind a counter. No doubt the thing was only an image of twisted india-rubber, but for the moment——! And his gesture was exactly that of a man who handles some petty biting bit of vermin. I glanced at Gip, but Gip was looking at a magic rocking-horse. I was glad he hadn't seen the thing. "I say," I said, in an under-tone, and indicating Gip and the red demon with my eyes, "you haven't many things like *that* about, have you?"

"None of ours! Probably brought it with you," said the shopman—also in an under-tone, and with a more dazzling smile than ever. "Astonishing what people *will* carry about with them unawares!" And then to Gip, "Do you see anything you fancy here?"

There were many things that Gip fancied there.

He turned to this astonishing tradesman with mingled confidence and respect. "Is that a Magic Sword?" he said.

"A Magic Toy Sword. It neither bends, breaks, nor cuts the fingers. It renders the bearer invincible in battle against anyone under eighteen. Half a crown to seven and sixpence, according to size. These panoplies on cards are for juvenile knights-errant and very useful; shield of safety, sandals of swiftness, helmet of invisibility."

"Oh, daddy!" gasped Gip.

I tried to find out what they cost, but the shopman did not heed me. He had got Gip now; he had got him away from my finger; he had embarked upon the exposition of all his confounded stock, and nothing was going to stop him. Presently I saw with a qualm of distrust and something very like jealousy that Gip had hold of this person's finger as usually he has hold of mine. No doubt the fellow was interesting, I thought, and had an interestingly faked lot of stuff, really *good* faked stuff, still——

I wandered after them, saying very little, but keeping an eye on this prestidigital fellow. After all, Gip was enjoying it. And no doubt when the time came to go we should be able to go quite easily.

It was a long, rambling place, that show-room, a gallery broken up by stands and stalls and pillars, with archways leading off to other departments, in which the queerest-looking assistants loafed and stared at one, and with perplexing mirrors and curtains. So per-plexing, indeed, were these that I was presently unable to make out the door by which we had come.

The shopman showed Gip magic trains that ran without steam or clockwork, just as you set the signals, and then some very, very valuable boxes of soldiers that all came alive directly you took off the lid and said——. I myself haven't a very quick ear and it was a tongue-twisting sound, but Gip—he has his mother's ear—got it in no time. "Bravo!" said the shopman, putting the men back into the box unceremoniously and handing it to Gip. "Now," said the shopman, and in a moment Gip had made them all alive again.

"You'll take that box?" asked the shop-man.

"We'll take that box," said I, "unless you charge its full value. In which case it would need a Trust Magnate——"

"Dear heart! *No!*" and the shopman swept the little men back again, shut the lid, waved the box in the air, and there it was, in brown paper, tied up and—*with Gip's full name and address on the paper!*

The shopman laughed at my amazement.

"This is the genuine magic," he said. "The real thing."

"It's a little too genuine for my taste," I said again.

After that he fell to showing Gip tricks, odd tricks, and still odder the way they were done. He explained them, he turned them inside out, and there was the dear little chap nodding his busy bit of a head in the sagest manner.

I did not attend as well as I might. "Hey, presto!" said the Magic Shopman, and then would come the clear, small "Hey, presto!" of the boy. But I was distracted by other things. It was being borne in upon me just how tremendously rum this place was; it was, so to speak, inundated by a sense of rum-ness. There was something a little rum about the fixtures even, about the ceiling, about the floor, about the casually-distributed chairs. I had a queer feeling that whenever I wasn't looking at them straight they went askew, and moved about, and played a noiseless puss-in-the-corner behind my back. And the cornice had a serpentine design with masks—masks altogether too expressive for proper plaster.

Then abruptly my attention was caught by one of the odd-looking assistants. He was some way off and evidently unaware of my presence—I saw a sort of three-quarter length of him over a pile of toys and through an arch—and, you know, he was leaning against a pillar in an idle sort of way doing the most horrid things with his features! The particular horrid thing he did was with his nose. He did it just as though he was idle and wanted to amuse himself. First of all it was a short, blobby nose, and then suddenly he shot it out like a telescope, and then out it flew and became thinner and thinner until it was like a long, red, flexible whip. Like a

And before I could do anything to prevent it the shopman had clapped the big drum over him.

I saw what was up directly. "Take that off," I cried, "this instant! You'll frighten the boy. Take it off!"

The shopman with the unequal ears did so without a word, and held the big cylinder towards me to show its emptiness. And the

"OUT IT FLEW AND BECAME THINNER AND THINNER."

thing in a nightmare it was! He flourished it about and flung it forth as a fly-fisher flings his line.

My instant thought was that Gip mustn't see him. I turned about and there was Gip quite preoccupied with the shopman, and thinking no evil. They were whispering together and looking at me. Gip was standing on a little stool, and the shopman was holding a sort of big drum in his hand.

"Hide and seek, dadda!" cried Gip, "You're He!"

little stool was vacant! In that instant my boy had utterly disappeared! . . .

You know, perhaps, that sinister something that comes like a hand out of the unseen and grips your heart about. You know it takes your common self away and leaves you tense and deliberate, neither slow nor hasty, neither angry nor afraid. So it was with me.

I came up to this grinning shopman and kicked his stool aside.

"Stop this folly!" I said. "Where is my boy?"

"You see," he said, still displaying the drum's interior, "there is no deception——"

I put out my hand to grip him, and he eluded me by a dexterous movement. I snatched again, and he turned from me and pushed open a door to escape. "Stop!" I said, and he laughed, receding. I leapt after him—into utter darkness.

Thud!

"Lor' bless my 'eart! I didn't see you coming, sir!"

I was in Regent Street, and I had collided with a decent-looking working man; and a yard away, perhaps, and looking a little perplexed with himself, was Gip. There was some sort of apology, and then Gip had turned and come to me with a bright little smile, as though for a moment he had missed me.

And he was carrying four parcels in his arm!

He secured immediate possession of my finger.

For the second I was rather at a loss. I stared round to see the door of the magic shop, and, behold, it was not there! There was no door, no shop, nothing, only the common pilaster between the shop where they sell pictures and the window with the chicks!...

I did the only thing possible in that mental tumult; I walked straight to the kerbstone and held up my umbrella for a cab.

"'Ansoms," said Gip, in a note of culminating exultation.

I helped him in, recalled my address with an effort, and got in also. Something unusual proclaimed itself in my tail-coat pocket, and I felt and discovered a glass ball. With a petulant expression I flung it into the street.

Gip said nothing.

For a space neither of us spoke.

"Dadda!" said Gip, at last, "that *was* a proper shop!"

I came round with that to the problem of just how the whole thing had seemed to him. He looked completely undamaged—so far, good; he was neither scared nor unhinged, he was simply tremendously satisfied with the afternoon's entertainment, and there in his arms were the four parcels.

Confound it! what could be in them?

"Um!" I said. "Little boys can't go to shops like that every day."

He received this with his usual stoicism, and for a moment I was sorry I was his

father and not his mother, and so couldn't suddenly there, *coram publico*, in our hansom, kiss him. After all, I thought, the thing wasn't so very bad.

But it was only when we opened the parcels that I really began to be reassured. Three of them contained boxes of soldiers, quite ordinary lead soldiers, but of so good a quality as to make Gip altogether forget that originally these parcels had been Magic Tricks of the only genuine sort, and the fourth contained a kitten, a little living white kitten, in excellent health and appetite and temper.

I saw this unpacking with a sort of provisional relief. I hung about in the nursery for quite an unconscionable time....

That happened six months ago. And now I am beginning to believe it is all right. The kitten has only the magic natural to all kittens, and the soldiers seem as steady a company as any colonel could desire. And Gip——?

The intelligent parent will understand that I have to go cautiously with Gip.

But I went so far as this one day. I said, "How would you like your soldiers to come alive, Gip, and march about by themselves?"

"Mine do," said Gip. "I just have to say a word I know before I open the lid."

"Then they march about alone?"

"Oh, *quite*, dadda. I shouldn't like them if they didn't do that."

I displayed no unbecoming surprise, and since then I have taken occasion to drop in upon him once or twice, unannounced, when the soldiers were about, but so far I have never discovered them performing in anything like a magical manner....

It's so difficult to tell.

There's also a question of finance. I have an incurable habit of paying bills. I have been up and down Regent Street several times, looking for that shop. I am inclined to think, indeed, that in that matter honour is satisfied, and that, since Gip's name and address are known to them, I may very well leave it to these people, whoever they may be, to send in their bill in their own time.

The labours of THE·XII·MONTHS set out in NEW PICTURES & OLD PROVERBS

WISE SHEPHERDS say that the age of man is LXXII years and that we liken but to one hole yeare for evermore we take six yeares to every month as JANUARY or FEBRUARY and so forth, for as the yeare changeth by the

twelve months, into twelve sundry manners so doth a man change himself twelve times in his life by twelve ages, and every age lasteth six yeare if so be that he live to LXXII. For three times six maketh eighteen & six times six maketh XXXVI And then is man at the best and also at the highest and twelve times six maketh LXXII & that is the age of a man.

OCTOBER

And then commeth OCTOBER: that all is into the foresaid house gathered both corne and also other manner fruits. And also the labourers soweth new seeds in the earth, for the year to come. And when he that soweth naught shall naught gather. And then in these other six yeares, a man shall take himself unto GOD for to doe penance and good works, and then the benefits the year after his death he may gather, and have spirit-

-tuall profit, and then is man full in the term IX yeare.

≡ Sts Simon & Jude on you I intrude, by this paring I hold- Without any delay & to tell me this day. - to discover. The first letter of my own true lover. (Oct 28≡) _____ On the first of MARCH, the crows begin to search . . . By the first o'APRIL, they are sitting still. . . . . . By the first o'MAY, they're a'flown away . - . . . . Goupin' greedy back again, wi'OCTOBER'S wind & rain.

English Illustrated Magazine 1890

Victorian Times

Vol. V, No. 11

November 2018

Happily Ever After

When I was a child, some of my best friends were Victorians. Granted, I didn't really think of them that way—I just looked forward to coming home from school and spending time with buddies like Sara Crewe of *A Little Princess*, or Heidi, or Mary and Colin and Dickon from *The Secret Garden*, or the Bastables of E. Nesbit. Even Dorothy of Oz and Tom Sawyer qualify, technically, as Victorians.

Flashing forward to a point in my childhood's future (though still more than 20 years in my past!), I can't help but recall (reluctantly) a book that holds the distinction of being the book I most sincerely wish I had never read. It was billed as a "sequel" to *The Secret Garden*. The cover had a lovely picture of flowers and reviews declaring the work to be "charming" and "delightful." A more accurate adjective would have been "icky."

I won't go into details. Suffice it to say that all the characters would have benefited from a massive dose of therapy—though I suspect the author might have benefitted even more. She seemed compelled to point out that, regardless of the progress made by the characters in the original novel, what lay ahead of them would literally shoot it all to heck. Because, of course, what lay ahead of a turn-of-the-century child was... World War I.

This comes to mind now because I've just come across another book in a similar vein. This one takes E. Nesbit's children from *Five Children and It*, and, through various convoluted methods, shows what will happen to them when *they* run smack dab into World War I.

Wow. Is it possible that living happily ever after is... gasp... a myth? Were Victorian authors truly so naïve as to imagine that everything was going to end well for our favorite characters, after we'd turned the last page on their "official" biographies? The tone of these "sequels" implies just that.

Well, here's the thing. Everyone dies, eventually. No matter how wonderful life is for Sara Crewe after she's rescued from her dismal garret, eventually she's going to get old. It's certainly possible that, after spending most of her life in the fog and smoke of London, she dies of tuberculosis by 65. Perhaps Oswald Bastable, whom you met in our March 2017 issue, dies in a car smash-up; he's the sort of boy who would love fast cars. Perhaps Dickon never reaches adulthood at all, having been bitten by a rabid fox on the moor. If so, I don't want to know.

Except... wait... that's *real* life. In real life, we don't reach "the end" until we literally reach *the end.* But the wonderful thing about fictional characters is that they do, literally, live forever. My grandmother, and probably my great-grandmother, read *A Little Princess.* My mother read it. I read it. I've passed a copy to my niece, and I hope she'll pass it on to her own children one day. And through, by that time, nearly two centuries, Sara will never change. She won't die a horrible death. Dickon won't be drafted. Heidi won't fall off an Alp. We won't live forever—but because *they will*, our lives and our children's and grandchildren's lives will the better for it.

I can't help but wonder what these authors are actually trying to kill. Is it merely a fictional character, or is it an idea? Is it the notion of hope, redemption, and triumph over adversity that troubles these writers? Are these elements lacking in the writers' own lives, so that they feel they must shatter our illusions by pointing out that "happily ever after" doesn't really exist? We know that! That's why we read fiction!

Conversely, were Victorian authors truly as naïve as their modern sequelizers imply? Was it foolish of them to "imagine" that their characters would not endure further horrors in life? I suspect that it is, in fact, today's authors who are naïve, for I doubt they can truly imagine the horrors Victorian authors were aware of. The children in Victorian novels weren't blithe innocents, unaware of the evils of life. They were survivors of a world that was brutal to children. Child mortality rates were astronomical. Victorian stories and poetry are filled with the reality of dead children—and dead parents. The fact that all the children I mention in the first paragraph are lacking at least one, if not both, parents wasn't an unusual characteristic in Victorian days; it was commonplace.

Victorian writers understood quite well the reality that surrounded their characters. So they wrote of children who managed to survive and "beat the odds." No, they probably never foresaw something as horrendous as World War I—but if they could have foreseen it, I doubt it would have changed the outcome of their books. For those children, life freezes when the book ends—and for us, they live forever. That's how it should be.

Today, when we write novels of our own, we can't foresee what lies in our future, or the future of our characters. It may be horrendous. Authors of the 22nd century may look back on our "happily ever afters" and shake their heads, thinking "how naïve" and "if they only knew..." But sufficient unto the day is the evil thereof... so thank goodness we *don't!*

—Moira Allen, Editor
editors@victorianvoices.net

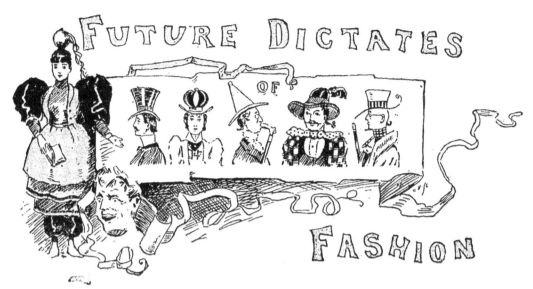

FUTURE DICTATES OF FASHION

BY W. CADE GALL.

AN elderly gentleman of our acquaintance, whose reading has been rather desultory than profound, and tending rather to the quaint and speculative, was astonished recently at coming across a volume in his library of whose very existence he had been completely unaware. This volume was oblong in shape, was bound in mauve morocco, and was called "Past Dictates of Fashion; by Cromwell Q. Snyder, Vestamentorum Doctor."

Glancing his eye downwards past a somewhat flippant sub-title, the elderly gentleman came, with intense amazement, to understand that the date of this singular performance was 1993. Other persons at a similar juncture would have pinched themselves to see if they were awake, or have tossed the book into the street as an uncanny thing. But our elderly gentleman being of an inquisitive and acquisitive turn of mind, despite his quaintness, recognised the fact that if he was not of the twentieth century the volume obviously was; seized pen and paper, and began to make notes with the speed of lightning. Being also something of a draughtsman he was able to embellish his notes with sketches from the engravings with which "Past Dictates of Fashion" was copiously furnished. These sketches appear with the present article.

Fashion in dress, according to the twentieth century author, notwithstanding its apparent caprice, has always been governed by immutable laws. But these laws were not recognised in the benighted epoch in which we happen to live at present. On the contrary, Fashion is thought a whim, a sort of shuttlecock for the weak-minded of both sexes to make rise and fall, bound and rebound with the battledore called—social influence. But it will interest a great many people to learn that Fashion assumed the dignity of a science in 1940. Ten years later it was taken up by the University of Dublin. By the science as taught by the various Universities later on were explained those points in the history, manners, and literature of our own ancestors which were formerly obscure and, in fact, unknown. They were also, by certain strict rules, enabled to foretell the attire of posterity. Here is a curious passage from the introductory chapter to the book :—

"Cigars went out of fashion twenty years ago. Men and women consumed so much tobacco that their healths were endangered. The laws of Nature were powerless to cope with the evil. Not so the laws of Fashion, which at once abated it. It will, however, return in thirty-one years. In 1790 Nature commanded men to bathe. They laughed at Nature. In 1810 Fashion did the same thing. Men complied, and daily cold baths became established. In 1900 it was pushed to extremes. The ultra-sect cut holes in the ice and plunged into the water. The fashion changed. For forty years only cads bathed."

The following table is also interesting, and should be borne in mind in considering the accompanying cuts. It professes to exhibit the sartorial characteristics of an epoch :—

TABLE OF WAVES.

	Type.	Tendency.
1790 to 1815	Angustorial	Wobbling
1815 ,, 1840	Severe	Recuperative
1840 ,, 1875	Latorial	Decided
1875 ,, 1890	Tailor-made	Opaque
1890 ,, 1915	Ebullient	Bizarre
1915 ,, 1940	Hysterical	Angustorial

The first plate in the book is dated 1893, and serves as a frontispiece. The costumes

1893

of the lady and gentleman are familiar enough, although we note with surprise that the gentleman's coat-tails seem to have a crinoline cast, and if the turned-up bottoms of his trousers are a little mortifying, it is

1908

atoned for by a triumphant attitude which disarms hypercriticism. Also the lady's posture makes it difficult for us to tell whether it is a stick or an umbrella she is carrying.

There is a pictorial hiatus of some years, but the text notes that crinoline for women enjoyed a sway of some years' duration. For, taking the tracings from the plates in the order in which they are given in the book, we find a subdued form of the article in the female costume for 1905. The ladies may well regard this plate as astounding. There is even a suggestion of "bloomer" about its nether portion, and if the hat is not without precedent in history, the waist is little short of revolutionary.

The next plate displays a gentleman's habit for the year 1908. The tailors, fifteen years hence, seemed to have borrowed, in the construction of the coat, very liberally from the lady's mantle of 1893. Apropos of this and the ensuing three plates, it is pleasing to be told, as we are by the author of this book, that the long reign of black is doomed.

1905

1910

1902

1911-12

and a flag at half-mast—were the items sacrificed. Knee-breeches enjoyed vogue for a time, but only for a time ; for they vanished suddenly in 1930 and were replaced by tights or shapes. Boots made way for Elizabethan slippers. Hats had long since gone the way of the superannuated. Taught by the Darwinian theory, society discovered whence its tendency to baldness originated. They had recourse by degrees to flexible tiles of extraordinary cut.

A further glance at the costume for the swells between 1902 and 1912 reveals the existence of an entirely novel adjunct to the male attire. Silk bows have been worn about the neck for nearly, if not quite, a century, but never in the body of the attire. It is true the gentleman as early as 1910 adorns his nether garments with a plain silk band, but in the elderly party of

Towards the close of April, 1898, Lord Arthur Lawtrey appeared in the Park attired literally in purple and fine linen, *i.e.*, in a violet coat, with pale heliotrope trousers.

Yet, in spite of the opposition to Lord Arthur, the wave was due, and the affection for colour spread. The new century, at its birth, saw black relegated to the past—also to the future. This was midway in the Ebullient Age. Pent up for decades, mankind naturally began to slop over with sartorial enthusiasm. In 1920 its *bizarrerie* became offensive, and an opposition crusade was directed against it. Something had to be conceded. Trousers, which had been wavering between nautical buttons and gallooned knees—or, in the vernacular of the period, a sail three sheets in the wind

1912

1912

1911 he has assumed gay ribbons for his shoes as well as at his knees and throat. In this plate we greet the presence of an unmistakable umbrella as a good omen. But it is only a short-lived rapture, for the spruce young party in the next sketch is balancing lightly between thumb and forefinger what we take to be nothing more or less than a shepherd's crook. This is hardly an edifying prospect. Yet if we do not altogether mistake the two wing-shaped objects projecting from his person, it is not the only feature of gentlemen's fashions twenty years hence which will occasion a shock. Nor must we overlook the frivolity of the lady of the same period who is doing her utmost to look pleasant under the most trying conditions. Yet it must be confessed that in spite of its intricate novelty and perplexity, the costume must still be called plain. One might be forgiven for surmising that the kerchief-shaped article covering a portion of the lady's bust is formed of riveted steel, for surely nothing else could support the intolerable load she is so blandly carrying off.

Female costume seems to have always been regulated by the same waves and rules which governed male costume, but in a different degree. In the Ebullient period it is chiefly distinguished by head-dress and the total abolition of stays. Crinoline, in spite of certain opposition, enjoyed a slight revival in the present day, and in 1897 the divided skirt threatened to spread universally. But it passed off, and nothing of a radical order was attempted in this direction until the revolution which brought in trousers for women in 1942.

Meantime, in the next plate of a lady's costume, which is dated 1922, we have presented a very rational and beautiful style

1922

of dress. The skirt, it is true, is short enough to alarm prim contemporary dames, and it is scarcely less assuring to find in the whole of the remaining plates only three periods when it seems to have got longer. But doubtless the very ample cloak, which is so long that it even trails upon the ground,

extenuated and in some degree justified its shortness.

The plate dated 1920 exhibits a very gorgeous and yet altogether simple set of

1920

garments for the male of that period. We are told that the upper portion was of crimson plush, and the lower part of a delicate pink, with white stockings and orange boots. It were well had the leaders of fashion stopped at this, but it would appear that either their thirst for novelty was insatiable or the Hysterical Wave too strong for them, for in the incredibly short space of six years fashion had reached the stage depicted in the following plate. Yet, even

1926

then, the depth of folly and ugliness does not appear to have been sounded, for three years later, in 1929, we are favoured with a plate of

1929

what is presumably a husband and wife on their way to church or perchance upon a shopping excursion. The lady is evidently looking archly back to see if anybody is observing what a consummate guy her spouse is making of himself, for with all her sartorial shortcomings she has certainly the best of the bargain. The prudes, too, seemed to have gained their point, for the skirt is considerably less scanty in the region of the ankles.

1935

This skirt seems to have been rather a weak point with our posterity of the female persuasion, for in the next three or four plates we find it rising and falling with the habitual incorrigibility of a shilling barometer. The Oriental influence is easily traced in the fashions from 1938 to 1945, but it cannot but make the judicious grieve to note that trousers seem to have been adopted by the women at the same time that they were discarded by the men.

A further detail which might interest

1938

the student concerns the revival of lace, which transpired so early as 1905. Curiously enough, this dainty adjunct to the attire had fallen into desuetude among women. More curiously still, it remained for the sterner sex to revive it. For it was in that year that the backbone of stiff white collars and cuffs was broken. A material being sought which would weather the existing atmospheric conditions, it was yielded in lace, which continued in vogue for at least two generations.

1940   1945

If we look for the greatest donkey in the entire collection, it is obvious that we shall find him in the middle-aged party of 1936, who is gadding about in inflated trunks and with a fan in his hand. If it were not for the gloves and polka-dot neck-wear we should

1936   1937   1945

assume that this costume was a particularly fantastic bathing-suit. The youth of the ensuing year, in the next plate, is probably a son of the foregoing personage, for it is not difficult to detect a strong family likeness. As to the costume itself for 1937, barring the shaved head and Caledonian cap, there is

plate for 1945. The confidently asinine demeanour of this youth is hardly relieved by the absurdity of a watch suspended by a chain from the crown of his hat. That society protested against this aspect of idiocy is evinced by the harmonious costume for 1950, in which a complete revolution is to

1950   1946   1948

nothing particular to be urged against it. It seems clearly a revival of the dress of the Middle Ages.

It is at least consoling to feel that only a very small minority of those who read this is destined to enliven our thoroughfares with such grotesque images as is furnished by the

be noted. We hasten to observe that the latter plate — the one for 1948 — is that of a clergyman.

There is very little beauty about the lady's costume for 1946, or in that of the child in the plate. That for 1950 is a great improvement. The exaggerated chignon has disap-

1950   1952   1955-6

peared, and two seasons later we find the costume fascinating to a degree, although certainly partaking more of the male than of the female order of dress. Without the cape it is not so captivating, as shown by the plate dated 1955–6, where both a lady and for no man's person can be considered in danger from the mob who habitually offers so many *points à saisir* as this policeman's head displays. We may likewise suspect the military gentleman depicted in the plate for 1965. It is not customary in the present

1960   1965   1965

gentleman are shown, although to accord praise to either's hideous style of head-dress would be to abandon permanently all reputation for taste.

The policeman shown in the drawing for 1960 seems to have a very easy time of it, day for army officers to affect umbrellas, but seventy years hence it may be found necessary to protect one's head-dress.

Mawkish describes the attire of the civilian of the same year, but in 1970 we notice a distinct change for the better, although personally many of us would doubtless strenuously object to wearing neckties of the magnitude here portrayed. In 1975 costume

1970

1978

seems to have taken a step backward, and the literary young gentleman, who is the hero of the engraving, may well be carrying about his MSS. inside his umbrella. Whatever may be the merits of the spring fashions for 1978,

are dressed precisely alike. Of the three remaining designs, that of 1984 appears to us to exhibit the contour of the lady's figure most generously, and to have certain agreeable and distinctive traits of its own which are not only lacking in the gentleman's apparel, but are absent from the inane conception which appears to have obtained vogue five years later.

As to the last plate in the series, we can only remark that if the character of our male

1975

1984

it would appear to have been universal (to speak of the future in the past tense), for both these young gallants

posterity after four or five generations is to be as effeminate as its attire, the domination by the fair sex cannot be many centuries distant. The gentleman appears to be lost in contemplation of a lighted cigar. If he possessed the gift of seeing himself as others now see him, he would probably transfer his nineteenth we term the black century. I am asked my opinion of the twentieth. It is motley. It has seen the apotheosis of colour. Yet in worshipping colour we do not confound the order of things. As is the twentieth, so was the fifteenth."

The author furthermore observes that

SPRING AND SUMMER FASHIONS, 1932.

attention to another and not less contiguous quarter.

In a general review of the costumes of the forthcoming century the Doctor observes:—

"The seventeenth is famous as the brown; the eighteenth is with us the yellow; and the "the single article of apparel which stands out most silhouetted against the background of the 19th century's dress is its hard, shiny, black head-gear. It is without a parallel. It is impossible for us to conceive of a similar article surviving for so long a period; and I venture to say, versed as I am in the science, nothing more absurd and irredeemably inappropriate, or more openly violating in texture and contour every rational idea on the subject, was ever launched. In 1962 the neck was left bare, in the négligé fashion, in imitation of Butts, the æsthete who the year previously had discovered the North Pole. In 1970, however, ruffs were resumed and are still worn, and I regret to say are growing in magnitude, until they threaten to eclipse precedent."

At this juncture the notes and nap together terminated, for our elderly gentleman woke up.

1989

1993

USEFUL RECIPES.

ORIENTAL FACE CREAM.

Six grains of powdered tragacanth, six drams of pure glycerine, nine ounces of triple rose water. Mix well, and add two drams of simple tincture of benzoin. This makes a splendid white emulsion, which leaves no greasy stain upon the skin.

HAIR RESTORER (IN POWDER).

Two drams of pure sugar of lead, three drams and a half of pure milk of sulphur, five grains of powdered cinnamon. Mix. To be added to twenty ounces of rose water.

LAVENDER PERFUME FOR SMELLING SALTS.

Six drams of oil of lavender aug., five drops of oil of cloves aug., ten drops of oil of rose geranium, ten drops of attar of roses, one dram and a half of essence of ambergris, two drams of essence of bergamotte, one dram and a half of essence of musk. Mix and shake well before dropping on the salts.

MACASSAR OIL.

Ten ounces of oil of sweet almonds, three drams of oil of bergamotte, two drams of oil of rose geranium, sufficient alkanet root to colour. Digest.

COCA TOOTH PASTE.

Four ounces of powdered precipitated chalk, three ounces of powdered orris root, one ounce of powdered white soap, half an ounce of powdered cuttle fish, two drams of powdered carmine, half an ounce of tincture of coca leaves, thirty drops of oil of ligu aloe, thirty drops of oil of peppermint, five drops of oil of castarilla, sufficient pure glycerine to make a paste.

BLOOM OF ROSES.

One dram of pure carmine, one dram and a half of strong solution of ammonia, three drams of pure glycerine, one dram and a half of white rose triple perfume. Sufficient triple rose water to make up four ounces; rub up the carmine with the ammonia and glycerine, add an ounce of rose water, and heat to drive off traces of ammonia. When cold add the white rose, and make up to four ounces with rose water, and filter.

FRECKLE LOTION.

One dram of sulpho-carbolate of lime, two ounces of pure glycerine, one ounce of spirits of wine, one ounce and a half of orange flower water, three ounces and a half of triple rose water. Mix well; to be applied morning and evening, and also after exposure.

LIME-JUICE AND GLYCERINE.

Two drams of white curd-soap, two ounces of distilled water, eight ounces of fresh lime-water, eight ounces of oil of sweet almonds, one dram of oil of bergamotte, half a dram of oil of lemon-grasse, half an ounce of essence of lemon. Well mix the oil and the lime-water in a large bottle, dissolve the soap in the distilled water by aid of heat, add the solution to the emulsion, shake well, and, lastly, add the essential oils.

MOUTH WASH.

Half an ounce of salts of tartar, four ounces of honey aug. opt., thirty drops of oil of peppermint, thirty drops of oil of wintergreen, two ounces of spirits of wine, ten ounces of triple rose water, sufficient liquid cochineal to colour. Mix well. To be used morning and evening.

WHITE HELIOTROPE.

(A). One dram of heliotropin, one ounce of extract of jasmine, one ounce of extract of white rose, two ounces of extract of ambergris, sixteen ounces of spirits of wine. (B.) Thirty drops of oil of bergamotte, three ounces of extract of neroly, three drops of essential oil of almonds. Mix. Allow (A and B) to stand separately for a week, then mix them and filter.

HOW TO COOK A PUMPKIN.

BY A HOUSEKEEPER.

PERHAPS few of my readers know how the pumpkin—that favourite article of food amongst the Americans—ought to be cooked; as it is very delicious as well as inexpensive, I will describe one or two good ways of using it. I must first tell you what the fruit is like. It resembles a very large round vegetable marrow, with a rather thick skin of a pale salmon - colour. The seeds, when ripe, can be sown in a frame, in the same manner as cucumbers are grown, and planted out in soil with plenty of manure in it, when the frosts are over. The fruit often grows to an enormous size, some specimens having been raised in this country weighing over 200 lbs. Of course in hot countries they are much larger. One very nice way of cooking it is to make it into a pudding. Take one pound of pumpkin, which costs about twopence, and boil it in water, with a very little salt, for an hour; then take it off the fire and mash it, as you would turnips, till it is smooth enough to rub through a colander; put the pulp into a pie-dish, add to it one egg, beaten very lightly, a table-spoonful of sugar, a piece of butter the size of a walnut, and a little grated lemon-peel, and pour in sufficient milk to fill the pie-dish. Bake in a moderate oven till it is a light golden colour. A little paste round the edge of the dish is a great improvement.

Pumpkin Pie.—Pare your pumpkin, cut it up into small pieces, and cook it gently over the fire, with a very little water, for about half an hour; then fill your pie-dish with it, sprinkle a little ground ginger and sugar over, and pour in some water. Have ready some nice puff paste, cover the fruit with it, and bake.

Pumpkin Tart.—Boil the pumpkin in the same way as for the pudding, and rub it through a colander, beat two ounces of butter, with a little sugar, to a cream, stir in the yolks of two eggs beaten lightly, the juice of one lemon and half the grated rind, and, last of all, the whites of the eggs beaten. Line a dish with pastry, pour in the mixture, and bake a nice brown.

If you wish to cook it as a vegetable, you must cut it in slices about six inches long, peal them, and boil them in a saucepan of water with a little salt and two ounces of fresh butter. When done sufficiently, drain them on a sieve, and serve them on a hot dish with some melted butter poured over them; or, after they are boiled, fry them in a little lard or dripping. Pepper and salt should be eaten with them. They are also very delicious mashed; they should be boiled, then drained, and mashed smoothly with a wooden spoon; heat them in a saucepan, add a seasoning of salt and pepper, and a small piece of butter, and serve them with small pieces of toasted bread placed round them.

In making preserve, take three pounds of pumpkin, peel it, and slice it into pieces about an inch thick, and two or three inches long; add the juice of two lemons, and the rind very finely grated, three pounds of loaf-sugar, and one ounce of ground ginger. Put all these ingredients into a preserving-pan, and boil all together till clear—about one hour. Put it in jars and tie it well down.

Soup made with Pumpkins.—Boil the pumpkin and rub twelve or thirteen ounces through a sieve; add gravy, soup, or good stock to it—it will take about one quart for the above quantity of pumpkin; mix it gradually, and season with salt and a little cayenne; let it boil up, add a very little corn-flour to it, and serve it very hot, with fried bread cut into small pieces.

The stock for the above receipt need not necessarily be made with meat, as this is expensive. The liquor in which a piece of meat has been boiled makes very good stock; bones of any kind can also be used. All sorts of bones may be mixed together—beef, mutton, veal, and game. Game bones give a very delicious flavour to soup. When large joints of meat are to be used for dinner, they will require a little trimming; take all these pieces of fat and gristle which have to be cut off, add a slice or two of bacon and some herbs and vegetables, with any bones you have left from other joints, and keep them over the fire a short time, taking care to shake the saucepan occasionally, that they may not set to the bottom. You must keep the pan closely covered. After it has been on the fire about ten minutes, pour in some boiling water, so as quite to cover the meat, &c., and let it stew gently till it is rich. Take off the fat when it is cold. This sort of stock will make very good pumpkin soup.

Before concluding, I must give you two more receipts to which pumpkins are a very great improvement. One is a "Buckland stew," and the other a "Trifle." This is how the "Buckland stew" is made:—Have ready a very clean pan, and some nice gravy; now take about a pound of meat—beef or mutton is the best for this purpose—cut it either in thin slices or square dice; peel a pound of potatoes, and cut them in small pieces, with two carrots, two turnips, and two onions, all cut up small, and half a pound of pumpkin which has been boiled for about half an hour previously. Put the meat and vegetables in the pan, season them well with pepper and salt, adding a little Worcestershire sauce, and pour in your gravy, which must have a little flour added to it to thicken it. Put the pan on one side of the fire ; then make some good suet crust, allowing four ounces of suet to one pound of flour, put in a little baking-powder, and mix it tolerably stiff ; roll it out an inch thick, and cut out a piece the size of the top of your pan, so as to exactly fit it, lay it over the meat and vegetables, cover the pan, and boil all together for three-quarters of an hour, or an hour. This is a very economical dish, as so little meat is required.

The " Trifle " is made in this way :—Scald six large apples, peel and pulp them ; boil one pound of pumpkin for an hour ; rub it through a colander, and mix it thoroughly with the pulped apple ; sweeten it well, and grate the rind of a lemon over ; then place this pulp in a deep glass dish, about half filling it ; scald half a pint of milk, half a pint of cream, and the yolks of two eggs over the fire, stirring it all the time till it boils ; add a little sugar ; let it stand till cold ; then pour it over the apples and pumpkin ; and, last of all, make a little whip, either with cream or white of egg, and lay it over the whole.

OUR BROTHERS AND SISTERS.

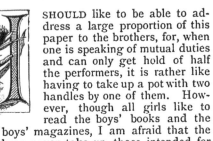

SHOULD like to be able to address a large proportion of this paper to the brothers, for, when one is speaking of mutual duties and can only get hold of half the performers, it is rather like having to take up a pot with two handles by one of them. However, though all girls like to read the boys' books and the boys' magazines, I am afraid that the boys never take up those intended for the girls except to jeer ; so there is no use my writing here, " My dear fellows, what are you thinking about in letting your sisters fetch and carry for you like that, and expecting them always to give in to your will and pleasure ? Don't you know that it is exactly in proportion as men are low down in the human scale that they allow women to wait on them, that it is the most debased class of peasantry who make their wives and sisters toil in the fields while they preserve a lordly idleness, and that it is the unmitigated savage who marches at the head of his tribe with his womankind following submissively, carrying the burdens ? "

No, my address can only be made to reach the girls, but before suggesting their own separate parts and duties I should like to sketch what I think the family relations should be, for am I not speaking to the future mothers of boys and girls ?

That there is something faulty about the long-accepted system of making the boy Number One in the house must, I think, be acknowledged when we reflect how universally it is allowed that men are selfish creatures, while self-abnegation and patience are considered the special prerogatives of women. Now, I think a great deal of the selfishness and domineering spirit of the average Englishman is in a large measure due to the way in which his sisters have been expected, as a matter of course, to do what their brothers want them to and put their convenience first, to be obliging and good-natured and set aside their own wishes for the wishes of Jack and Tom, while anything the brothers do for them is looked on as an exceptional favour—" so good of the dear fellows ! "

Very unselfish women are produced by this means, no doubt, but I am too fond of boys not to resent their being so completely sacrificed to the girls—their characters I mean, the importance of which stands surely on a higher level than that of their comfort.

So it comes about that nearly all the nicest men I have known, those really unselfish, courteous and considerate to women, have either had no sisters at all, or selfish sisters, or sisters so few in comparison with the brothers that they occupied the position of importance in the household attendant on rarity.

Do I want the sisters to give up being unselfish and good-natured to their brothers ? you will ask. Not at all, for there would be again the sacrificing of one half of the family to the other ; what I urge is that these things should be mutual. By all means let the girls mend their brothers' socks, and be always ready cheerfully to perform any little feminine office asked of them ; let them allow their own especial pursuits to take a secondary place for the short time that Jack and Tom are at home ; let them write their brothers the long chatty letters everyone loves to get, when they are away again.

But why should not Jack and Tom answer these letters ? Why should not they consider whether, while they are with their sisters, they cannot make life more cheerful for them, and devise such festivities or expeditions as would make a pleasant break in the comparative monotony of a girl's existence ?

Boys have generally more pocket-money than girls. Might not a little of this be spent on their sisters, instead of all on their own gratifications ? When Molly has spent her morning putting new pockets in Jack's trousers, why shouldn't Jack take her over in the afternoon to the golf links and introduce some of his friends to her, and give her tea ? If Grace leaves the reading-up for her exam. till Tom has gone back to Oxford, because he likes to have her cycle and play tennis with him, and she is sure she can make up for it afterwards with a little extra work, why shouldn't Tom arrange to get her up there for " eights," and let her have a little fun ?

And if the girls show so much consideration—which means the highest form of courtesy—to them, would it not show nicer feeling in the brothers if they were more considerate, more courteous, in fact, more gentlemanly to the girls ? The ideal sister would have all the affectionate thoughtfulness for her brother she would have for the man she loved. The ideal brother would show his sister all the little attentions he would to the woman whose preference he wanted to win.

It is a generally acknowledged privilege of brothers to be brutally frank, and the process is usually considered good for the sisters as tending to " take the nonsense out of them." Unfortunately, it is not only the nonsense that is apt to be knocked out of women by brutality of any kind, but some desirable qualities as well. Rough treatment on the part of brothers, as of parents, brings out a roughness in return. Girls accustomed to receive it learn to hide and suppress not only their sensitiveness, which may often be the better for keeping under, but all their feelings ; they adapt themselves to their environment, adopt manners as anti-sentimental, off-hand and downright as the boys. " And very sensible too," will be said. True, but sense is not the only excellent attribute of woman ; there are also tenderness, sympathy, graciousness, all that is comprehended under the term *womanly*, and which gives to womanhood its greatest charm. The girl who grows up with these characteristics dwarfed and stunted, as every characteristic systematically suppressed is almost certain to become, will be lacking in one of the essential qualities of an ideal wife and mother. According to my experience this especial womanly charm is rarely possessed to any marked extent except by brotherless girls. The girl who has no " brutal " brother, but is the companion of masculine cousins, "almost the same as brothers," is, to my mind, the one most happily situated for the development of her attractive womanliness, for, in the case of cousinhood there is just that touch of difference which generally prevents that familiarity excluding respect, at least of outer bearing, which is apt to make the intercourse between brothers and sisters a common, unlovely thing.

The relations between *nice* cousins who see a good deal of each other without being under the same roof, and " get on capitally together," are precisely those I should like to see established between brothers and sisters. There is the intimate knowledge of each other—so good for both sexes, so necessary in this world, where men and women are made to live together—the exchange of ideas, the interest in each other's pursuits, the recognition of the lines of demarcation between the boy's sphere and the girl's, the mutual consideration, kind offices, and unselfish ways that give the brightness and beauty to life.

So much for the two handles of the pot. But if Jack and Tom have never learnt to do their part, how about that of Grace and Molly ?

Well, as far as one can see, that cannot be greatly altered. The attempt to get things out of people for oneself, even if it be only fair dealing and common courtesy, is but poor work, and apt to be destructive of more than it acquires. But there is no reason Grace should not use her influence to make Tom more considerate of Molly's feelings in the kind of things he says to her. There is no reason Molly should not suggest to Jack—her own especial brother—that Grace would be pleased if he asked her to go out riding with him sometimes ; there is no reason either should not occasionally say with a laugh to the boys, " Yes, I will do this for you, if you will do that for her," and the plan is not unlikely to succeed. After all, the boys are rude and selfish mainly from habit and from some vague impression that to be so is the manly thing. And brothers are much less apt to resent an attempt to influence them on the part of their sisters than on that of their parents, just as sisters are generally better pleased to acknowledge themselves under the influence of their brothers.

And now comes the question of influence, that most important point in the whole subject of the relation between the different members of a family. There is an old tradition that the woman at home, be she wife, mother or sister, should be the man's good angel ; it has been taken for granted that that is her *rôle*. In these days, when all the old traditions are being broken up and accepted ideas required to be tested, the question is asked why should this be the relative position of the man and woman ? What right has he to expect her to be any better than himself and take her saintly conduct towards him as a matter of course ? And in consequence of these questionings the modern woman is inclined to decide to go her own way and leave her mankind to sink or swim as it pleases without relying on any influence from her.

Now, as it seems to me, it is an insult to Him who made man in His own Image to take it as the right and natural thing that men should be less good than women, and the accepting of any lower standard for them than for us is fundamentally wrong. It is no more right for a boy to torture an animal, or in any way act cruelly to the weak than it would be for a girl, just as—for in certain points the male standard is higher than ours, one must not forget this—it is just as despicable for a girl to do a dishonourable thing or say a spiteful one as it would be for a boy.

But the fact that our brothers, or lovers, or husbands, are not so good as we should like them to be is no reason that we should level ourselves to their standard. On the contrary, it makes the duty the more pressing for us to hold the torch of faith and hope aloft, to be living witnesses of the beauty of holiness, of the possibility and the grandeur of an ideal life. Who is to do it if not we, the women who have been brought up in refined loving homes, taught from childhood the highest principles, the purest forms of belief, sheltered from the temptations into which our brothers are thrust so early, kept from contaminating influences, encouraged in religious habits, where our brothers can only keep to the saying of their prayers and reverent conduct in church in the teeth of that form of opposition most unendurable to the boy or young man ? The English girl, of a rank above that subject to the temptations incident to ignorance and poverty, brought up in a religious house and by loving parents, is surely the possessor of the ten talents from whom much shall be required. So let us set ourselves to our task.

Home influence, the influence of mothers, wives and sisters is, as most men will acknowledge, the most valuable there is in life, and like most valuable things, it is not to be had cheap. In the influence exercised at home nothing but the absolutely solid and genuine will pass muster. There is no question here of fine preaching on Sundays and pleasing ourself for the rest of the week. The religion that tells at home must have " more deeds than words to grace it." Those who live in the same house with us are painfully sharp in detecting any pretence or unreality. We may impose upon the nice, pleasant friends who see us occasionally and think us very unselfish when our kind deeds and sacrifices for others happen always to be exercised in a direction where they finally will pay, very sweet-tempered if we have enough self-control to hide for the moment our vexation, while we make up for it afterwards in grumbles or well-directed reproaches. Our love of religious observances and a habit of speaking authoritatively in matters of faith may gain for us an outside credit for being " good," while formal self-denials on certain days do not prevent our being greedy on others, and our defence of dogmas goes hand in hand with a painful lack of charity, but we cannot take in those who live in the house with us, who see us every day at all times of the day. It is only when they see us—not faultless, of course, for that nobody ever will—but so far as in us lies thorough, with self-knowledge enough to be humble and throughout wholly genuine and sincere, that we begin to have any influence for good. But under these conditions influence always does exist ; it may be resisted, in fact, any member of a family who sets herself to live up to a higher standard than contents the rest is almost certain to meet with some opposition, to her own benefit and strengthening if she only knew it, as vegetation is benefited by the keen winds of spring, but she becomes a quiet power. Little by little the power begins to make itself felt ; one brother or sister perhaps follows the example of the first, and then another. It is curious to watch how, in the progress of years, every member of a family more or less assimilates the lived, if unspoken, teaching of the pioneer, who at first was in her spiritual life alone with her Master.

Some time of especial stress arrives and the courage and unselfish devotion of the religious girl, learnt imperceptibly in the quiet of ordinary life, shows what her religion has made of her. A heavy sorrow falls, and all instinctively turn to her who knows the secret of transforming sorrow into peace. The brothers have gone forth into the world, but they have their hold on home in the lovely memory of sweetness and purity and faith, the certainty of sympathy, whatever life may bring, the knowledge that someone is praying for them, to be their inspiring influence, their shelter in moments of overwhelming temptation. The brother, with a sister worthy of the name, can never feel that, now he is away in the world, he may do what he likes with his life, throw it away as he will, since it now concerns nobody. He can never lose the respect for women, which forms the very salt of the character of a man, he cannot learn to believe the theories which meet him that religion is a pretence, and the creeds an old superstition that has no power left over men's hearts and lives : for has he not at home—his sister !

"WE'LL COME BACK AFTER THANKSGIVING."

Youth's Companion, 1898

PAPER MODELING.

BY H. J. VERNON.

This elegant and useful art is but little known and practiced, owing, we imagine, to the want of a simple, practical, and illustrated account of its manipulation; and yet it has several qualities which recommend it, which are not possessed by some other branches of imitative and decorative art. Its cleanliness, for instance. Instead of the oils, colors, and varnishes, needed by the artist; the glue, wet leather, and coloring matter required by the leather modeler; the various pigments, balsams, plaster-of-paris, moulds, &c., used in the manipulation of wax fruit; and the powders, patterns, leaves, and other expensive adjuncts, required by those who work in wax flowers; all that is wanted in Papier-Plastique, is a penknife, a ruler, a few punches, a piece of lead, and a little thick gum, and clean card-board. Again, there is no disagreeable smell to contend with, arising from the nature of the materials employed, and yet ornaments of a first-class description may be produced, the production of which is neither difficult nor costly; the value of any piece of modeling being propor-

tionate to the time spent upon it. One other advantage paper modeling possesses, is its durability. Leather work is, generally, too large to cover with glass shades, and soon the dust takes off its freshness and beauty. Wax flowers, alas! soon "fade as a leaf," and their leaves are always falling; but an article once made in card-board is liable to none of those disadvantages.

The sketch introduced (fig. 1,) represents a neat Gothic Lodge or Cottage, and can be executed in about a day. We shall proceed to speak of the tools and materials needed for its formation, and describe its construction, so as to enable any one possessing ordinary taste and intelligence to form it for themselves.

THE MATERIALS AND IMPLEMENTS.—1. Provide yourself with a penknife which is fast in its handle when opened, and not what is called "ricketty." The blade should be shaped thus (fig. 2,) for a straight-edged beveled front cuts

2.

with greater certainty and precision than any other shape.

2. Have a piece of willow (or soft pine wood will do) planed perfectly flat and smooth: it should be about one foot wide and two feet long.

3. A piece of hard wood should be procured for a straight-edge, otherwise the knife would be apt to cut it when the work is being executed: it should be about one foot long and two inches broad with the edges beveled down thus ⬡ .

4. Procure a piece of lead, cast in a mould, about four inches square and half an inch thick.

5. In modeling church work a few round punches, like fig. 3, are required to pierce the

3.

foil-work of the windows. They may be obtained from No. 1 to any desired size.

6. Dissolve one ounce of the best white gum in as much water as will cover it. It should be rather thick, or considerable annoyance may arise from it not adhering well and quickly.

7. The card-board used is either "Bristol" or "Turnbull's," the latter is a little the whitest. It may be had in various thicknesses to suit the purpose for which it is required. Three leaves thick will do for small models, but four thicknesses are best for larger ones. It is best to have two, three, and four, for the thin is required for light ornamentation.

The cottage may thus be formed. Take clean white card-board, No. 3, and draw upon it a representation of the pattern, as fig. 4, only double every dimension (the size of our pages does not admit of full-sized drawings.) The lines which are dotted thus .... are to be half-cut through from the outside. The lines marked thus ...... are to be half-cut from the inside. The black

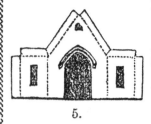

5.

portions are to be cut entirely out. The dotted lines, where the porch comes, are not to be cut, but they merely show where the porch which is to be formed, as fig. 5, is put on. The marginal pieces serve to secure it to the larger building when bent into form, as well as to secure the roof to it.

The window and door openings are to be backed by pieces cut to fit, as figs. 6, 7, 8, 9, 10, 11, 12:

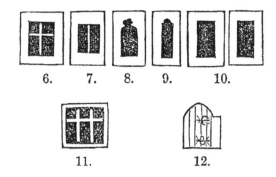

6.   7.   8.   9.   10.

11.   12.

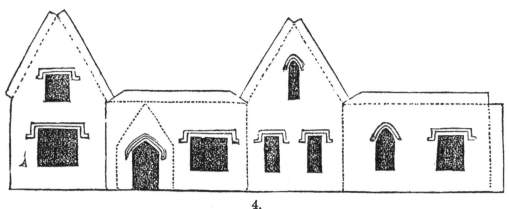

4.

Care must be taken that the hands are always dry and clean on commencing work, and too much attention cannot be paid to the manner of joining the different pieces of board together; the manipulator should not put on so much gum as will ooze out when the pieces to be joined are pressed together, but by applying the brush to portions along the intended joint, these portions may be lightly spread by drawing the finger along. The gum should appear to cling to the finger rather than to wet it only.

the black portions of which are also cut out, and behind them small pieces of glass, or what answers much better, thin talc—the diamond panes being scratched lightly upon it previous to fixing, as in fig. 13. When these are dry, they are to be placed in the four elevations, and weighted down in their proper place until dry; the labels over the windows are to be cut as represented and gummed on. Then, when all is dry, mark the quoin-work round the

13.

windows, fig. 14, in a very irregular way, as also at the angles of the building; and then it

may be bent at the angles and the flap, A. joined to the back of B. and secured thus by setting the house on end, inserting the straight edge over the joint, and leaving it for ten minutes undisturbed. The porch may now be fixed to the main building; its doorway is open, but the door shown in the drawing must be put to the house, being bent a little open; it can be secured by the flange.

14.

The next thing to be done is to form the roofs to porch and to main building, which is done thus: procure a piece of card double the size of fig. 15, half-cut through the centre, but only

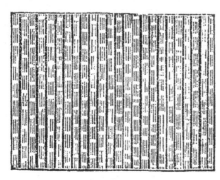

15.

very faintly; cut the lines which are intended to represent the tiles or slates; these slight scratches are to be reversed, as shown on fig. 15. A similar piece should be made for the porch of the requisite size (see fig. 16); these may now be secured to the side walls and gables, to the flanges left, and suffered to dry. During this time cut four patterns, like fig. 17, and

when ready put them on the ends or rather a little under the projections of the roof, as shown in the perspective drawing; a pendent should be cut of the shape shown, of tolerably thick board, and inserted at the point where the barge-boards mitre. These small things are best applied by a pair of spring pincers, similar to fig. 18, which can be

16.

formed of a piece of tin or brass, bent into the required form.

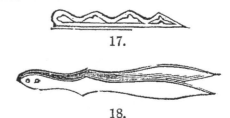

17.

18.

We now come to the chimneys. These are formed of No. 2 board, half-cut, like fig. 19, doubled, and gummed. Small portions like these are best secured while the gum is drying, by wrapping round them a piece of cotton.

19.

As many of these must be formed as will represent the number of flues. A base must then be cut (fig. 20,) making the sides C D, so large as to admit the number of flues; this is to be bent round the flues, the portions notched out being fitted to the pitch of the roof, before bending. A small fillet ▭, half cut at the corners, is now to be put near the top of the chimney; and, when the whole is dry, it is to be secured to the roof. A small band, to represent the plinth of the building, must be neatly put round the whole; but care must be taken that it should stand on a level surface while this is being done; this will give a neatness to its finish, for should the building not be exactly true on its lower edge, it may be rendered so by the plinth. The whole should now be fixed on crimson velvet, or on a black polished stand.

20.

Never color any portion of the work; it is not æsthetic in principle, nor good as a matter of taste. Many a tolerably good model has been spoiled by color being put upon the slates, doors, &c.

The work is done in card-board; and no attempt should be made to make it appear what it is not. No skill will ever make the card-board roof convey to the mind the idea of its being slate, nor the doors wood: indeed, the beauty of the work is its whiteness and sharpness of outline.

FIG. 1.—EGYPTIAN SANDALS.

THAT costume is incomplete if due attention has not been paid to the clothing of the feet, is an admitted fact; yet, I think that our ancestors would be filled with astonishment, could their superbly clad feet carry them again through the stately homes, halls, and courts in which they once had their place, so that they might be enabled to observe the simplicity of design and material, in the *chaussure* which satisfies the *élégantes* of the present day; unless, indeed, they were to be carried back to those remote ages, when their forefathers had only just discovered the inconvenience of going barefoot. The date of this discovery I have been unable to arrive at, but that sandals were worn by the Egyptians more than three thousand years ago, is amply proved by the fact that they have been found upon the feet of mummies preserved since that time, and that they were evidently worn by Moses, for he was commanded, "Loose thy shoe from off thy foot," &c. There is an even earlier mention of the shoe than that just quoted, when Abram declared to the King of Sodom, "I will not take from a thread even to a shoe-latchet" (Gen. xiv. 23). The Egyptian shoe alluded to in Exodus was doubtless a sandal, as the one word used in the original is translated both ways. It was probably made from the same preparation of papyrus as that used for writing upon, examples of this primitive foot-gear being still in existence; sandals were also worn made from palm-leaves—they must have been delightfully cool and light for a hot climate—(the idea is recommended to the notice of shoemakers of the present day for the soles of indoor shoes for summer wear, and although the material might possibly not be found very durable, yet that would hardly be regarded as a disadvantage from their point of view). These sandals were kept in place by two thongs, one across the instep, and another passing between the great and second toe, and joining the first at the instep: not a very perfect method of attaining the desired object, but adopted, probably, that the feet

might be easily withdrawn from them: a custom denoting reverence to Deity and respect to superiors —practised in the East even now—which has been so ably and humorously illustrated by Robertson's "The Shoes of the Faithful," a picture that attracted a good deal of attention from visitors to the Academy Exhibition of '82.

The sandal of the Egyptians denoted the caste of the wearer; that reserved for the upper classes being

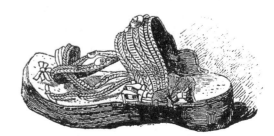

FIG. 2.—ROMAN SANDAL.

long, pointed, and turned up at the toe, not unlike the skate of the present day. The lower classes were forbidden to wear them shaped in this manner, but what they lost in the supposed elegance of the fashionable foot-gear, was compensated by the greater convenience of the commoner short-toed sandal. The Egyptian belles seem, after a time, to have paid great attention to the beauty of their sandals, which we find made of rushes, palm-tree bark, and even leather, dyed and variously ornamented.

An extremely curious custom was practised by the men of Egypt in order to gratify their hatred of their enemies; upon the cloth lining of the sandal a figure was painted representing the hated nation or person,

FIG. 3.—ROMAN SOLDIER'S SANDAL.

"that so they might continually tread the enemy underfoot" (Fig. 1).

The Romans ordinarily went barefoot indoors, and the earliest examples of the sandals used by them are extremely simple, until their far-reaching conquests introduced them to the luxurious foot-gear of other nations, which they adopted and improved upon to such an extent that Cato, as a protest against the usage which compelled their wear, and the extravagance of decoration his countrymen indulged in, often went barefoot. The ancient Greeks, as well as the Romans, shod themselves with great simplicity, except in time of war, until they, too, advanced as they increased in riches and luxury, to an elaboration of style, and richness of decoration in their foot-gear,

FIG. 4.—ROMAN PATRICIAN'S SHOE.

(From an Iron Statue of Hadrian in the British Museum.)

which raised shoe-making to the dignity of an important and artistic handicraft.

Amongst them, as well as the Egyptians, the foot-gear indicated the class of the wearer. Slaves were not allowed to wear anything on their feet. Priests and philosophers often adopted the foot-gear of the lower orders as a sign of humility. One of the kinds in use amongst rustics was called the *crepida*, on account of the noise (*crepitus*) made by the wearers in walking. Fig. 2 represents a very curious kind of sandal belonging, it is supposed, to the period of the conquest of Britain; the high soles are of cork, and the straps are most wonderfully elaborate. In the time of Caligula, the Roman soldiers wore a kind of shoe, the sole of which was studded with spikes, to give them a firm foot-hold when marching over rugged ground, or climbing steep places : a device the value of which cricketers of the present day can appreciate (Fig. 3). It was because he wore a lighter and more elegant variety of this kind of shoe (*caliga*) while with the army of his father Germanicus, that the soldier gave to the young Caius the surname of Caligula.

FIG. 5.—PYKES.

The shoe was so called from the number of straps (*ligulæ*) used to fasten it round the leg.

The *campagus*, a sort of half-boot not unlike the *caliga* in shape, was usually worn by the Emperors, but it was adorned with the embroidered figure of an eagle, and enriched with jewels. Heliogabalus is said to have worn exquisite cameos on his shoes ; and as it is related of him that he never wore a pair twice, it is to be hoped that the costly adornments of the cast-off shoes were sometimes transferred to the new ones. Cyrus, the great Persian monarch—who, by the way, must have been rather a fop—advises short men to wear something between the sole of the sandal and the foot, in order to increase the dignity of their appearance ; a hint which was adopted, centuries later, by the Roman ladies, who also copied the example set them by Heliogabalus, of adorning their *chaussures* with gold, silver, and precious stones, some having even the soles made of gold. It is difficult to understand why they were at length forbidden by him to ornament their shoes in this costly fashion, unless he wished to establish a monopoly of the privilege.

When luxury and extravagance in the adornment of the feet had arrived at its greatest height, the wealthy and fashionable Romans began to prefer half-boots made of purple leather, to those enriched with gold and precious stones ; but these were by no

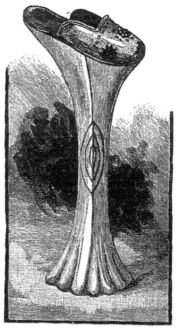

FIG. 6.—CHOPINE.

means inexpensive, on account of the enormous cost of the dye used to give the desired tint, and the time taken to produce the exquisite embroidery with which they were embellished. It is said that the shoes of the Roman maidens were so ornamental, that lovers preserved the soles of those worn by the beloved one, in the same manner as they now treasure locks of hair, ribbons, &c.

I have said that the foot-gear indicated the wearer's rank ; this indication was made decisive by sumptuary laws, the senators wearing black shoes, with a crescent of gold or silver, or other elaborate ornament on the top (Fig. 4), the patricians being allowed shoes with four straps, while the plebeians were forbidden to wear more than one.

We must pass on to the eleventh century, when the Normans began to wear long, sharp-toed shoes—a fashion which was carried to such an extent, that Archbishop Anselm deemed it necessary to preach furiously against it. His eloquence seems to have been wasted, for we find one of the courtiers of the day improved upon the prevailing mode, by stuffing the toes of his shoes with tow, and having them twisted like rams' horns. Amongst the eccentricities of the Plantagenet period, was the fashion of wearing a differently coloured stocking on each leg, the shoes being adorned with designs cut from the upper leather, to show the stocking, each shoe itself being of a different colour; thus the right leg and foot would be clothed with a red stocking and a white shoe, while the left would display a purple stocking and a green shoe. The long-toed shoes then reappeared, the common people being permitted by law, to wear "pykes on their shoon" half a foot, rich citizens a foot, and princes two and a half feet long (Fig. 5); those who could afford it fastened them to the

FIG. 7.—CAVALIER'S BOOT.

knee with gold or silver chains. It was in vain that Popes and Councils remonstrated against this absurd fashion —that "persons of any condition whatsoever" were forbidden, "on pains of being mulcted in a penalty of ten florins," from using the "long-peaked shoon, as contrary to good manners, and a mockery of God and His Church," until Parliament in 1643 prohibited shoemakers from making them with "beakes" more than two inches long, enforcing their prohibition with heavy fines, and the curse of the clergy. Fashion then ran to the opposite extreme, requiring the shoe to be a foot in breadth across the toes. One of the greatest follies ever perpetrated by the *beau monde* was the adoption, during the sixteenth century, of the "chopine," a device for increasing the wearer's stature. Shakespeare alludes to it when he makes Hamlet address one of the lady actors thus: "Your lady-ship is nearer heaven than when I saw you last by the altitude of a chopine." These chopines, as worn by the ladies of Venice, were "made with wood covered with leather of various colours . . . many of them curiously painted . . . some gilt. . . . and by how much nobler a woman is, by so much higher are her chopines. All . . gentle-women . . that are of any wealth, are assisted and sup-ported either by men or women, when they walk abroad . . . otherwise they might quickly take a fall." Raymond says they wore these "wooden scaffolds" as "high as a man's leg." One writer says that "one being asked how he liked the Vene-tian dames," he laughingly an-swered "that they were *mezzo carro, mezzo ligno* (half flesh, half wood), and he would have none of them." (Fig. 6.) During the seventeenth cen-tury high boots were worn, the tops of which were turned down when walking, to display the costly lace with which they were lined. The top of one style of boot worn at this time was so broad as to compel the wearer to assume a most ridiculous "straddle when walking." (Fig. 7.) Then high red heels, and buckles of an enormous size, became fashionable, which subse-quently were worn richly ornamented, sometimes with real diamonds. After a time the heels became lower, and were slanted towards the middle of the foot; the discomfort of this mode was probably the reason why heels for a time almost vanished. Then came a period which was marked by nothing very remarkable in the history of foot-gear, until the introduction of ma-chinery for the manufacture of boots and shoes.

The Rainy Day.

BLEST drizzle that keeps prudent people
  Shut tight in-doors,
And blots the town roofs and the steeple,
  And builded shores,
Wipes out all bounds and limitations,
And leaves but vaguest intimations
Of his or thine! My old vexations
  Depart by scores;
Abstract, I am, without relations,
  Whene'er it pours.

What are to me the wretched changes
  Of human life?
Here, hemmed by mists, my being's range is
  All closed to strife.
Despair may tackle me to-morrow,
And I may share the whole world's sorrow,
Or others woe from me may borrow,
  But not to-day,
The sphere I walk in is too narrow
  To breed dismay.

The woods and fields I roam about in,
  Wet as an eel,
At every step the water spouting
  From toe and heel,
The traveling seeds of weeds and grasses
I furnish gayly with free passes,
They board me singly and in masses,
  By hook and crook,
And, being of the clinging classes,
  Cannot be shook.

But night comes on; I'm stiff and weary,
  The storm grows rude,
The landscape all is wild and dreary,
  And so's my mood;
The task assigned by the Creator
To me, as weed-disseminator,
Is done; I'm ready now my fate for,
  And I would fain
A gust of wind exchange my state for,
  Or drift of rain.

Roger Riordan.

THE SUMMER'S AFTERMATH.

No more above its verdant robe, like dainty jewels pink and blue,
The morning-glory's slender cups are held to catch the shining dew;
No more the lily's graceful stalk holds bells which every zephyr rings,
No longer in the happy breeze the rose her fragrant censer swings.

But purple pansies, here and there, uplift brave faces toward the sky,
And mignonette its perfume flings, like gold, among the passers-by;
The cardinals in sheltered spots disclaim the coming winter's gloom,
And autumn asters, many-hued, make bright the garden-beds with bloom.

The stately corn in regiments uplifts its serried blades on high,
And ghosts of summer's thistle flowers on gauzy wings go sailing by;
The white-robed frost has not yet laid, with chilling touch, his mantle brown
On solidago's golden head, or meadow clover's crimson crown.

Still sings the robin in the wood, and, from some corner out of sight,
The quail his mellow call repeats for that unknown, long-lost "Bob White."
The blackbirds chatter in the tree, the crickets chirp beside the path
Where drowsily the cattle stand knee-deep in fragrant aftermath.

A darker green is on the pine, a deeper blue is in the sky,
From where embowering willows bend, with sweeter song the stream slips by.
In shadowy hollows by its side the partridge beats his muffled drum,
And autumn apples blush beneath the lusty kisses of the sun.

The gold that binds the birch's brow, the rubies from the maple's crown,
Through mellow depths of slumb'rous air in lazy spirals settle down;
The Autumn trails her azure robe across the mountain's ample breast,
And overlays the level land with blessedness of perfect rest.

BETH DAY.

NOVEMBER GRAY NOW SAUNTERS FORTH
AND BIDS US MIDST OUR PLEASURE
OUR GRATITUDE TO GOD POUR FORTH
FOR BLESSINGS WITHOUT MEASURE

A CHRISTMAS CARD FROM LIFE.
By permission of Hon. and Rev. F. Dutton.

DOGS AND CATS AS SITTERS.

By NELLIE HADDEN.

To many people there is no greater ordeal than that of sitting for a portrait—yet very few ever take into consideration the fact that it may be even more of a trial to the artist. Anxious, as he may well be, to do the utmost justice both to his subject and to his art, what can the artist find more dispiriting than a sitter who speedily becomes restive or easily bored?—and, alas! the majority of people fall easily under one of these two headings.

My own experience goes to prove that animals on the whole are far more satisfactory sitters than human beings. For instance, what elderly gentleman could you keep not merely awake, but also exhibiting a lively intelligence, by so simple a device as a live hedgehog rustling beside him in a paper bag? True, it might make him sit up at first, but the novelty would soon wear off. Whereas I found this device most successful in the case of a phlegmatic little terrier, "Bobbie," who was once posed in my studio. He was a keen sportsman, with a marked predilection for hedgehogs; hence it

I.—"BOBBIE": A SPORTING CHARACTER.
By permission of Lady Isabella Keane.

was brought by Sir William Gatacre from Chitral in 1895. She was the only cat discovered in that place. I found her a most difficult subject to deal with, as she had none of the reserve and dignity of the home-made article. She was all life and activity, and would run up the curtains with a zest that was distinctly distracting—from the artist's point of view. At other times she would give vent to the most pitiful little cries, more like those of an infant than of an animal. She soon succumbed to our climate, dying in little over a year, despite the utmost care bestowed on her by her devoted mistress.

For studio purposes cats are much more difficult to manage than dogs. They have an exasperating habit of curling themselves up in a comfortable position, when the mood seizes them, and turning their backs on the portrait painter with a most perfectly studied show of indifference; or they will look contemptuously at any dainty that may be placed

II.—THE ONLY CAT FOUND IN CHITRAL.
By permission of Sir William Gatacre.

was an easy matter to keep him on the *qui vive* throughout the whole length of each sitting, without actually gratifying his curiosity; moreover, the animal in the paper bag unconsciously played its part with praiseworthy perseverance, leaving me free to devote myself to the work in hand.

Though I have had many odd experiences with animal sitters in general, I have only space now to refer to the dogs and cats of my acquaintance. Perhaps one of the most interesting of these was a curious little cat, with a mole-like skin, that

III.—"BOGIE," OR "WHO KILLED COCK ROBIN?"
By permission of Miss H. G. Williams.

IV.—"CORINNE."

By permission of Mrs. Lockwood.

before them, and walk off nonchalantly, as though their habitual attitude were a bland disregard of food. I tried an experiment with our own cat, "Bogie," which proved most successful. He was a splendid specimen of a silver-grey chinchilla (stolen, alas! and never since recovered). The first time he sat to me I put him on a table and attached him, by means of a collar and a string, to a bar running across the studio ceiling. After a while he got bored and jumped down, only to find himself swinging in mid-air. Of course, I rushed to the rescue; but "Bogie"

took the lesson promptly to heart, and never again attempted to jump down after he had been posed. I doubt whether a dog would have taken in the situation quite as quickly.

As a general thing I have found it much easier to manage animals in the absence of their owners. There are, however, exceptions to this rule. "Corinne," the handsome poodle whose portrait I painted in miniature on ivory, turned her back on me the moment we were left alone, and howled dismally without stopping. Could anything be more disconcerting? In the end her master or mistress had to assist at every sitting.

A model sitter was the dog I have designated "Jock No. I." He was well known in many parts of London, sedately trotting after his master in Piccadilly, or giving a *ton* to St. James's Street. He had a paw in all his master's pies—this busy

VI.—"JOCK NO. I."
By permission of William Sayer, Esq.

had a pathetic little face, but he was not so interesting as my own old friend and model, "Jock No. III." The latter began to sit at the early age of six weeks, and how he hated

V.—"JOCK NO. II."
By permission of Miss Lucy Hadden.

"Jock." Until that master married, he saw him to his work every morning. He accompanied him on his wedding tour (after being shown the marriage lines), and on their return felt it his duty to remain at home and guard the house which contained his mistress. After his portrait was finished, he would sit up and "pose" every time he met me, for sitting meant biscuit. "Jock No. II."

VII.—"JOCK NO. III.": "THE HAPPY HUNTING GROUNDS."

VIII.—BLUE PERSIAN KITTENS, "PROMISING BUDS."
By permission of John M. Wood, Esq.

IX.—"GAMBOGE, THE BIRD-FANCIER."
By permission of Miss H. G. Williams.

X.—" VENUS."

By permission of John Deverell, Esq.

"Gamboge" is a large yellow gentleman, like a tawny tiger. Most cats object to walking in snow, and when compelled to do so from the force of necessity they shake each paw as they lift it, with an air of marked disgust at finding themselves in such circumstances. But "Gamboge" is an exception, and looks particularly handsome against the white background when prowling stealthily after the birds.

"Venus" was one of three beautiful bulldogs. Whether seated in a row in their respective baskets or rushing out barking at the chance caller, this trio invariably struck terror to the heart of the timid stranger. In reality "Venus" was the most good-natured and confiding of dogs, and became so much attached to me that when I left the house she wanted to come with me. "Victor" was a perfect

it at first! Later he became so accomplished in the art, and was so jealous of other sitters, that I had to shut him up when they arrived. He loved his food, as most dogs do, and a greedy dog is the easiest to keep quiet and alert; but he would also sit and "look on" (as in the illustration on page 300) while his friends lapped, in spite of the remarks published with a reproduction of this picture in one of the papers to the effect that no dog could be made to look on while a cat fed. Good little "Jock"! He is gone to the "happy hunting grounds!"

Perhaps one of the most difficult subjects I ever had to paint was the handful of Blue Persian kittens shown in illustration VIII. "Promising Buds" they were called; but to the artist they were anything but promising, for the little electric atoms were all over the place.

XI.—" VICTOR."

By permission of Col. J. C. Dalton, R.A.

XII.—"THE WITCH OF BRIGHTON."
By permission of H. Senior, Esq.

XIII.—" ROMETTA."
By permission of Lady Willes.

XIV.—"THE ONE WHO LOOKED ON."
By permission of Mrs. Whitfield.

gentleman. He usually sat "with his arms crossed," as an old servant described him. He and I lunched together during the sittings at an A. B. C. shop in London, and his manners, as he gravely mounted a chair opposite me and partook of sponge cake, might be copied with advantage by some humans.

The "Witch of Brighton" was well known there, and quite a professional beauty. It is a great pleasure to paint a beauty who is not self-conscious, and this lady gave herself no airs, though she was most openly flattered and praised to her very face.

Another very dainty sitter was "Rometta,"

a native of Rome. She would pose with all the ease of an Italian model. Perhaps no greater contrast could be presented than this graceful little foreigner and the bulldog "Venus." It seems strange that both should come under the heading "dog"; yet each in its way was equally interesting. And it is amazing what character and individuality will reveal itself in animals as one cultivates their personal acquaintance and devotes all one's attention to their idiosyncrasies during a number of sittings. With their lack of affectation, and their general intelligence, it would be difficult to find more entertaining sitters than cats and dogs.

"THE BLACK WATCH."
By permission of W. P. Ker, Esq.

Illustrated London Almanack, 1851

HOUSEHOLD HINTS.

If the hands are stained with fruit juice, do not wash in hot water and soap, but only rinse in cold water, when the stains will disappear.

The best way to light a kitchen fire, is to pack the coals and cinders carefully and closely, and then light it on the top with a fire-wheel or wood and a little small coal. This will then burn downwards and make a glowing fire which will need no further attention for a long time. If the bottom of the grate is not fitted with a shaped piece of tin or iron to stop the bottom draught, a piece of brown paper should be cut to shape and put in position before the coals are laid.

To cut a piece of indiarubber easily, wet the knife with water before using it.

Whalebone may be very easily cut if warmed first over a lamp-glass or by the fire, when it will become quite soft.

To remove fruit-stains from linen, pour boiling water over the stain as soon as possible.

When passing a bad smell in the road, do not open the mouth to speak of it, but close it immediately and pass quickly on. Children should be taught to do this.

When making an open treacle tart or tartlets, mix two tablespoonfuls of very fine breadcrumbs with the treacle. It makes it much nicer and prevents the treacle soaking into the paste and making it sodden.

Stewed fruit is nicer if a small quantity of sago is boiled separately and then mixed with the stewed fruit before sending it to table. The proportions should be two ounces of sago boiled in a pint of water to a quart of fruit.

Eggs that are to be kept should be stood on the small end of the egg, and not the broad end.

To prevent made mustard from drying and caking in the mustard pot, mix a little salt when making it, and it should always be made with boiling water.

Chamois leather should never be washed in hot water, which hardens it, but in cold water, with either a little ammonia or a lather of soap.

Boots and gloves wear longer and better if kept for some time before wearing them. It is well to have a pair or pairs of each kept for some months before use.

Suet puddings are much lighter and better if plunged into boiling water if they are to be boiled.

To keep the feet warm in cold weather, cut a sole to the size of the boot or shoe in thick brown paper and wear it.

Baking powder of superior quality can be made of three ounces of tartaric acid, four ounces of carbonate of soda, and half a pound of ground rice. Pound the tartaric acid in pestle and mortar till quite smooth; do the same separately with the carbonate of soda; mix all three well together in a basin and keep in a close-fitting tin in a dry place.

A tear in a dress, or the worn seams of umbrellas, may be neatly and effectually mended by bringing the edges together and putting over them on the under-side a piece of sticking-plaster, or tissue made for the purpose, cut in a strip to the size of the tear. In the case of thin muslin being torn, only gum or thin paste need be used.

Flannel should not be used in needle-books for sticking needles into, as flannel is often prepared with sulphur, which will rust the needles; a piece of fine linen or chamois leather is better.

The best lemonade is made with one lemon, one quart of water, and ten lumps of sugar. Peel the lemon, taking great care not to get any of the white under-skin, cut the lemon in half, take the pips out and squeeze out all the juice, add the sugar, and pour the water over it quite boiling, adding the thin yellow peel at the last. This can be drunk hot or cold.

Aberdeen sausage is a very nice breakfast- or supper-dish, made according to the following recipe:—One pound of lean buttock-steak, half a pound of fat bacon, two small teacupfuls of grated bread-crumbs, one dessertspoonful of Harvey or Worcester sauce, one egg, one teaspoonful of salt, and half a teaspoonful of pepper. The beef and bacon to be finely minced and well mixed, then add the bread-crumbs and other ingredients, and lastly the egg. Form it all into a roll, not too long, and boil in a floured cloth tied at the end (not too tightly) for two hours. When done, cover it while hot with crisp bread-crumbs, and serve cold at the table.

When hanging meat in the larder, it is well not to put the metal hook through the meat itself, but through a loop of string tied on to the joint.

Too much care cannot be taken about constant changing of the water in which cut-flowers are placed in rooms, as also to empty out and clean the ornamental china bowls in which flower-pots are placed, and these should always be a couple of sizes larger than the pots, so as to allow of free ventilation; they are non-porous, and are not good for the plants unless there is room for ventilation. Plants should never stand in stale water.

To keep off rats, put tar round the holes they come out of. They are very clean creatures, and will not tolerate anything dirty or sticky on their fur.

A DETECTIVE ON DETECTIVE STORIES.

E was an expert in crime. There was no doubt about that. But he regarded it not from the point of view of the criminal, habitual or otherwise. His was the vantage-ground of a member of the detective force at headquarters, and he was of rank in this calling—a skilled man, with admirable patience, a knowledge of men and matters, a cool courage and a ready wit which had many times saved him. The rules of the service prevent my naming him, and he would not himself like it. Our conversation had turned on detective stories and some glaring legal absurdities which I had remarked in one of the tales I had picked up for a railway journey.

My friend stretched himself still more luxuriously in the club chair, hugely enjoying his after-dinner cigar and a lengthened moment of leisure, and proceeded to reason with me on my fondness for reading that class of literature. "Not," he said, "that I suppose you would call those stories literature any more than I would call them true accounts of a detective's methods."

"Every man to his trade. I don't believe they are entitled to be called literature, not even when they are written by Conan Doyle. Not that my opinion is worth much on the subject ; still, I feel pleased he has stopped writing them. You should know best about their other side, for I am friendly enough to be aware of your experience and your constant success in a difficult branch. That is for your private ear ; publicly, I shall feel bound to say that New Scotland Yard is an utter failure in the more delicate line of rogue-catching. It's a genial fashion of the newspapers."

"I know it is, and I don't mind it. No matter ; if we don't go hunting about for criminals with a microscope, nor write essays on the varieties of tobacco ash, we get our men much more frequently than the public choose to imagine."

"You don't read detective stories?" I said, with a touch of malice, for I thought I had him.

"Have I time?" he said reproachfully. "I have seen some of them, and they have given me an amount of amusement which their authors didn't intend when they wrote them—at least, not in that direction."

"For instance ? " I said inquiringly.

"They magnify crime too much ; they make it *grand*. Now I read a story the other day in which the mystery turned on the proceedings of a gang of coiners. There were three of them in the gang, two men and a young woman, and they were described to have taken a big country house, say, in Kent. Here they had fitted up a hydraulic press with a chamber big enough to hold a man, which was used for stamping. Now the whole thing is impossible. The hydraulic press will never be heard of in that business, because it is useless. Coining is a mighty small and ill-paid occupation, and is only done in one way. It has gone down to very small dimensions in this country. The chief coiners here—it is a curious story, and you may hear it—were a family named Kelly. They all died in prison—father, mother, and son."

"And what of them ? "

"They made a discovery which put them in the front rank. It was how to make false money ring. I won't tell you what the secret was. It is not a very great secret, but you would put it in a paper, or perhaps try the game on yourself——"

"Thanks. Have another cigar ? "

When this was well lighted he went on.

"It's a certain substance which is cheap enough and readily got. All that is needed apart from the various moulds to enable hundreds of pounds' worth of bad money to be made is an ordinary crucible. That is easily got. The chief and most difficult things to get are the moulds, of which no mention is made in this famous story. They are made of plaster-of-Paris, and are subsequently baked and pass through another process, after which they can be filled with the metal in a molten state. Clamps are used to keep the two heads of the moulds together, and when these are released the coin is ready for the milling process—you know, that which gives the serrated edge to the coins."

"Could the press not have been used as a stamper to press the coins out of metal ? "

"They would not need a die stamper of that size. Besides, there are a great many substantial reasons why a stamp could not be used. No, it could not be used to compress the alloy. The truth is the author did not study his facts."

"Well, but apart from that, the idea is feasible enough?"

"I fail to see its feasibility. Take another point. You have a powerful hydraulic press fitted up in a private house in the country, and nobody takes any notice of it or is aware of its existence. Why, such a thing would not have been there for twenty-four hours in a small country place without everybody knowing of it. Workmen must have been employed for some time to fit it up, and they must have lodged close by. Gossip, my friend, is a great institution. It's been the key to the convict establishments to many a clever criminal. Nobody knows how great is gossip, and how useful to society, as does the detective."

"You forget the London correspondent, but go on."

"Note this, that here are two men working a powerful hydraulic press, and yet neither of them has sense enough to put a collar right on one of the working parts, and has to call in an engineer for the purpose. Mind you, I don't say the story is not a good one. All I say is that the author has no practical knowledge of the subject. Besides, there is the money to be disposed of. It is no easy thing to get rid of bad coins. There is a regular procedure involved. It is notorious that the man who makes the money never passes it unless under very rare circumstances. The business is in the hands of a very low class, and is not a flourishing means of living, I assure you. The trade is dying out. Ever since Inspector Brennan set himself to stamp it out it has been dying down every year. About twenty-five years ago he cleared the country of the best of the gangs. It was a noticeable thing that at that time the trade ran in certain families, of which the Kellys I mentioned were the biggest operators. Each group had its own little secret of making the coins; but they were all a very low class. The care that has to be taken of the coins is very great. Each has to be wrapped in tissue paper so that it will not 'rust.' The chief place of 'parting,' as they call it, with it is, and was, Seven Dials. It's a most instructive fact that none of those engaged in the trade were ever very successful. I have never found that they were ever able to hire a house, and few have got beyond one room, and a miserable one at that."

"A great deal is often made in these stories of forged notes. I believe that is a more difficult art even than coining?"

"It is. The great difficulty is to get the paper, and certainly bank-note forgers have displayed great ingenuity in getting over that trouble. We have not had many cases lately, and they have been mostly forgeries on foreign banks. It is only recently that Dombroski was sentenced at Winchester to ten years for the offence, and there have been others from time to time; but in our own country note-forgery is largely defeated by the use of special paper, which only one firm is allowed to make, and if a note is not of that paper, it can be detected even by the most inexpert. It is many years ago since Austin succeeded in forging a Bank of England note, and since then we have been free from that class of forgeries."

"Your reference to a Russian rouble-note forger reminds me of another detective story in which the forger leaves his trade and takes to stealing the plans of a new torpedo which is going to play Rule Britannia among the enemy's ships next war."

"I fancy I remember the story; you sent it me when I made the capture of that foreigner," referring to an arrest of a man wanted abroad, which had attracted the attention of two nations to his captor.

"Yes, that was the case. If you will recollect, the plans were hid in an iron rod, painted to resemble a malacca cane, such as I carry when I can afford to brave the risks of the weather, owing to having hopes of possessing sixpence next day wherewith to pay a hat ironer. They were taken away in the cane, photographed, and brought back, and left in the office umbrella-stand. I thought the idea rather smart."

"Now I didn't, nor would you if you had thought for a minute. Just imagine what the plans for a torpedo of that sort would be like. I am reminded that the writer himself lays stress on their minutiæ, and yet he would pack them into the inside of a sham malacca cane. They would be too bulky to go near the inside. It is too absurd to be thought of seriously. Those stories, to me, always fail in one crucial point, and that spoils them for my enjoyment."

"But look at the romance, my dear sir; think how able all these criminals are!"

"That is another thing. All the high falutin' about crime and criminals is so much wasted breath. I have told you before that there is no romance about crime. It is a very rare occasion indeed in which a man of any education whatever has been engaged in ordinary crime. What has attracted them has been such things as embezzlement and trifling forgeries. These are chiefly done by clerks led away by betting and drinking."

"Don't they join the criminal classes after their first experience?"

"I should say not. As far as I have observed, they very often rejoin the ranks of honest citizens and do well, probably not where they made their lapse from honesty, but elsewhere, free of old surroundings. It is quite different with the man who has been a common thief. I really think you never can reform him. He goes back to his old games as soon as he is released, in spite of prison-gate organisations. I have known many cases where men just out after a seven years' sentence have been back in prison within a week. A moment's carelessness, after his first spree with his old comrades, and he is back again."

"That is rather a striking notion about men of education. Nearly all the detective-story law-breakers are rather romantic, in-telligent persons, and, of course, now I think of it, you don't hear of them in real life."

"Very seldom indeed, and then it is im-pressed on your memory by the fuss the newspapers make about it."

"Still, there have been many cases."

"Yes, but they have always been in the direction of swindles. A man with a decent education may be engaged in bigger things, so to speak, when he does take up crime ; often he swindles very meanly, but it does not follow that he escapes."

"Any real story on the point ? "

"Yes, I can give you one of a clergyman and his son. The Rev.—well, after all, never mind his name. It's enough to say he was the rector of a church in Brixton. He was committed the first time for stealing money from collecting boxes. He was caught more than once, and then, plunging deeper, he forged a name to a cheque, for which he got a long sentence. Then his smartness came in. Soon after going into prison he managed to ingratiate himself with the prison doctor, and the doctor—how, I really don't know—consented to be a party to an attempt to get him freed. The parson induced the doctor to bring in some sheep's liver. He then com-plained of blood-spitting, managing the symptoms by chewing the liver, and the doctor ordered him to the hospital. There he pretended to be very ill indeed, and the doctor wrote to the authorities, representing the man as dying and not having many hours to live. He recommended that he should be released at once and conveyed home to die, the doctor offering to attend him to the bosom of his family. It was done, and the parson taken carefully home. As soon as he arrived there he turned on the doctor and demanded £20 as the price of his silence. He pointed out how easily he could ruin the doctor, and perhaps benefit himself by doing so, and the doctor weakly yielded. That parson, sir, bled the doctor dry, till the poor man died broken-hearted. It was a smart trick, but an ungrateful one."

"What happened to the smart parson ? "

"It was another case of clever tricks. He went to Islington and started in the money-lending line. There he became known to ladies as ready to lend money on their jewellery without their husbands knowing of it. A great many, naturally, have objec-tions to going to the ordinary pawnshop. The rev. gentleman raised his money by putting everything into the pawnshop and letting it remain there. Pawn-tickets expire in time. He would be pressed to return the articles, and then he wrote something in this strain—

"'Dear Madam,—If you again annoy me with regard to the article to which you refer I shall be under the painful necessity of dis-closing the whole of our intimacy to your husband.'"

"Yes, that was what you would call a mean swindle."

"You see, none of them would say a word for fear of what the old villain might write to their husbands. His son turned out in a similar way. I had him in custody myself. And as a contrast, if you like, I will tell you how I caught him. He was a collector for a sewing-machine company. He was found to have been cheating the firm and was dis-charged, but managed to keep a book, and still went on collecting. He was a most slippery customer, and I had great difficulty in catching him. I got him finally through a woman he had collected money from, and who was not afraid, as so many of them are, to assist the police. I saw her and arranged with her that she should tell him to call at one o'clock another day because her husband was in the country, and she would not have money till he returned. Now the trick with those fellows is to go to the place before the time appointed ; they never keep the exact time. This woman was equal to the occasion. He called at eleven o'clock, and I turned up at twelve. But the woman knew what she was about, for she seemed surprised at his calling so soon, reminded him that she said her husband would not be there before one, and told him to come back. I thought I had lost my man, but he had been taken in, and the woman showed him into the little front room, and ostensibly called her husband downstairs. I had nothing to do except put the handcuffs on. It was marvellous how that man collapsed when I appeared. Both father and son were in the dock together."

"By the way, what sort of man was this criminal parson in appearance ? "

"Tall, with a fine figure and a beautiful

voice—a clever man and a good preacher, the sort of man women like to hear. He could look very pleasing when inclined, to smooth his own way to roguery, and could produce a good impression before he spoke."

"Well, he seems to have had a curious warp in him and apparently some versatility."

"There is another thing for which little or no allowance is made by detective story writers, and that is the specialisation of crime. It is a most noticeable fact that criminals generally keep to the same line. I knew one man, a fellow named Amos, whom I had under observation for years. I have followed that man and his wife for a whole day, from nine in the morning till eight at night, when I knew they had nothing in their pockets and were hungry, thinking they would have done a little shoplifting. But no. They would stand outside shops where goods were displayed and look at them or gaze in windows, yet they never touched a thing. They were watch-snatchers, and I captured them red-handed at the end of the day, and the man got ten and the woman seven years. It has always struck me as strange that they should have gone about a whole day hungry and yet never attempted to steal handkerchiefs or clothing, of which they could have readily disposed, to buy food. They just stuck to their one line. There are few all-round felons. All try to strike a special line."

"It's the nature of things, I suppose. Everybody is a specialist now."

"Yes; and there is another fact in the nature of things which knocks spots out of the detective story as a transcript from life. It is that crime is nearly always as low and squalid as the criminal. Their ways are as nasty as their lives, and no magazine would admit the true story of crime into its pages. It's a story of wretchedness, worry of mind, and often disease of body. I have seen them by the thousands, and I know. I assure you there is no man so much to be pitied as the criminal, no matter whether he is successful or not."

My detective friend expressed himself with emphasis and some indications of disgust. "Not that there have been no exceptions— notable exceptions—but that is the general rule. Crime is not romantic, but squalid. I did know a case where an element of romance might be imagined. It was that of a man who robbed the mails between Ostend and Dover. He devoted time, money, and address to the job. It occupied him two or three years. He travelled frequently during that time, as an independent gentleman, between London and Ostend and Paris. He was friendly and chatty, and in time became

well known to the people who were in charge of the strong boxes. He managed to sound them, and was enabled to rob the mails of a large sum. He was almost immediately suspected, and in the end arrested."

"The result—penal servitude, I suppose?"

"A curious point of law arose about the case. It was made a plea that it could not be proved where the crime was committed, whether in English or Belgian waters, and the question of jurisdiction was raised. The same plea could have been raised in Belgium, and the man, had it been successful, would have got off. He got seven years. He lived, I found, in good style, kept a ten-roomed house, and had a fine library."

"And what on earth was he?"

"He had been trained as an engineer. Very soon after being out of his time he turned to crime, mixing up with some of the worst characters. It was long before he was found out, for he performed his exploits, principally burglaries, at a distance from his home."

"You did not say how he was arrested. I should like to hear how so able a man was trapped."

"You should know that in England we only take account of facts. The law won't allow us to imagine much, and, I think, rightly, because I am sure the result would be disastrous. This man was suspected and watched. There was nothing more romantic or mysterious about it than that. He was watched for months very close, for the booty had not turned up. He was traced to a firm of jewellers in a big way in the City. They were a firm about which I don't wish to say anything. They were known to the police, and it was arranged that the man should call there at a certain time. When he did call, and was making his purchase, he was arrested and was in actual possession of the bulk of the proceeds of the robbery. It was no more than that, but it was effective enough."

"It would not read so prettily as some of the elaborate arrests of which I have read."

"I dare say not. There was one story I was rather struck with, because it fitted together. Mr. Springfield was the author, and he gets his mystery by causing a secretary guilty of forgery to attempt to poison his employer. The employer drinks the poison, but is unharmed, while the secretary dies. The employer has a fad for collecting curios, and has some poison used by Indians somewhere to poison their arrows. It is pretty harmless taken into the stomach, but fatal in a wound. The secretary puts it into a glass of port, and in getting it out of the jar has some enter a wound on his hand and dies."

"Yes, that is not an improbable mystery, which would work up into a pretty story, and the post-mortem would reveal the facts."

"It is facts we have to deal with all the time. We must not hearsay or fancy, and it is always 'from information received' unless the prisoner is there. All the favour is shown on the side of the accused—a marked contrast to the state of things in France, where the *juge d'instruction* makes it his business to drag the very inside out of an accused man. They go further and hear everything. It is good enough evidence if 'a woman told me that a woman told her.' But there is no room for romance in our system. It fits crime, for in that also there is no room for romance. We have no parrots trained to steal jewellery, and have not to trace the thief by the marks of a bill on a wooden match. I think there is no reason to complain because of that. We are as successful as most men, and crime is year by year going down in amount. I am afraid if it was all on the lines of the detective story it would be going up."

Whereat my friend departed the smoke-room to resume his duties, whether in or out of the New Central Offices it was no business of mine to ask.

W. E. GREY.

A MOTOR IN THE BULL RING

By R. B. TOWNSHEND

"AH, you do not like the sight?" said the marquesa, with a flash of her dark eyes. "You have no taste for our *toreros*."

There was a touch of supercilious coldness in her tone that stung the American. "It is the horses, marquesa," he said, briefly. "I can't stand that."

He was sitting in the marquesa's box in the bull-ring, envied of most men, for the marquesa was as difficult as she was beautiful, and her victims were more in number than those of the most celebrated *torero*. Perhaps it was a sort of fellow-feeling that made the beautiful woman so fond of her national sport. Perfect skill and perfect courage might win anything in the ring, and only such qualities could find favour in her eyes—and both in the bull-ring and in the marquesa's drawing-room it was *væ victis!*

The visitor turned to face her with his back to the plaza. Out there in the sunshine one of Spain's most distinguished *espadas*, with the red cloak in one hand and his long, straight sword in the other, was coolly luring a sullen bull to his death. The marquesa put up her fan as if to shut off a view of a part of the bull-ring where three horses were lying.

"Oh," she answered, indolently, "life is not long enough to let one dwell on the disagreeables. If you look for them," she shut her fan with a click, "you can find them in the house as well as out there— but why look for them?"

It was rumoured that the lady had learned philosophy during the life of the late lamented marquis, who had not been a model husband.

"But, my friend," she continued, "the skill and the courage of the man, can you not even admire them?"

"Oh, the men, of course," returned the American. "I'm not saying anything against them. They're all right. Besides, it's their trade, anyway; and I will say they're real smart—quick as cats, and their nerve just splendid."

"Well," she took him up quickly, "what more would you have? What is there more admirable than address and courage? And where can we see it as in the bull-fight?"

A thrill passed through him at the proud challenge in her eyes.

"What would I have?" he answered, quickly. "I'd have them show their courage by something better than forcing blindfolded plugs only fit for the knacker on to a bull's horns. I'd have them come in on fancy cow-ponies and beat the bull at his own game of twisting and turning. That's worth doing, and I guess our Texas cowboys could do it, too."

"Ah, I knew you were right at heart," she smiled, with a look that for the first time seemed to admit him to the secret intimacy of her soul. "You should have been here when our King was crowned. Then the proudest nobles in Spain themselves rode their best steeds into the ring and met the bull with the lance in full career. Ah! that was a truly splendid sight!"

"Did they, by gum?" said the Transatlantic millionaire. "Wal, I'd have given a thousand dollars to see that. Wish I'd been here. Why, if I'd only known it was on I'd have hired Colonel Cody's best vaqueros to enter for the show and keep our end up."

"You would not then have ridden in the ring yourself?" she said, with a drop of her eyelids. "Before the King no one was allowed to ride but the nobility—no vaqueros could have entered. I suppose you great millionaires are the nobles of America?" she added, with a tinge of malice.

He flushed darkly. "No," he answered, "I'm no nobleman; we don't keep a nobility in my country. And I don't brag that I'd have ridden in the ring myself. I was raised in New York and didn't get much of a chance to ride when I was young. If I'd been raised a cowboy out in Texas, it would have been different with me. You see, I wasn't born rich, and I didn't inherit any millions. I had to rustle around and make them for myself, every solitary cent."

"It appears, then," she insinuated, "that in America the men who make the millions are too busy to be heroes, and so it is your cowboys who have the horsemanship and the—how do you call it?—nerve?"

"I guess in America a man without nerve don't gather many millions," he retorted.

"And if our city folks don't ride much they kin drive. It takes some nerve to drive a two-twenty trotter, and heaps more to drive a sixty horse-power motor. Nerve!" he laughed, scornfully. "There's more kinds of nerve than one, but they all mean that a man's got grit."

"Someone said you had a stable full of motors," she observed. "Do you, then, guide them yourself, or sit beside your chauffeur and let him steer the teuf-teuf?"

"Wal, that's as may be," he returned. "Sometimes one drives and sometimes the other. But if you ask me what I really like it's a sixty horse-power Panhard, a clear track, and a mile every fifty-five seconds. And I prefer my own hand on the steering-wheel every time."

He was interrupted by a roar of cheers from all round the ring. The gaily-harnessed mule-team had already dragged out the carcass of the bull whom the *espada* had duly dispatched and also those of the three horses who had fallen in the fray. Was it not Théophile Gautier who said of the steeds slain in the bull-ring, "They are not carcasses; they are corpses"?

Ringing cheers greeted the advent of a second bull, full of fire, who dashed round the ring like a tornado, sending the gold-bespangled *toreros* flying to the barrier.

"Ah, what a lively bull!" cried the lady, her eyes sparkling. "He moves like a whirl-wind. Even your Texas cowboys might find it hard to evade his swift rush—that is, sup-posing they had the nerve to enter and challenge him." He met her eyes, as hard as steel and as bright, and found there a challenge to his nation. Was there a per-sonal one to himself, too? A sudden in-spiration darted through his mind.

"I can rack that little ten horse-power Daimler round and turn it on a blanket just as good as a cow-pony. And a golden key, they say, opens any gate in Spain, including even that of the *Toril*. B'gosh, I believe a thousand dollars wadded at the man who keeps the door will let me inside, and, once in, I guess I can find the nerve for the rest of the show. 'Twill take lightning steering, but I reckon I can show her a thing or two, if I am a New Yorker." He was watching the sharp rushes of the bull as the *toreros* called him and played him with their dexterous turns and twists. "Anyway, there's no great chance of my wheels skidding on that sandy surface, and I'll gamble I can do the quick turning and dodging as well as those fancy-dressed fellers." He turned to the lady. "Marquesa," he said, aloud, "I've got to ask you to excuse me a few minutes. See you again soon. What's the pretty phrase you have? '*Hasta otra vista*,' and '*Beso sus manos.*'" And like a flash he was gone.

Five bulls had entered one after another the floor of that wide amphitheatre, round which rose to the sky row upon row of eager faces and bright costumes, and after their

innovation on the sacred traditions of the great national institution of Spain; while others yelled "*Olé! Bravo! viva!*" ("Well done, bravo, hurrah!") cheering the novelty of this entirely unexpected turn given to the performance. The puzzled *toreros* ran this way and that, for they were more taken aback than the bull. They were used to bulls, but not to a wild motor driven by a mad American. An enraged *banderillero*

" HIS HOOTER GAVE THREE LOUD, DERISIVE TOOTS."

brief madness of rage and desperate fighting had in turn sunk on the sand before the unerring thrust of the great *espada*.

But as the sixth and last bull bounded from the darkness of his pen into the bright arena and stood there a moment bewildered by the light, the circling crowd, and the cheering, a new thing happened. Another door was hastily half opened and then closed again, and through it in that half-second there darted in, not a gaily caparisoned *torero* on horseback, but a very small motor-car with a single occupant. The swiftly whirling wheels were so low, and the whole machine so tiny, that the man, who held a red flag in one hand and the guiding-wheel in the other, seemed almost as exposed as if he had been on a bicycle. As he rushed past the bull his hooter gave three loud, derisive toots, the motor swung swiftly round the centre of the arena, and then came back full speed straight at the astonished beast. A great clamour went up from the no less astonished audience, some shouting "*Fuera, fuera*" ("Out with him"), indignant at this most unheard-of

made a spurt for the car as if actually meaning to plant his barbed darts in the bold charioteer; but avoiding him by a rapid swerve the American left him behind as if he were standing still, and the yells and cheers of the audience changed in a moment into a burst of laughter. It tickled the spectators to see how the skill of the *torero*, trained solely to baffle the bull, had been as skilfully baffled in turn by the adroitness of the intruder. And now again the laughter ceased and the audience held their breath as the little motor, heading for the bull, speeded straight on to what seemed certain destruction. It came close, the red flag shot out at arm's length to the left, the bull charged blindly at the flag, and with the least possible swerve to the right the motor sped triumphantly past, and again swung round in swift obedience to the guiding hand of the American, now safe in the rear of the outmanœuvred bull.

Round the edge of the barrier were being held hasty and excited conferences of the *toreros*. Taken at a disadvantage like this they hardly knew what to do. The laws of the Spanish bull-ring have come down from antiquity as sacred and as inviolable as those of cricket in England ; doubtless there may indeed have been certain variations tolerated in bygone days, such as the use of bulldogs, nay, even of the lasso. But this dreadful intrusion of the motor-car was a thing utterly beyond precedent. What was to be done? It was all very well to say, "Arrest the intruder," but to run in between a motor going thirty miles an hour and a furious bull was like running in between the devil and the deep sea.

But while the *toreros* hesitated, the audience made up its mind. It had been used to seeing six bulls killed, in the regular fashion, once a week from time immemorial, and it had seen five so killed to-day Now there was offered the novel chance of seeing an up-to-date motor demolished by a bull. and the audience rose to the occasion. Shouts of "*Bravo, motorero ; bravo, motorero,*" rent the air. The childish pun in "mo torero" caught their fancy, and their laughter was as loud as their cheers. The American *motorero* had succeeded in tickling the imagination of the people, and those ten thousand shouts spoke their decision in his

multitude of spectators, and steering for a moment with his left hand he took off his hat and bowed right and left. The cheers were redoubled, and he heard innumerable cries of "*Otra vez ! que se repita !*" ("Encore, encore") while the jesters of the audience encouraged his car with the Madrid cab man's cry of "*Arre, arre !*" ("Gee up !") Never before in his life had Mr. Elihu P. Hanks performed on the public stage, and the effect on him of these cries was curious He suddenly was aware that he, by nature the most masterful, self-controlled, and independent of men, was rapidly becoming the mere slave of a crowd. He was conscious of an insane desire to obey—yes, to please them, to do any mortal thing they wanted. Individually he rather despised, or even disliked them—all but one ; as a mass, they set alight in his heart a new fire—the love of applause ; and he half-hated himself for feeling it.

Round swung the car till it once more headed straight for the bull and at its highest speed. The bull saw it coming, knew his enemy, and with a savage roar charged headlong forward to meet it Swiftly the gap between them closed up, as the gap might

"THE AMERICAN GAVE HER FULL SPEED AGAIN, AND A DESPERATE RACE ENSUED."

favour. In Spain, above all places, it is a dangerous thing to thwart the fancy of the people, and the much and justly irritated authorities (authorities are always irritated by a change of programme) saw that the people must be allowed to have their way.

As the American swung his "teuf-teuf" round in a large circle on the far side of the arena he divined in a flash the new feeling towards him that had come over that great

close between two locomotives encountering on a single rail : but just before the crash came the motor-car slowed up, swerved, and curled away to the left. But the bull, not hampered this time by the flag in his face, turned almost as quickly, and in a moment was galloping right at the tail of the little car. The American, with one hasty glance over his shoulder, gave her full speed again, and a desperate race ensued. For fifty yards there was nothing in it, and the bull, barely two feet behind, was furiously trying to gore the petrol tank at the rear. The little car was one of those for only two people, where both sit right in front. But inch by inch the car drew away and the American signalized his success by a volley of derisive toot-toot-toots on his hooter. Nearing the barrier the car swerved sharp to the right and the bull dashed past it and almost into a stately but startled municipal guard who, hesitating between his duty as a public official and his extreme disgust at this monstrous irregularity, had ventured inside the barrier. He was absolutely grazed by the unexpected swerve of the car, but a quick leap aside saved him by a hair's breadth, and springing to the barrier he went up it like a lamp-lighter, having had quite enough of the unwonted combination, while the bull, who had suddenly turned after him, roared with disappointed rage as he dashed his horns against the solid wood just below the fugitive.

At this same instant the bull was astonished to find himself spanked from behind with a flag. The American had turned instantly to succour, if need be, the hunted official, and, seeing him already safe, dashed past the bull's heels and flapped him as he went by. A round of cheers greeted the neatness of the trick, which the American acknowledged by another volley of toots; to the bull it seemed as if those toots were the challenge of a rival, and, forgetful of the municipal guard, he sped once more after the motor. For a moment it seemed as if he must catch the audacious *motorero* this time. The motor was running in a circular course close to the barrier, and the bull, who cut straight across and ran on the inner circle, had the advantage of a shorter track, an advantage which practically more than equalized their speeds. Now, now, he was all but up with the motor, which was, as it were, penned between the bull and the barrier, when lo! on went the brake hard, the car stopped within twice its length, the bull shot helplessly past, and the car glided gracefully out behind him into the middle of the arena. The *motorero* had scored again.

Then at last the American ventured to take his eyes from the ring and glance up at the box where he had been sitting half an hour before. The marquesa had risen and come forward and was leaning over the edge of the box. He had interested her. She would not hint again that American millionaires had no nerve. And yet was she pleased?

Was not that look upon her beautiful face one of mere expectancy, as if she were waiting for the real business to begin? Could it mean that she was unsatisfied because the final business of the *espada*, the death of the bull, was lacking? Did she expect him to produce a weapon and thrust home with it to win her favour? If so, he would be no *matador*—she might expect.

But while he thus debated in his own mind other people were active. The *espada* himself in particular was furious at this invasion, and his first wrath had fallen upon the unlucky wight at the gate, on whom he fixed the responsibility of having admitted the stranger and whom he trounced soundly therefor. Now, followed by his whole *cuadrilla*, he sprang into the ring, determined at once to stop the unseemly performance and to take ample vengeance for what he looked on as an insult to himself and his profession. But before he and his men could reach the middle of the arena there was a startling change. Hanks had started off after the bull again and had been waltzing round him in a sort of secure ecstasy. He had now found out exactly how near he could shave a collision without being caught; the car flickered this way and that under his sure touch on the steering-wheel, and the exhibition of his amazing dexterity brought cheer after cheer from the crowd. He had skilfully drawn the bull to the far side of the arena just below where the marquesa sat, and proud of his success glanced up at her once more. But just in front of him there stood one of the sweepers, those humble servants of the arena whose inglorious duty it is to rake smooth the sand and hide the gory traces left by the last victim. Theirs is no fancy gold and velvet costume; they win no plaudits from the excited crowd. They only sweep the floor. The man sprang aside to avoid the car, and in so doing put himself right in the path of the bull.

In a moment the unhappy victim was tossed high in the air, and as he fell the furious animal turned, to gore him through and through as he lay. Hanks heard the stricken man's cry of despair and, whirling his car, took in the situation in a flash. The *toreros*, as he perfectly well understood, had entered the arena after him and not after the bull, and in any case they were too far off to be of any use for a rescue. There was only one thing to be done and he did it. Without an instant's hesitation he headed the car full speed straight at the bull, and this time there was no swerving aside. He had no sword, no lance in his hand ; but to save the life of the poor *chulo*, imperilled by the American's rash action, he would dare the uttermost. Right headlong into the bull he drove the car full smash, just as the

with the presence of the King of Terrors. Was he not claiming this rash foreigner as his own ? One man shook his head, another shrugged his shoulders, as they skilfully raised the senseless form to bear it out of the

" RIGHT HEADLONG INTO THE BULL HE DROVE THE CAR."

terrible horns were within a yard of the prostrate sweeper. There was a terrific thud as they collided. The bull's legs were knocked clean from under him, and his great body crashed heavily down upon the car and its occupant. The farce had ended in a tragedy. The petrol from the burst tank caught fire and a great tongue of flame and smoke went up as from a holocaust.

The *toreros* darted to the spot, eager now not to punish, but to save. Some bore away the unconscious sweeper, others hastened to put the crippled but struggling bull out of his pain with the puntilla or dagger before they were able to drag out from under him and from under the burning wreck of the shattered car a piteous figure.

As they disengaged the stricken man with careful swiftness and raised him from the ground, his hanging head and nerveless limbs filled them with dismay. These men had spent their lives in the bull-ring and were familiar

ring. " It is possible," said one to the other ; " he is tough ; he still breathes ; by a miracle he may live. But I do not believe it. Look at his face "; for indeed the ghastly pallor that overspread it was but too like the ashen hue of death.

The marquesa watching from her box saw it, and the ring of admiring young Madrileños who were gazing at her feared for a moment that her cheek grew paler.

Then she furled her fan languidly.

" I think, on the whole," she said, " that the old fashions please me best. They are more artistic."

Yet some people ventured to doubt the marquesa's artistic taste when, three months later, she petrified society by giving her hand to a bridegroom with a cork leg ; but the disappointed gallants finally consoled themselves by swearing that she did it for the honour of Spain, for no one could doubt that it needed more daring to marry a mad Americano than even to take a motor into the bull-ring.

ROUND THE LONDON RESTAURANTS.

By W. J. Wintle.

Illustrated by Will Owen.

Nation newspaper of New York ventured thirty years ago upon the statement: "There are no restaurants in England. There are one or two eating-houses in London which have the air of restaurants, until a fair trial shows the hollowness of their pretensions. There is no nation in Europe where there is so much bad cookery and so little good as in England." If this were ever true—and the writer apparently held a brief for a famous American house—thirty years have made a change, and to-day the catering of London has no need to fear comparison with that of any city in the world.

To estimate the number of establishments devoted to the replenishment of the outer man is a bewildering task indeed. The

ROMANO'S.

London Directory gives a list of 414 refreshment-rooms, 762 dining-rooms, and 1712 coffee-houses, making a total of 2888 eating-houses, without including the great host of

hotels and public-houses. Allowing each of these establishments two hundred customers a day—a very moderate estimate—we find ourselves faced with the startling total of nearly 600,000 meals a day supplied by the London caterers. That this estimate is but a fraction of the reality there is abundant evidence.

The houses are as varied as they are numerous. Between the turtle soup of Romano's and the humble kipper of Shadwell are many stages and degrees of culinary excellence, or its reverse. A hungry man may lounge in marble halls and dine to the

IN SHADWELL.

tune of high-class music and a five pound note, or he may wedge himself between the table and the straight high-backed partition of a coffee-house in Pentonville, and feast his eyes upon a flaming placard bearing the equivocal inscription, "Dine here once, and you'll never dine anywhere else." If his purse be a long one he may relieve its weight at any of the restaurants in Regent Street or Piccadilly; if he suffer from the *res angusta domi* he may test the qualities of Harris's sausages or Lockhart's cocoa. But if he has any pretensions to a working knowledge of the great metropolis he will wend his way to Soho and take his place at a modest *table d'hôte*, where for a shilling he will get five courses admirably served and plentiful in quantity. It is a pleasant little place, is the *Restaurant aux Bons Frères*—though that is not its real name—and the company remind one of the Latin Quarter as they chat with Madame, who presides behind the tiny bar, while Monsieur waits upon his patrons. But I must not give away its real name, for I sometimes go there myself, and have no wish to see the "Good Brothers" crowded out by the inrush of a London multitude.

How London feeds is a problem wreathed in mystery. The attempt to solve it ends in desperation and brings one to the state of mind to which I reduced a caterer by the single question, "What is a Vienna steak?" When he recovered from the shock he piously replied, "Heaven only knows." One cannot measure up the sea, but one may deal with samples of it, and so the catering of London may be dealt with in departments.

Resolving to make a good beginning, I called on Messrs. Buszard of Oxford Street,

OUTSIDE BUSZARD'S.

and was soon deep in conversation with their genial representative Mr. Ansell. The air was redolent of cake. Stacks upon stacks of bridecakes stood around us piled upon shelves from floor to ceiling. Some were disguised in wondrous robes of gleaming sugar, others were simply coated with thick layers of almond icing, and some were still *in puris naturalibus.* They were of all sizes, though uniform in shape, and ranged in price from 13s. 6d. to infinity. Towering in the midst stood a replica of Princess Beatrice's wedding cake. Built in tiers and weighing half a ton, it was a perfect marvel of confectionery. Passion-flowers formed the staple decoration, and the leaves,

which numbered several thousands, were each one carved from solid sugar. The monograms and heraldic designs, all wrought in many-coloured sugar, bore witness to the fact that genuine artists had employed their skill upon them. Hard by were several assistants busily packing pieces of bridecake in the familiar three-cornered boxes. In answer to a question Mr. Ansell said, "No, we never have complaints of the cake disappearing in the post. Our method is very simple; we cut a slice that will fill the box and so make a solid parcel. Now most people put a morsel in a large empty box, tie a piece of ribbon round it, and then consign it to the post. Of course the box breaks beneath the stamping process, the fragment escapes, and the disappointed recipient talks about the dishonesty of postmen. The trouble is entirely due to the carelessness of the public. I may add that we have sent pieces of bridecake to all the Courts of Europe. The custom shows no sign of becoming obsolete in exalted circles."

Upstairs we found the large refreshment saloon, a place much frequented by lovers of turtle soup. Many come solely to taste the dish beloved of aldermen. Occasionally a novice is disappointed, and once in a way remarks have been overheard about "such a confounded lot of beastly fat," much to the amusement and contempt of the initiated. The soup here is made exclusively from fresh turtle, the dried article being strictly tabooed, and as a consequence it is greatly in demand for city banquets. Notwithstanding the reputation for solid feasting which attaches to these occasions the caterers find but little call for substantial old English fare. Light made dishes and entrées have displaced the time-honoured joints, and men eat less than did their fathers.

Descending to the public department we found a vast assortment of sweet things on every side. Piles of chocolates of many flavours, forty kinds of *petits fours,* rout biscuits in endless variety, crystallised fruits and flowers, ices designed to closely mimic fruits and vegetables, and cakes without number were spread before us, mingled with side dishes of every kind. There is a busy scene here at eight o'clock on week-day mornings. Sometimes as many as 200 children and poor folk attend for the purpose of buying yesterday's pastry and the odds and ends of dainty food for trifling sums.

Le haut en bas. It is a long stride from Buszard and turtle soup to Pearce and Plenty, though the distance is not great from

Oxford Street to Farringdon Road. Here I found Mr. John Pearce, the managing director of Pearce's Refreshment Rooms, Limited, and of the British Tea-Table Company.

THE BEGINNING OF "PEARCE AND PLENTY."

Sitting in the board-room, surrounded by framed photographs of the forty-six houses under his control, Mr. Pearce was very willing to chat about his remarkable career.

"You see," he said, "I went to work when I was nine years old, through the loss of both my parents, and I have had to work hard all my life. In 1866 I started with a coffee-stall at the corner of East Road and the City Road, and for thirteen years I was there every week-day morning at four o'clock. I always had a notion of trying to attract the working classes, so I called my stall ' The Gutter Hotel,' and the name caught on famously. You see I keep a drawing of the concern hung up in my office to remind me of the pit from whence I was digged. Well, by being very careful I managed to save a little money, and in 1879 I opened a shop in Aldersgate Street, but moved in 1882 to Farringdon Street, where I started the big place with the two bent mirrors in front, to show the public how they looked before and after trying my beef-steak puddings.

"I ran this place myself for four years, and supplied 6000 meals a day, so I fancy I know a little about how the working-classes feed. But in 1886 a few wealthy gentlemen,

who were interested in the experiment, formed a company, and now we have twenty-two houses, while the British Tea-Table Company, which is an outgrowth of Pearce's Refreshment Rooms, Limited, and is under the same management, has twenty-four houses, making a total of forty-six establishments. Fourteen of these have temperance hotels connected with them.

"In Pearce's Refreshment Rooms we supply 50,000 persons every day, consisting almost entirely of workmen. You will be interested to know that my experience proves that they live up to their income. Here is a curious fact. If you show me our takings for any day, I can at once tell the day of the week. On Monday we get plenty of large silver, but it gradually dwindles from day to day, until on Friday we take more half-pence than anything else. Monday is our worst day, because so many of the men bring cold meat with them to their work, but the next worst day is Friday, when we find a great demand for haddocks and eggs. I used to put this down to religion, for many of our customers are Irish Catholics, until I noticed that the men who have such a light dinner on Friday often come back in the evening after paytime and indulge in a good square meal. So it is evidently more poverty than piety.

"In our class of business we find no falling off in the demand for solid food. The

THE COMIC MIRRORS.

working-man likes to know what he is eating. Though our sausages are home-made and thoroughly genuine, we have comparatively little call for them. Our customers prefer to see their dinner cut from the joint. We make a speciality of beef-steak puddings, of which we sell an enormous number during the year. We give our customers half a pound of thoroughly good beef and a well-made crust for fourpence, and if you were to try one you would find it filling at the price. When I first commenced in a shop the largest of the three urns was kept for coffee, but now we find that tea is the favourite beverage, probably because, owing to its greater cheapness, we are able to supply a better article. The demand for cocoa has also largely increased of late years. You will notice that we only use Fry's Concentrated Cocoa, and at first our customers thought it was poor stuff because the spoon would not stand up in it, but they have learnt better now.

"Of course the weather makes a great difference in such a business as ours. A fall in the temperature means a rise of twenty-five per cent. in the sale of bread and butter. So much is this the case that we take careful note of the temperature every morning, and regulate our supplies accordingly. Our annual output is scarcely credible. The weight of beef, mutton, pork and veal consumed by Pearce's Refreshment Rooms during the course of a year would equal the weights of a drove of oxen numbering 995, a flock of sheep numbering 1002, a herd of pigs numbering 1415, and 121 calves. Here are some more startling figures for the year. We consume 990 tons of potatoes and 902 tons of flour. The eggs total up to 1,870,000, and as we sell them slightly under cost price, taking the year as a whole, this represents a very considerable loss in our annual accounts. We use 99,000 gallons of milk, $13\frac{1}{4}$ tons of cocoa, 58,300 pounds of tea, and 385,000 pounds of sugar, while we get through 110 tons of jam, $2\frac{1}{4}$ tons of pepper, $4\frac{1}{2}$ tons of mustard, and 2640 gallons of vinegar. As a small offset against the profit of all this I may mention that we break 30,060 cups, 27,432 plates, and 12,648 saucers every year. You will bear in mind that these figures refer to Pearce's Refreshment Rooms only, and do not include the British Tea-Table establishments.

"As to order, we rarely have any trouble with the genuine working-man. When difficulty occurs it is usually with someone who fancies himself a little superior to the ordinary run of the community."

"And now, Mr. Pearce, will you tell the readers of the WINDSOR MAGAZINE something about the British Tea-Table Company?"

"Yes; that was started in September 1892 in order to cater for young City clerks and others who, while requiring something superior to the arrangements of 'Pearce and Plenty,' yet found themselves unable to pay high prices. We have now twenty-four houses, and supply 15,000 meals every day. The catering is distinctly lighter than in the other establishments. Eggs on toast, ham, and salad, are most in demand during the summer, while in winter we do a brisk trade in soup, chops and steaks.

"Most of our cooking for both companies is done at Farringdon Road, where we keep forty bakers hard at work. Our total staff numbers over 800, and I am proud to say, from close personal observation, that there are not two idle ones amongst them. We try to treat them well, and they repay us by faithful service. On an average we have twelve fresh applicants for positions as waitresses every day, most of them from domestic service, and I should like to take this opportunity of saying to the public, as the result of a long experience with young women of this class, that the one great reason why they so often neglect their work and finally go to the bad is that their lives are spent in practical slavery. If they had more time for themselves they would devote far more energy to their employers' service.

AT RAMSGATE.

"One other fact may be of interest," Mr. Pearce added in parting, "we take all our employés to Ramsgate for a day in July, and the whole of the funds are provided by the sale of our kitchen refuse, grease, bones, and the rest. There is a lesson in domestic economy for you!"

From the heat and bustle of the crowded establishment in Farringdon Road it was a decided change to find myself in the spacious coolness of Olympia. The afternoon performance had commenced in the arena, and the long arched corridors and the gaily-decorated gardens were well-nigh deserted.

Outside, in the crystal walk, many thousands of cut-glass lustres kept up a musical tinkling as they were stirred by the breeze, and in the lofty grill-room the many waiters were enjoying a welcome rest after the exertions of the luncheon hour.

Here I found Mr. Isidore Salmon, the enterprising secretary of Messrs. J. Lyons and Co., whose great reputation for popular catering in London seems to have sprung up in a single night. Every *habitué* of the London streets is familiar by this time with the graceful arrangement in white and gold which distinguishes the restaurants of the firm. Though fifteen years old in the provinces, they have only appeared in London during the present decade, yet already the refreshment houses number seventeen, in addition to Olympia and the Trocadero.

Mr. Salmon had some interesting figures ready to hand. It was in the height of summer when our talk took place, and at that time the daily consumption of strawberries reached 900 lbs., while 3000 lemons were converted into squash and 500 quarts of ices were disposed of every day. One may call to mind in passing that no part of the business of a caterer yields a more surprising profit than does this. A recent case in the courts showed that a profit of from 200 to 300 per cent. can easily be made from ice cream and ginger beer. To return to Messrs. Lyons, they very justly pride themselves upon the vast resources which enable them to undertake, at short notice, feats of catering which are fairly astonishing. Last year they arranged practically all the great balls in connection with the University of Cambridge. At Trinity College they actually built a bridge across the river for the convenience of the 5000 guests, while at the opening of the Imperial Institute at South Kensington they catered for 25,000 guests at a bar 500 feet in length, and served by 400 waitresses. At Olympia they are able to boast that they cater for the public at lower rates than is the case at any other high-class place of entertainment in the country.

Three times a day the various refreshment houses are supplied with goods from the bakeries at Cadby Hall, Kensington, notably with the far-famed batons of bread which are regularly used by the Prince of Wales and the Duke of York. For private catering the firm possess an immense stock of silver and other goods, and are prepared at a few days' notice to undertake anything, from serving light refreshments at a small reception to carrying out the enormous preparations for a Lord Mayor's banquet. They have indeed performed the latter feat with great *éclat* on the last two occasions.

Reminding Mr. Salmon of this, he at once produced a large folio volume of statistics and plans, from which the entire romance of the great civic festivity, from its inception to its triumphant consummation, might be compiled. Selecting only a few of the many startling figures, it may be noted that on the last occasion the thousand guests consumed 100 gallons of turtle soup, 500 lobsters, 120 turkeys, 200 partridges, 100 pheasants, 300 plovers, 200 chickens, and 20 hams. 700 calves' feet were used for jelly, 2400 ices were in readiness, 350 lbs. of grapes were consumed, and 250 dozen of choice wines proved not greatly in excess of the demand. The service required 15,000 plates, 10,000 silver forks, 9000 knives, and 6500 glasses, while the tables were decorated with 3000 yards of smilax, besides countless roses and lilies.

Once more the scene changes. Not very far from the Guildhall, where the civic banquet takes place, stands a modest restaurant with windows filled with fruits and pulse, and near the door a conspicuous inscription, "Three courses for sixpence." This is one of the vegetarian restaurants, of which there are now thirty in London, supplying 20,000 luncheons daily. As the oldest of them started only fifteen years ago it is evident that the kind of diet they provide has largely grown in popularity. From conversations with the managers I learn that this is not due to any very widespread acceptance of vegetarian principles, but simply to a preference for light and economical luncheons, the heavier meal being taken in the evening. When the vast number of suburban residents who spend their days in City houses is taken into account, it is evident that the luncheon question is one of no small importance and magnitude. The fact that a satisfying if not very stimulating meal can be obtained

AT SLATER'S.

for a trifling sum is necessarily a recommendation to those who have to watch closely their expenditure.

At one of these establishments I tried the experiment, and received in return for sixpence a plate of oatmeal porridge, a savoury omelette with green peas, and a portion of raspberry jelly with two slices of tinned pineapple. Yet somehow, after one of these meals, a man never quite feels that he has dined, and we are not surprised to learn that twelve out of the thirty vegetarian restaurants have found it advisable to set apart a room in which those who look back with sighing to the flesh-pots of Egypt may solace their backsliding appetites. The general experience seems to be that customers attend regularly for about a fortnight, and then relapse for awhile, and that the favourite dishes are those which are most disguised to resemble meat, as for example, Vienna steaks, vegetarian ducks, and food reform turkeys. But it is some consolation to know that there is a profit of considerably over a 100 per cent. on vegetarian catering.

In St. Martin's Lane stands a restaurant called St. George's House, mainly frequented by officials from the Government and County Council offices, which offers a kind of half-way house between the two extremes of diet.

Neither fish, flesh nor fowl can be obtained, and yet the bill of fare differs widely from that of the vegetarian restaurant. Egg cookery and Italian dishes are the speciality here, and the coffee claims to be the best in London. It is made on the Vienna system, and a well-known Austrian count may be seen here any morning sipping his favourite beverage. The courteous proprietor, Mr. Hodges, claims that the customers who crowd the house to inconvenience at midday are brought together solely by the lightness of the food and the excellence of the *cuisine*, while certain dishes of tropical origin and fiery character attract a good many Anglo-Indians. In Lent especially the tables are well filled.

We have but space to mention the Cyprus restaurants, now becoming better known as Slater's. Started seventeen years ago by Mr. W. Kirkland, who still manages them with great success, the four City houses now provide 2000 luncheons daily. Each seat is filled six times between 1 and 3 p.m., showing that City men do not linger long over their meals. The houses are conducted on strictly temperance lines, and the manager announces with gratification that the sale of non-intoxicating beverages has increased three-fold during the past ten years.

We have been the round, and our task is ended. If anything more than another will help the problematical New Zealander to appreciate the vast population which

THE NEW ZEALAND EXPLORER.

once filled the City upon whose ruins he will gaze, it will surely be the great collections of cups and saucers, plates and dishes, knives and forks, *et hoc genus omne*, which he will dig up from the crumbling remains of the erstwhile busy restaurants of London.

Animal Actualities.

NOTE.—*These articles consist of a series of perfectly authentic anecdotes of animal life, illustrated by Mr. J. A. Shepherd, an artist long a favourite with readers of* THE STRAND MAGAZINE. *While the stories themselves are matters of fact, it must be understood that the artist treats the subject with freedom and fancy, more with a view to an amusing commentary than to a mere representation of the occurrence.*

XVII.

Cuckoo, The Little Police Constable

 ISS EDITH HAWTHORN, a very well-known bird lover, has a cockatoo which once upon a time distinguished itself brilliantly in police duty, and repelled single-handed—if one may say so when the bird used both claws and a beak—the attack of a burglar ; more, the gallant bird arrested and kept prisoner as much of the criminal as he could manage to detain—that is to say, a good large piece of his ear.

"Cuckoo" was the cockatoo's name, and

THE BIRD-ROOM.

THE ATTACK.

he lived, mostly, in Miss Hawthorn's bird-room—a sitting-room on the third floor, containing an aviary and several cages—all left wide open—certain perches, and many birds; parrots, love-birds, and various others, as well as "Cuckoo" himself.

It chanced on a gloomy November day, just before six at the beginning of a dark evening, that the enterprising housebreaker made his attack on Miss Hawthorn's house, choosing, such was his ill-luck, the bird-room as a convenient place wherein to start business. He came silently in at a window, when the house was quiet, and when the birds were all composing themselves for a pleasant sleep. Mrs. Midge, also, the bird-room cat, was taking her repose among the many birds, against not one of whom had

THE ALARM.

THE BATTLE.

she ever lifted the paw of anger. At the sound of the intruder, however, every head was raised, every eye was opened, and every feather stood on end. The next instant Mrs. Midge had sought refuge under the sofa, and every bird had crammed itself into what corner it could ; all except " Cuckoo," who met the foe right stoutly, pecked and clawed, and buffeted like twenty fiends incarnate in one cockatoo. The burglar fought also, though it is something of a surprise for any burglar of quiet habits to find himself suddenly attacked in the dark by such an amazing Thing as was clawing at him now. But " Cuckoo " triumphed, and when the noise brought help he was found, exhausted and bloodstained, but victorious, in a disordered room, with the piece of burglarious ear already mentioned and several locks of grey hair as trophies of his hard-fought battle. And that is why they call " Cuckoo " the Policeman.

THE VICTOR.

Autumn. By W. H. Boot.

Chatterbox, 1875

CONDUCTED BY LAURA LATHROP.

HOME COOKERY.

AS the days of chill November creep along, the busy housewife, ever on the alert, thinks of the coming anniversary, our national Thanksgiving; and recognizing all the causes for thankfulness enumerated in the presidential proclamation — her own heart, meanwhile, glowing with gratitude and pleasure as she thinks of the coming re-union of dear friends, remote and near — bestirs herself to provide betimes the necessary good cheer, which shall form one means of expressing that gratitude.

Allowing her the traditional bill of fare, as established by our New England ancestors, and without which no Thanksgiving feast would be deemed worthy the name, we give one containing all the regulation requisites, but formulated with more latitude than would have accorded with the rigorous customs of our Puritan forefathers.

THANKSGIVING DAY MENU.

Raw Oysters on the Half Shell.

Cream Soup.

Boiled Fish, Egg Sauce.   Boiled Potatoes.

Roast Turkey, Brown Sauce.

Cranberry Jelly.

Baked Sweet Potatoes.

Whipped White Potatoes.

Mashed Turnips.   Beets.

Scalloped Chicken.

Celery.   Cheese.

Mince Pie.   Pumpkin Pie.

Orange Pudding.   Almond Cake.

Fruit.   Nuts.   Raisins.

Coffee.

RAW OYSTERS. — Raw oysters are nice served on the half shell, previously cleaned to a nicety, or on little shell-shaped majolica plates for the purpose. These brighten the table wonderfully.

CREAM SOUP. — Take a quart of either good mutton or veal stock, cut an onion in quarters, slice three potatoes very thin, and put them into the stock with a small piece of mace. Boil gently for an hour, then pass through the strainer. Add a pint of rich milk (half milk and half cream) with enough corn starch added to make the soup almost as thick as cream. Add a piece of nice, fresh butter, and just before serving, a little finely chopped parsley.

EGG SAUCE. — Egg sauce is simply drawn butter (butter, flour, water, salt, and pepper, boiled together) with a few hard-boiled eggs cut up and added, after removing from the fire.

BOILED POTATOES. — Small boiled potatoes, peeled, dropped into hot lard to brown quickly, and drained.

BROWN SAUCE. — The gravy should be strained, returned to the fire, and thickened with nicely browned flour. Add finely chopped giblets, previously boiled tender in salted water.

BAKED SWEET POTATOES. — Sweet potatoes are much nicer to be steamed until they can be penetrated with a silver fork, then browned for fifteen minutes in a quick oven.

WHIPPED POTATOES. — Peel, quarter, and boil, until tender, in salted water. Beat until light and creamy; then, with a heavy fork, whip in a large spoonful of melted butter and enough hot milk to soften to the desired consistency. Pile lightly on a dish, and place in oven to keep hot. If lightly browned, it makes a very pretty dish.

BEETS. — Boil nice red beets until tender; scrape off the skins, chop quite fine, and pour over them a tablespoonful of melted butter. Add vinegar, salt and pepper to the taste, and serve hot.

SCALLOPED CHICKEN. — For one cold boiled chicken, use one egg, beaten light, one cup cracker crumbs, half a cup drawn butter, pepper and salt. Mince the chicken fine, removing all bits of bone; stir in the egg and seasoning, and then beat the chicken into the hot drawn butter. Fill an earthen baking dish with this mixture, cover with the cracker crumbs; pour half a cup of cream or very rich milk over the top; dot with bits of butter, and brown lightly in the oven.

CELERY AND CHEESE. — Celery is now passed with dishes of grated cheese, into which the celery is dipped while being eaten. In England, this forms the last course at dinner.

ORANGE PUDDING. — One pint of milk, nine eggs, nine oranges, half a cupful of nice butter, one large cupful of granulated sugar, three heaping tablespoonfuls of powdered sugar, and a tablespoonful of ground rice. Mix the ground rice with a little of the cold milk, heat the remainder to the boiling point, stir in the moistened rice, and continue stirring for five minutes; add the butter, stirring it in well, and set aside to cool. Beat together the granulated sugar, the yolks of nine eggs and whites of five; squeeze the juice of the oranges into this, add the cooked mixture, and pour the whole into a pudding dish holding about three quarts, and previously lined with a nice paste. Bake forty minutes in a moderate oven. Beat the whites of the four eggs to a stiff froth, and then beat in, slowly, the powdered sugar. Cover the pudding with this, place in the oven for about ten minutes to cook, being careful to leave the oven door open. It should be very cold when served.

ALMOND CAKE. — Two cups sugar, three-fourths of a cup of butter, one cup of sweet milk, two cups of flour and one cup of corn starch mixed together, whites of six eggs, two teaspoonfuls of cream tartar in the flour, one teaspoonful of soda dissolved and added to the milk. Cream the butter and sugar by beating well together, add the milk gradually, then the stiffly beaten whites of eggs, and gradually the mixture of flour, corn starch and cream tartar, all having been passed through a sieve together. Bake in jelly tins. *Filling.* — Take two pounds of almonds, blanch and pound fine in a mortar, or beat fine in a stout cloth; beat whites and yolks of two eggs together lightly, add a cup and a half of powdered sugar, then the almonds with one teaspoonful of vanilla. This is a delicious cake. Shelled almonds are more economical for use in cakes. One pound of unshelled almonds makes only six and one-half ounces, or one coffee-cupful when shelled, while the shelled are generally only double the price per pound, and sometimes not that.

GARNISH. Before using parsley as a garnish for meats, place in ice water for a while, then dip quickly in and out of very hot lard, when it will be found

> " As crisp as glass,
> And green as grass."

Seasonable Hints.

BEFORE the ground is frozen for the winter, everything about the home, both inside and out, should have most careful attention. Whatever repairing needs to be done, should be done at once; all rubbish of every description should be cleared away, so that untidiness may not be added to the bleakness of winter. Now is the time to cover with coarse litter or straw the beautiful pansy beds, which are still green in spite of frost and straying snowflakes. Let the half hardy roses and other plants of the same class be well cared for.

In the general clearing up the cellar must not be forgotten. Whatever collects dirt or breeds offensive odors, should be removed, for the air of the cellar penetrates the whole house, sometimes quite noticeably, as one may perceive in the shaking of draperies, the removal of carpets, etc.

Let the little ones at this season be warmly clad, their little feet enveloped in good, warm hose to prevent frost-bitten toes, and sent out into the bracing November air to grow rosy and strong with healthful exercise, and to become gradually accustomed to the now rapidly changing atmosphere.

In looking over the supply of warm and comfortable clothing, that which is outgrown or a trifle overworn should not be left as food for the moths, but given to some less favored creature than yourself, some poor, pinched child of adversity. For "the poor have we always with us." Amid all our busy cares, let us not forget to be charitable.

THE BIRDS' FAREWELL.

By O. Herford.

OUR DEAR LITTLE MAID:
            We must bid you good-bye,
For November is here, and it 's time we should fly
To the South, where we have an engagement to
    sing.
    But remember this, dear, we 'll return in the spring.
And if, while abroad, we hear anything new,
We 'll learn it, and sing it next summer to you
In the same little tree on the lawn, if you 'll let us.
So, good-bye, little maiden! Please do not forget us.
We 're sorry to leave you — too sorry for words,
And we 'll always remain,
                Yours sincerely,
                    " THE BIRDS."
P. S.— Please don't mind if this letter sounds flat,
And present our respectful regards to your cat.

The labours of **THE·XII·MONTHS**
set out in **NEW PICTURES & OLD PROVERBS**

WISE SHEPHERDS say that the age of man
is LXXII years and that we liken but to one
hole yeare for evermore we take six yeares to
every month as JANUARY or FEBRUARY and
so forth , for as the yeare changeth by the

twelve months, into twelve sundry manners so
doth a man change himself, twelve times in
his life by twelve ages, and every age lasteth
six yeare if so be that he live to LXXII. For three
times six maketh eighteen & six times six
maketh XXXVI And then is man at the
best and also at the highest. and twelve times
six maketh LXXII & that is the age of a man .

H.S.

NOVEMBER

Then cometh NOVEMBER that the daies
be very short, and the sun in manner giveth
little heat, and the trees loseth their leaves.
The fields, that were greene looke horye and
grey . When all manner of herbs bee hid in
the ground . And then appeareth no flowers.
And then winter is come that a man hath
understanding of age, and hath lost his
kindly heat and strength . His teeth begin

to rot, and also to chatter , and then hath hee no
more hope of long life , but desireth to come
to the life everlasting, for this month maketh
him LX and six yeares .
— He that by the plow would thrive
Himself must either hold or drive.
— There belongs more than whistling to going
to plow.
GOD speed the plow & give us corn eno.

English Illustrated Magazine 1890

Victorian Times

Vol. V, No. 12

December 2018

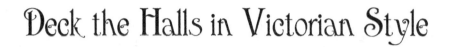

Deck the Halls in Victorian Style

Do you love Victorian Christmas? Chances are, you do even if you don't know it; a host of our best-beloved holiday traditions have their roots in Victorian days. But perhaps you'd like to go a bit farther, and bring an authentic Victorian touch to your celebration. Here are some ways to do that.

First, when thinking "Victorian Christmas," there are two primary themes to consider: "Nature" and "Handmade." While Victorians did have glass balls and other factory-made ornaments for their trees, many households emphasized decorations based on natural elements. Holly, ivy and mistletoe were available from street-sellers, while those who lived in the country might go into the woods and fields to gather their own. Children joined in the festivities by creating hand-made ornaments and decorations. One charming advantage of this approach is that, each year, most of the decorations would be new and fresh.

For the tree, think about decorating with fruits, nuts, pine cones, seed-pods, gum-tree balls and any other object that will keep for a reasonable period of time. Victorians often decorated their trees with oranges and apples. Sometimes these were gilded; oranges might also be pierced with cloves. (When creating a clove orange pomander, you can either completely cover the orange in cloves, or arrange cloves in attractive patterns on the orange. The more covered the orange is, the more it is likely to dry into a pomander that you can keep to scent your closet.) Nuts and seed-pods were gilded or painted.

Another common decoration was sweets. Consider hanging real candy canes directly on your tree. Cornucopias were popular; this is a bit of colorful paper rolled into a small cone and filled with candy and hung upon the tree. While Victorians didn't have the wealth of shimmery, glittery papers that we have today, there's no reason not to take advantage of those! Cornucopias can also be decorated with ribbon, lace, doilies, etc. (A nice approach is to form the basic cone of a colorful paper and then wrap a paper doily around that.)

Garlands were made of popcorn, cranberries, and paper. To make a popcorn garland, you'll need to be able to pop some plain popcorn with no butter or salt. (Consider investing in a microwave glass popcorn popper and plain kernels.) You can also create popcorn balls for the tree using popcorn and sugar syrup. This is a delightful way to thoroughly burn your hands; the sugar syrup must be hot to form the balls, but then hardens when it cools.

As a child I tried a popcorn string *once,* in our little farmhouse in the woods of Mendocino, which we visited only on weekends. When we returned the week after Christmas, we discovered that the resident mouse population had been very grateful for their Christmas treat; a few fragments of thread and a handful of kernels were all that remained. Children also enjoy making paper chains, which are assembled from thin strips of paper that can be glued, taped or stapled together.

Natural elements were key in decorating the rest of the home for the holiday as well. Of course, one needed a bit of mistletoe; I've read that the custom is that for every kiss taken beneath it, one removes a berry, and once all the berries are gone, the forfeits end. Picture frames were often wreathed with branches of greenery and holly. Since Victorian pictures were often hung not from the wall but from the picture rail that ran around the ceiling, this meant they were suspended from fairly long wires, and tended to tilt forward a bit on the wall. One form of décor was to put a small vase of water behind the picture and arrange greenery in it to hang over the frame.

Consider, as an alternative to plain mistletoe, a "kissing ball." Traditionally this was made from two iron hoops (e.g., barrel or wheel hoops) arranged to create a ball shape and then filled and wrapped with greenery and suspended from a ceiling or doorway. You can accomplish the effect by using a ball of florist's clay and covering it with sprigs of greenery. Hang it with a ribbon, with strips of ribbon falling over the greens—and of course add a sprig of mistletoe at the bottom. An advent wreath with four candles, placed on a horizontal wheel, makes another nice addition.

Victorians simulated the effect of snow on branches by dipping the branches in water and then in flour or Epsom salts. Some actually used crushed glass, but I don't recommend this (nor do most Victorian articles!).

One final note on Victorian décor: Since it often involves food items and sweets, be sure to keep the safety of your pets in mind. It's one thing for the mice to nibble a popcorn string, and quite another for your dog to do the same and possibly ingest the string itself. Keep candy and other edibles well out of reach of pets (and make sure small children understand that these are off limits until Christmas Day)!

—Moira Allen, Editor
editors@victorianvoices.net

MERRY CHRISTMAS IN THE TENEMENTS.

BY JACOB A. RIIS.

WITH PICTURES BY JAY HAMBIDGE.

IT was just a sprig of holly, with scarlet berries showing against the green, stuck in, by one of the office boys probably, behind the sign that pointed the way up to the editorial rooms. There was no reason why it should have made me start when I came suddenly upon it at the turn of the stairs; but it did. Perhaps it was because that dingy hall, given over to dust and drafts all the days of the year, was the last place in which I expected to meet with any sign of Christmas; perhaps it was because I myself had nearly forgotten the holiday. Whatever the cause, it gave me quite a turn.

I stood, and stared at it. It looked dry, almost withered. Probably it had come a long way. Not much holly grows about Printing-House Square, except in the colored supplements, and that is scarcely of a kind to stir tender memories. Withered and dry, this did. I thought, with a twinge of conscience, of secret little conclaves of my children, of private views of things hidden from mama at the bottom of drawers, of wild flights when papa appeared unbidden in the door, which I had allowed for once to pass unheeded. Absorbed in the business of the office, I had hardly thought of Christmas coming on, until now it was here. And this sprig of holly on the wall that had come to remind me,—come nobody knew how far,—did it grow yet in the beech-wood clearings, as it did when I gathered it as a boy, tracking through the snow? «Christ-thorn» we called it in our Danish tongue. The red berries, to our simple faith, were the drops of blood that fell from the Saviour's brow as it drooped under its cruel crown upon the cross.

Back to the long ago wandered my thoughts: to the moss-grown beech in which I cut my name, and that of a little girl with yellow curls, of blessed memory, with the first jack-knife I ever owned; to the story-book with the little fir-tree that pined because it was small, and because the hare jumped over it, and would not be content though the wind and the sun kissed it, and the dews wept over it, and told it to rejoice in its young life; and that was so proud when, in the second year, the hare had to go round it, because then it knew it was getting big,—Hans Christian Andersen's story, that we loved above all the rest; for we knew the tree right well, and the hare; even the tracks it left in the snow we had seen. Ah, those were the Yule-tide seasons, when the old Domkirke shone with a thousand wax candles on Christmas eve; when all business was laid aside to let the world make merry one whole

Christmas Mottos.

chatting gaily, and elbowing the jam of holiday shoppers that linger about the big stores. The street-cars labor along, loaded down to the steps with passengers carrying bundles of every size and odd shape. Along the curb a string of peddlers hawk penny toys in push-carts with noisy clamor, fearless for once of being moved on by the police. Christmas brings a two-weeks' respite from persecution even to the friendless street-fakir. From the window of one brilliantly lighted store a bevy of mature dolls in dishabille stretch forth their arms appealingly to a troop of factory-hands passing by. The young men chaff the girls, who shriek with laughter and run. The policeman on the corner stops beating his hands together to keep warm, and makes a mock attempt to catch them, whereat their shrieks rise shriller than ever. «Them stockin's o' yourn 'll be the death o' Santa Claus!» he shouts after them, as they dodge. And they, looking back, snap saucily, «Mind yer business, freshy!» But their laughter belies their words. «They gin it to ye straight that time,» grins the grocer's clerk, come out to snatch a look at the crowds; and the two swap holiday greetings.

At the corner, where two opposing tides of travel form an eddy, the line of push-carts debouches down the darker side-street. In its gloom their torches burn with a fitful glare that wakes black shadows among the trusses of the railroad structure overhead. A woman, with worn shawl drawn tightly about head and shoulders, bargains with a peddler for a monkey on a stick and two cents' worth of flitter-gold. Five ill-clad youngsters flatten their noses against the frozen pane of the toy-shop, in ecstasy at something there, which proves to be a milk-wagon, with driver, horses, and cans that can be unloaded. It is something their minds can grasp. One comes forth with a penny goldfish of pasteboard clutched tightly in his hand, and casting cautious glances right and left, speeds across the way to the door of a tenement, where a little girl stands waiting.

«A Large-sized Santa Claus for Ten Cents.»

week; when big red apples were roasted on the stove, and bigger doughnuts were baked within it for the long feast! Never such had been known since. Christmas to-day is but a name, a memory.

A door slammed below, and let in the noises of the street. The holly rustled in the draft. Some one going out said, « A Merry Christmas to you all!» in a big, hearty voice. I awoke from my reverie to find myself back in New York with a glad glow at the heart. It was not true. I had only forgotten. It was myself that had changed, not Christmas. That was here, with the old cheer, the old message of good-will, the old royal road to the heart of mankind. How often had I seen its blessed charity, that never corrupts, make light in the hovels of darkness and despair! how often watched its spirit of self-sacrifice and devotion in those who had, besides themselves, nothing to give! and as often the sight had made whole my faith in human nature. No! Christmas was not of the past, its spirit not dead. The lad who fixed the sprig of holly on the stairs knew it; my reporter's note-book bore witness to it. Witness of my contrition for the wrong I did the gentle spirit of the holiday, here let the book tell the story of one Christmas in the tenements of the poor.

It is evening in Grand street. The shops east and west are pouring forth their swarms of workers. Street and sidewalk are filled with an eager throng of young men and women,

«It's yer Chris'mas, Kate,» he says, and thrusts it into her eager fist. The black doorway swallows them up.

Across the narrow yard, in the basement of the rear house, the lights of a Christmas tree show against the grimy window-pane. The hare would never have gone around it, it is so very small. The two children are busily engaged fixing the goldfish upon one of its branches. Three little candles that burn there shed light upon a scene of utmost desolation. The room is black with smoke and dirt. In the middle of the floor oozes an oil-stove that serves at once to take the raw edge off the cold and to cook the meals by. Half the window-panes are broken, and the holes stuffed with rags. The sleeve of an old coat hangs out of one, and beats drearily upon the sash when the wind sweeps over the fence and rattles the rotten shutters. The family wash, clammy and gray, hangs on a clothes-line stretched across the room. Under it, at a table set with cracked and empty plates, a discouraged woman sits eying the children's show gloomily. It is evident that she has been drinking. The peaked faces of the little ones wear a famished look. There are three—the third an infant, put to bed in what was once a baby-carriage. The two from the street are pulling it around to get the tree in range. The baby sees it, and crows with delight. The boy shakes a branch, and the goldfish leaps and sparkles in the candle-light.

«See, sister!» he pipes; «see Santa Claus!» And they clap their hands in glee. The woman at the table wakes out of her stupor, gazes around her, and bursts into a fit of maudlin weeping.

The door falls to. Five flights up, another opens upon a bare attic room which a patient little woman is setting to rights. There are only three chairs, a box, and a bedstead in the room, but they take a deal of careful arranging. The bed hides the broken plaster in the wall through which the wind came in; each chair-leg stands over a rat-hole, at once to hide it and to keep the rats out. One is left; the box is for that. The plaster of the ceiling is held up with pasteboard patches. I know the story of that attic. It is one of cruel desertion. The

Holly.

woman's husband is even now living in plenty with the creature for whom he forsook her, not a dozen blocks away, while she «keeps the home together for the childer.» She sought justice, but the lawyer demanded a retainer; so she gave it up, and went back to her little ones. For this room that barely keeps the winter wind out she pays four dollars a month, and is behind with the rent. There is scarce bread in the house; but the spirit of Christmas has found her attic. Against a broken wall is tacked a hemlock branch, the leavings of the corner grocer's fitting-block; pink string from the packing-counter hangs on it in festoons. A tallow dip on the box furnishes the illumination. The children sit up in bed, and watch it with shining eyes.

«We're having Christmas!» they say.

The lights of the Bowery glow like a myriad twinkling stars upon the ceaseless flood of humanity that surges ever through the great highway of the homeless. They shine upon long rows of lodging-houses, in which hundreds of young men, cast helpless upon the reef of the strange city, are learning their first lessons of utter loneliness; for what desolation is there like that of the careless crowd when all the world rejoices? They shine upon the tempter, setting his snares there, and upon the missionary and the Salvation Army lass, disputing his catch with him; upon the police detective going his rounds with coldly observant eye intent upon the outcome of the contest; upon the wreck that is past hope, and upon the youth pausing on the verge of the pit in which the other has long ceased to struggle. Sights and sounds of Christmas there are in plenty in the Bowery. Juniper and tamarack and fir stand in groves along the busy thoroughfare, and garlands of green embower mission and dive impartially. Once a year the old street recalls its youth with an effort. It is true that it is largely a commercial effort—that the evergreen, with an instinct that is not of its native hills, haunts saloon-corners by preference; but the smell of the pine-woods is in the air, and—Christmas is not too critical—one is grateful for the effort. It varies with the opportunity. At «Beefsteak John's»

A CHRISTMAS «TURKEY-SHOOT» ON THE BOWERY.

it is content with artistically embalming crullers and mince-pies in green cabbage under the window lamp. Over yonder, where the mile-post of the old lane still stands,—in its unhonored old age become the vehicle of publishing the latest «sure cure» to the world,—a florist, whose undenominational zeal for the holiday and trade outstrips alike distinction of creed and property, has transformed the sidewalk and the ugly railroad structure into a veritable bower, spanning it with a canopy of green, under which

dwell with him, in neighborly good-will, the Young Men's Christian Association and the Gentile tailor next door.

In the next block a «turkey-shoot» is in progress. Crowds are trying their luck at breaking the glass balls that dance upon tiny jets of water in front of a marine view with the moon rising, yellow and big, out of a silver sea. A man-of-war, with lights burning aloft, labors under a rocky coast. Groggy sailormen, on shore leave, make unsteady attempts upon the dancing

The Man with Mechanical Insects.

balls. One mistakes the moon for the target, but is discovered in season. « Don't shoot that,» says the man who loads the guns; «there's a lamp behind it.» Three scared birds in the window-recess try vainly to snatch a moment's sleep between shots and the trains that go roaring overhead on the elevated road. Roused by the sharp crack of the rifles, they blink at the lights in the street, and peck moodily at a crust in their bed of shavings.

The dime-museum gong clatters out its noisy warning that « the lecture » is about to begin. From the concert-hall, where men sit drinking beer in clouds of smoke, comes the thin voice of a short-skirted singer warbling, « Do they think of me at home? » The young fellow who sits near the door, abstractedly making figures in the wet track of the « schooners,» buries something there with a sudden restless turn, and calls for another beer. Out in the street a band strikes up. A host with banners advances, chanting an unfamiliar hymn. In the ranks marches a cripple on crutches. Newsboys follow, gaping. Under the illuminated clock of the Cooper Institute the procession halts, and the leader, turning his face to the sky, offers a prayer. The passing crowds stop to listen. A few bare their heads. The devoted group, the flapping banners, and the changing torch-light on upturned faces, make a strange, weird picture. Then the drumbeat, and the band files into its barracks across the street. A few of the listeners follow, among them the lad from the concert-hall, who slinks shamefacedly in when he thinks no one is looking.

Down at the foot of the Bowery is the « panhandlers' beat,» where the saloons elbow each other at every step, crowding out all other business than that of keeping lodgers to support them. Within call of it, across the square, stands a church which, in the memory of men yet living, was built to shelter the fashionable Baptist audiences of a day when Madison Square was out in the fields, and Harlem had a foreign sound. The fashionable audiences are gone long since. To-day the church, fallen into premature decay, but still handsome in its strong and noble lines, stands as a missionary outpost in the land of the enemy, its builders would have said, doing a greater work than they planned. To-night is the Christmas festival of its English-speaking Sunday-school, and the pews are filled. The banners of United Italy, of modern Hellas, of France and Germany and England, hang side by side with the Chinese dragon and the starry flag—signs of the cosmopolitan character of the congregation. Greek and Roman Catholics, Jews and joss-worshipers, go there; few Protestants, and no Baptists. It is easy to pick out the children in their seats by nationality, and as easy to read the story of poverty and suffering that stands written in more than one mother's haggard face, now beaming with pleasure at the little ones' glee. A gaily decorated Christmas tree has taken the place of the pulpit. At its foot is stacked a mountain of bundles, Santa Claus's gifts to the school. A self-conscious young man with soap-locks has just been allowed to retire, amid tumultuous applause, after blowing « Nearer, my God, to thee » on his horn until his cheeks swelled almost to bursting. A trumpet ever takes the Fourth Ward by storm. A class of little girls is climbing upon the platform. Each wears a capital letter on her breast, and has a piece to speak that begins with the letter; together they spell its lesson. There is momentary consternation: one is missing. As the discovery is made, a child pushes past the doorkeeper, hot and breathless. « I am in ‹Boundless Love,›» she says, and makes for the platform, where her arrival restores confidence and the language.

The Toy-monkey Seller.

In the audience the befrocked visitor from up-town sits cheek by jowl with the pigtailed Chinaman and the dark-browed Italian. Up in the gallery, farthest from the preacher's desk and the tree, sits a

CHRISTMAS EVE IN MULBERRY BEND.

Jewish mother with her three boys, almost in rags. A dingy and threadbare shawl partly hides her poor calico wrap and patched apron. The woman shrinks in the pew, fearful of being seen; her boys stand upon the benches, and applaud with the rest. She endeavors vainly to restrain them. « Tick, tick! » goes the old clock over the door through which wealth and fashion went out long years ago, and poverty came in.

Loudly ticked the old clock in time with the doxology, the other day, when they cleared the tenants out of Gotham Court down here in Cherry street, and shut the iron doors of Single and Double Alley against them.

Never did the world move faster or surer toward a better day than when the wretched slum was seized by the health officers as a nuisance unfit longer to disgrace a Christian city. The snow lies deep in the deserted passageways, and the vacant floors are given over to evil smells, and to the rats that forage in squads, burrowing in the

IN THE ATTIC.

the plate» hails the Yule-tide season with a pyramid of green made of two coffins set on end. It has been a good day, he says cheerfully, putting up the shutters; and his mind is easy. But the «good days» of the Bend are over, too. The Bend itself is all but gone. Where the old pigsty stood, children dance and sing to the strumming of a cracked piano-organ propelled on wheels by an Italian and his wife. The park that has come to take the place of the slum will curtail the undertaker's profits, as it has lessened the work of the police. Murder was the fashion of the day that is past. Scarce a knife has been drawn since the sunlight shone into that evil spot, and grass and green shrubs took the place of the old rookeries. The Christmas gospel of peace and good-will moves in where the slum moves out. It never had a chance before.

The children follow the organ, stepping in the slush to the music,—bareheaded and with torn shoes, but happy,—across the Five Points and through «the Bay,»—known to the directory as Baxter street,—to «the Divide,» still Chatham street to its denizens though the aldermen have rechristened it Park Row. There other delegations of Greek and Italian children meet and escort the music on its homeward trip. In one of the crooked streets near the river its journey comes to an end. A battered door opens to let it in. A tallow dip burns sleepily on the creaking stairs. The water runs with a loud clatter in the sink: it is to keep it from freezing. There is not a whole window-pane in the hall. Time was when this was a fine house harboring wealth and refinement. It has neither now. In the old parlor down-stairs a knot of hard-faced men and women sit on benches about a deal table, playing cards. They have a jug between them, from which they drink by turns. On the stump of a mantel-shelf a lamp burns before a rude print of the Mother of God. No one pays any heed to the hand-organ man and his wife as they climb to their attic. There is a colony of them up there—three families in four rooms.

neglected sewers. The «wall of wrath» still towers above the buildings in the adjoining Alderman's Court, but its wrath at last is wasted.

It was built by a vengeful Quaker, whom the alderman had knocked down in a quarrel over the boundary line, and transmitted its legacy of hate to generations yet unborn; for where it stood it shut out sunlight and air from the tenements of Alderman's Court. And at last it is to go, Gotham Court and all; and to the going the wall of wrath has contributed its share, thus in the end atoning for some of the harm it wrought. Tick! old clock; the world moves. Never yet did Christmas seem less dark on Cherry Hill than since the lights were put out in Gotham Court forever.

In «the Bend» the philanthropist under-taker who «buries for what he can catch on

«Come in, Antonio,» says the tenant of the double flat,—the one with two rooms,—«come and keep Christmas.» Antonio enters, cap in hand. In the corner by the dormer-window a «crib» has been fitted up in commemoration of the Nativity. A soap-box and two hemlock branches are the elements. Six tallow candles and a night-light illuminate a singular collection of rarities, set out with much ceremonial show. A doll tightly wrapped in swaddling-clothes represents «the Child.» Over it stands a ferocious-looking beast, easily recognized as a survival of the last political campaign, —the Tammany tiger, — threatening to swallow it at a gulp if one as much as takes one's eyes off it. A miniature Santa Claus, a pasteboard monkey, and several other articles of bric-à-brac of the kind the tenement affords, complete

SHOPPERS IN A JEWISH METAL SHOP, CHRISTMAS EVE.

the outfit. The background is a picture of St. Donato, their village saint, with the Madonna, «whom they worship most.» But the incongruity harbors no suggestion of disrespect. The children view the strange show with genuine reverence, bowing and crossing themselves before it. There are five, the oldest a girl of seventeen, who works for a sweater, making three dollars a week. It is all the money that comes in, for the father has been sick and unable to work eight months, and the mother has her hands full: the youngest is a baby in arms. Three of the children go to a charity school, where they are fed, a great help, now the holidays have come to make work slack for sister. The rent is six dollars—two weeks' pay out of the four. The mention of a possible chance of light work for the man brings the daughter with her sewing from the adjoining room, eager to hear. That would be Christmas indeed! «Pietro!» She runs to the neighbors to communicate the joyful tidings. Pietro comes, with his new-born baby, which he is tending while his wife lies ill, to look at the maestro, so powerful and good. He also has been out of work for months, with a family of mouths to fill, and nothing coming in. His children are all small yet, but they speak English.

« What, » I say, holding a silver dime up before the oldest, a smart little chap of seven— « what would you do if I gave you this? »

« Get change, » he replies promptly. When he is told that it is his own, to buy toys, his eyes open wide with wondering incredulity. By degrees he understands. The father does not. He looks questioningly from one to the other. When told, his respect increases visibly for « the rich gentleman. »

They were villagers of the same community in southern Italy, these people and others in the tenements thereabouts, and they moved their patron saint with them. They cluster about his worship here, but the worship is more than an empty form. He typifies to them the old neighborliness of home, the

A Prayer of Thanksgiving that he « lives in a Free Country. »

spirit of mutual help, of charity, and of the common cause against the common enemy. The community life survives through their saint in the far city to an unsuspected extent. The sick are cared for; the dreaded hospital is fenced out. There are no Italian evictions. The saint has paid the rent of this attic through two hard months; and here at his shrine the Calabrian village gathers, in the persons of these three, to do him honor on Christmas eve.

Where the old Africa has been made over into a modern Italy, since King Humbert's cohorts struck the up-town trail, three hundred of the little foreigners are having an uproarious time over their Christmas tree in the Children's Aid Society's school. And well they may, for the like has not been seen in Sullivan street in this generation. Christmas trees are rather rarer over here than on the East Side, where the German leavens the lump with his loyalty to home traditions. This is loaded with silver and gold and toys without end, until there is little left of the original green. Santa Claus's sleigh must have been upset in a snow-drift over here,

and righted by throwing the cargo overboard, for there is at least a wagon-load of things that can find no room on the tree. The appearance of « teacher » with a double armful of curly-headed dolls in red, yellow, and green Mother-Hubbards, doubtful how to dispose of them, provokes a shout of approval, which is presently quieted by the principal's bell. School is « in » for the preliminary exercises. Afterward there are to be the tree and ice-cream for the good children. In their anxiety to prove their title clear, they sit so straight, with arms folded, that the whole row bends over backward. The lesson is brief, the answers to the point.

« What do we receive at Christmas? » the teacher wants to know. The whole school responds with a shout, « Dolls and toys! » To the question, « Why do we receive them at Christmas? » the answer is not so prompt. But one youngster from Thompson street holds up his hand. He knows. « Because we always get 'em, » he says; and the class is convinced: it is a fact. A baby wails because it cannot get the whole tree at once. The « little mother »—herself a child of less than a dozen winters—who has it in charge cooes over it, and soothes its grief with the aid of a surreptitious sponge-cake evolved from the depths of teacher's pocket. Babies are encouraged in these schools, though not originally included in their plan, as often the one condition upon which the older children can be reached. Some one has to mind the baby, with all hands out at work.

The school sings « Santa Lucia » and « Children of the Heavenly King, » and baby is lulled to sleep.

« Who is this King? » asks the teacher suddenly, at the end of a verse. Momentary stupefaction. The little minds are on ice-cream just then; the lad nearest the door has telegraphed that it is being carried up in pails. A little fellow on the back seat saves the day. Up goes his brown fist.

« Well, Vito, who is he? »

« McKinley! » shouts the lad, who remembers the election just past; and the school adjourns for ice-cream.

It is a sight to see them eat it. In a score of such schools, from the Hook to Harlem, the sight is enjoyed in Christmas week by the men and women who, out of their own pockets, reimburse Santa Claus for his outlay, and count it a joy—as well they may: for their beneficence sometimes makes the one bright spot in lives that have suffered of all wrongs the most cruel—that of being despoiled of their childhood. Sometimes they are little Bohemians; sometimes the children of refugee Jews; and again, Italians, or the descendants of the Irish stock of Hell's Kitchen and Poverty Row; always the poorest, the shabbiest, the hungriest—the children Santa Claus loves best to find, if any one will show him the way. Having so much on hand, he has no time, you see, to look them up himself. That must be done for him; and it is done. To the teacher in this Sullivan-street school came one little girl, this last Christmas, with anxious inquiry if it was true that he came around with toys.

«I hanged my stocking last time,» she said, «and he did n't come at all.» In the front house, indeed, he left a drum and a doll, but no message from him reached the rear house in the alley. «Maybe he could n't find it,» she said soberly. Did the teacher think he would come if she wrote to him? She had learned to write.

Together they composed a note to Santa Claus, speaking for

THE SCHOOL FOR ITALIAN CHILDREN—AN ICE-CREAM FEAST.

a doll and a bell—the bell to play «go to school» with when she was kept home minding the baby. Lest he should by any chance miss the alley in spite of directions, little Rosa was invited to hang her stocking, and her sister's, with the janitor's children's in the school. And lo! on Christmas morning there was a gorgeous doll, and a bell that was a whole curriculum in itself, as good as a year's schooling any day! Faith in Santa Claus is established in that Thompson-street alley for this generation at least; and Santa Claus, got by hook or by crook into an Eighth-Ward alley, is as good as the whole Supreme Court bench, with the Court of Appeals thrown in, for backing the Board of Health against the slum.

But the ice-cream! They eat it off the seats, half of them kneeling or squatting on the floor; they blow on it, and put it in their pockets to carry home to baby. Two little shavers discovered to be feeding each other, each watching the smack develop on the other's lips as the acme of his own bliss, are «cousins»; that is why. Of cake there is a double supply. It is a dozen years since «Fighting Mary,» the wildest child in the Seventh-Avenue school, taught them a lesson there which they have never forgotten. She was perfectly untamable, fighting everybody in school, the despair of her teacher, till on Thanksgiving, reluctantly included in the general amnesty and mince-pie, she was caught cramming the pie into her pocket, after eying it with a look of pure ecstasy, but refusing to touch it. «For mother» was her explanation, delivered with a defiant look before which the class quailed. It is recorded, but not in the minutes, that the board of managers wept over Fighting Mary, who, all unconscious of having caused such an astonishing «break,» was at that moment engaged in maintaining her prestige and reputation by fighting the gang in the next block. The minutes contain merely a formal resolution to the effect that occasions of mince-pie shall carry double rations thenceforth. And the rule has been kept—not only in Seventh-Avenue, but in every industrial school—since. Fighting Mary won the biggest fight of her troubled life that day, without striking a blow.

It was in the Seventh-Avenue school last Christmas that I offered the truant class a four-bladed penknife as a prize for whittling out the truest Maltese cross. It was a class of black sheep, and it was the blackest sheep of the flock that won the prize. «That awful Savarese,» said Miss Haight, in despair. I thought of Fighting Mary, and bade her take heart. I regret to say that within a week the hapless Savarese was black-listed for banking up the school door with snow, so that not even the janitor could get out and at him.

Within hail of the Sullivan-street school camps a scattered little band, the Christmas customs of which I had been trying for years

MRS. BENOIT.

to surprise. They are Indians, a handful of Mohawks and Iroquois, whom some ill wind has blown down from their Canadian reservation, and left in these West-Side tenements to eke out such a living as they can weaving mats and baskets, and threading glass pearls on slippers and pincushions, until, one after another, they have died off and gone to happier hunting-grounds than Thompson street. There were as many families as one could count on the fingers of both hands when I first came upon them, at the death of old Tamenund, the basket-maker. Last Christmas there were seven. I had about made up my mind that the only real Americans in New York did not keep the holiday at all, when, one Christmas eve, they showed me how. Just as dark was setting in, old Mrs. Benoit came from her Hudson-street attic—where she was known among the neighbors, as old and poor as she, as Mrs. Ben Wah, and believed to be the relict of a warrior of the name of Benjamin Wah—to the office of the Charity Organization Society, with a bundle for a friend who had helped her over a rough spot—the rent, I suppose. The bundle was done up elaborately in blue cheese-cloth, and contained a lot of little garments which she had made out of the remnants of blankets and cloth of her own from a younger and better day. « For those,» she said, in her French patois, « who are poorer than myself»; and hobbled away. I found out, a few days later, when I took her picture weaving mats in her attic room, that she had scarcely food in the house that Christmas day, and not the car-fare to take her to church! Walking was bad, and her old limbs were stiff. She sat by the window through the winter evening, and watched the sun go down behind the western hills, comforted by her pipe. Mrs. Ben Wah, to give her her local name, is not really an Indian; but her husband was one, and she lived all her life with the tribe till she came here. She is a philosopher in her own quaint way. « It is no disgrace to be poor,» said she to me, regarding her empty tobacco-pouch; « but it is sometimes a great inconvenience.» Not even the recollection of the vote of censure that was passed upon me once by the ladies of the Charitable Ten for surreptitiously supplying an aged couple, the special object of their charity, with army plug, could have deterred me from taking the hint.

Very likely, my old friend Miss Sherman, in her Broome-street cellar,—it is always the attic or the cellar,—would object to Mrs. Ben Wah's claim to being the only real American in my note-book. She is from down East, and says «stun » for stone. In her youth she was lady's-maid to a general's wife, the recollection of which military career equally condones the cellar and prevents her holding any sort of communication with her common neighbors, who add to the offense of being foreigners the unpardonable one of being mostly men. Eight cats bear her steady company, and keep alive her starved affections. I found them on last Christmas eve behind barricaded doors; for the cold that had locked the water-pipes had brought the neighbors down to the cellar, where Miss Sherman's cunning had kept them from freezing. Their tin pans and buckets were even then banging against her door. « They're a miserable lot,» said the old maid, fondling her cats defiantly; « but let 'em. It's Christmas. Ah!» she added, as one of the eight stood up in her lap and rubbed its cheek against hers, « they 're innocent. It is n't poor little animals that does the harm. It's men and women that does it to each other.» I don't know whether it was just philosophy, like Mrs. Ben Wah's, or a glimpse of her story. If she had one, she kept it for her cats.

In a hundred places all over the city, when Christmas comes, as many open-air fairs spring suddenly into life. A kind of Gentile Feast of the Tabernacles possesses the tenement districts especially. Green-embowered booths stand in rows at the curb, and the voice of the tin trumpet is heard in the land. The common source of all the show is down by the North River, in the district known as «the Farm.» Down there Santa Claus establishes headquarters early in December and until past New Year. The broad quay looks then more like a clearing in a pine-forest than a busy section of the metropolis. The steamers discharge their loads of fir-trees at the piers until they stand stacked mountain high, with foot-hills of holly and ground-ivy trailing off toward the land side. An army-train of wagons is engaged in carting them away from early morning till late at night; but the green forest grows, in spite of it all, until in places it shuts the shipping out of sight altogether. The air is redolent with the smell of balsam and pine. After nightfall, when the lights are burning in the busy market, and the homeward-bound crowds with baskets and heavy burdens of Christmas greens jostle each other with good-natured banter,—nobody is ever cross down here in the holiday season,—it is good to take a stroll through the Farm, if one has a spot in his heart faithful yet to the hills and the woods in spite of the latter-day city. But it is when the moonlight is upon the water and upon the dark phantom forest, when the heavy breathing of some passing steamer is the only sound that breaks the stillness of the night, and the watchman smokes his lonely pipe on the bulwark, that the Farm has a mood and an atmosphere all its own, full of poetry, which some day a painter's brush will catch and hold.

Into the ugliest tenement street Christmas brings something of picturesqueness as of cheer. Its message was ever to the poor and the heavy-laden, and by them it is understood with an instinctive yearning to do it honor. In the stiff dignity of the brownstone streets up-town there may be scarce a hint of it. In the homes of the poor it blossoms on stoop and fire-escape, looks out of the front window, and makes the unsightly barber-pole to sprout overnight like an Aaron's rod. Poor indeed is the home that has not its sign of peace over the hearth, be it but a single sprig of green. A little color creeps with it even into rabbinical Hester street, and shows in the shop-windows and in the children's faces.

The very feather-dusters in the peddler's stock take on brighter hues for the occasion, and the big knives in the cutler's shop gleam with a lively anticipation of the impending goose « with fixin's » —a concession, perhaps, to the commercial rather than the religious holiday. Business comes then, if ever. A crowd of ragamuffins camp out at a window where Santa Claus and his wife stand in state, embodiment of the domestic ideal that has not yet gone out of fashion in these tenements, gazing hungrily at the announcement that « A silver present will be given to every purchaser by a real Santa Claus. — M. Levitsky.» Across the way, in a hole in the wall, two cobblers are pegging away under an oozy lamp that makes a yellow splurge on the inky blackness about them, revealing to the passer-by their bearded faces, but nothing of the environment save a single sprig of holly suspended from the lamp. From what forgotten brake it came with a message of cheer, a thought of wife and children across the sea waiting their summons, God knows. The shop is their house and home. It was once the hall of the tenement; but to save space, enough has been walled in to make room for their bench and bed. The tenants go through the next house. No matter if they are cramped; by and by they will have room. By and by

WAITING FOR A PEEP AT A « REAL SANTA CLAUS. »

comes the spring, and with it the steamer. Does not the green branch speak of spring and of hope? The policeman on the beat hears their hammers beat a joyous tattoo past midnight, far into Christmas morning. Who shall say its message has not reached even them in their slum?

Where the noisy trains speed over the iron highway past the second-story windows of Allen street, a cellar-door yawns darkly in the shadow of one of the pillars that half block the narrow sidewalk. A dull gleam behind the cobweb-shrouded window-pane supplements the sign over the door, in Yiddish and English: « Old Brasses. » Four crooked and moldy steps lead to utter darkness, with no friendly voice to guide the hapless customer. Fumbling along the dank wall, he is left to find the door of the shop as best he can. Not a likely place to encounter the fastidious from the Avenue! Yet ladies in furs and silk find this door and the grim old smith within it. Now and then an artist stumbles upon them, and exults exceedingly in his find. Two holiday shoppers are even now haggling with the coppersmith over the price of a pair of curiously wrought brass candlesticks. The old man has turned from the forge, at which he was working, unmindful of his callers roving among the dusty shelves. Standing there, erect and sturdy, in his shiny leather apron, hammer in hand, with the firelight upon his venerable head,

A CHRISTMAS WEDDING AT LIBERTY HALL.

strong arms bared to the elbow, and the square paper cap pushed back from a thoughtful, knotty brow, he stirs strange fancies. One half expects to see him fashioning a gorget or a sword on his anvil. But his is a more peaceful craft. Nothing more warlike is in sight than a row of brass shields, destined for ornament, not for battle. Dark shadows chase each other by the flickering light among copper kettles of ruddy glow, old-fashioned samovars, and massive andirons of tarnished brass. The bargaining goes on. Overhead the nineteenth century speeds by with rattle and roar; in here linger the shadows of the centuries long dead. The boy at the anvil listens open-mouthed, clutching the bellows-rope.

In Liberty Hall a Jewish wedding is in progress. Liberty! Strange how the word echoes through these sweaters' tenements, where starvation is at home half the time. It is an all-consuming passion with these people, whose spirit a thousand years of bondage have not availed to daunt. It breaks out in strikes, when to strike is to hunger and die. Not until I stood by a striking cloak-maker whose last cent was gone, with not a crust in the house to feed seven hungry mouths, yet who had voted vehemently in the meeting that day to keep up the strike to the bitter end,—bitter indeed, nor far distant,—and heard him at sunset recite the prayer of his fathers: « Blessed art thou, O Lord our God, King of the world, that thou hast redeemed us as thou didst redeem our fathers, hast delivered us from bondage to liberty, and from servile dependence to redemption! »—not until then did I know what of sacrifice the word might mean, and how utterly we of another day had forgotten. But for once shop and tenement are left behind. Whatever other days may have in store, this is their day of play. The ceremony is over, and they sit at the long tables by squads and tribes. Those who belong together sit together. There is no attempt at pairing off for conversation or mutual entertainment at speechmaking or toasting. The business in hand is to eat, and it is attended to. The bridegroom, at the head of the table, with his shiny silk hat on, sets the example; and the guests emulate it with zeal, the men smoking big, strong cigars between mouthfuls. « Gosh! ain't it fine? » is the grateful comment of one curly-headed youngster, bravely attacking his third plate of chicken-stew. « Fine as silk, » nods his neighbor in knickerbockers. Christmas, for once, means something to them that they can understand. The crowd of hurrying waiters make room for one bearing aloft a small turkey adorned with much tinsel and many paper flowers. It is for the bride, the one thing not to be touched until the next day—one day off from the drudgery of housekeeping; she, too, can keep Christmas.

A group of bearded, dark-browed men sit apart, the rabbi among them. They are the orthodox, who cannot break bread with the rest, for fear, though the food be kosher, the plates have been defiled. They brought their own to the feast, and sit at their own table, stern and justified. Did they but know what depravity is harbored in the impish mind of the girl yonder, who plans to hang her stocking overnight by the window! There is no fireplace in the tenement. Queer things happen over here, in the strife between the old and the new. The girls of the College Settlement, last summer, felt compelled to explain that the holiday in the country which they offered some of these children was to be spent in an Episcopal clergyman's house, where they had prayers every morning. « Oh, » was the indulgent answer, « they know it is n't true, so it won't hurt them. »

The bell of a neighboring church-tower strikes the vesper hour. A man in working-clothes uncovers his head reverently, and passes on. Through the vista of green bowers formed of the grocer's stock of Christmas trees a passing glimpse of flaring torches in the distant square is caught. They touch with flame the gilt cross towering high above the « White Garden, » as the German residents call Tompkins Square. On the sidewalk the holy-eve fair is in its busiest hour. In the pine-board booths stand rows of staring toy dogs alternately with plaster saints. Red apples and candy are hawked from carts. Peddlers offer colored candles with shrill outcry. A huckster feeding his horse by the curb scatters, unseen, a share for the sparrows. The cross flashes white against the dark sky.

In one of the side-streets near the East River has stood for thirty years a little mission church, called Hope Chapel by its founders, in the brave spirit in which they built it. It has had plenty of use for the spirit since. Of the kind of problems that beset its pastor I caught a glimpse the other day, when, as I entered his room, a rough-looking man went out.

« One of my cares, » said Mr. Devins, looking after him with contracted brow. « He has spent two Christmas days of twenty-three out of jail. He is a burglar, or was. His daughter has brought him round. She is a seamstress. For three months, now, she has been keeping him and the home, working nights. If I could only get him a job! He won't stay honest long without it; but who wants a burglar for a watchman? And how can I recommend him? »

A few doors from the chapel an alley runs into the block. We halted at the mouth of it.

« Come in, » said Mr. Devins, « and wish Blind Jennie a merry Christmas. » We went in, in single file; there was not room for two. As we climbed the creaking stairs of the

rear tenement, a chorus of children's shrill voices burst into song somewhere above.

«This is her class,» said the pastor of Hope Chapel, as he stopped on the landing. «They are all kinds.

laps, or squatting on the floor; in the midst of them, a little old woman with heavily veiled face, and wan, wrinkled hands folded in her lap. The singing ceased as we stepped across the threshold.

«Be welcome,» piped a harsh voice with a singular note of cheerfulness in it. «Whose step is that with you, pastor? I don't know it. He is welcome in Jennie's house, whoever he be. Girls, make him to home.» The girls moved up to make room.

«Jennie has not seen since she was a child,» said the clergyman, gently; «but she knows a friend without it. Some day she shall see the great Friend in his glory, and then she shall be Blind Jennie no more.»

The little woman raised the veil from a face shockingly disfigured, and touched the eyeless sockets. «Some day,» she repeated, «Jennie shall see. Not long now-- not long!» Her pastor patted her hand. The silence of the dark room was broken by Blind Jennie's voice, rising cracked and quavering:

THE SCRUBWOMEN'S FESTIVAL.

We never could hope to reach them; Jennie can. They fetch her the papers given out in the Sunday-school, and read to her what is printed under the pictures; and she tells them the story of it. There is nothing Jennie does n't know about the Bible.»

The door opened upon a low-ceiled room, where the evening shades lay deep. The red glow from the kitchen stove discovered a jam of children, young girls mostly, perched on the table, the chairs, in each other's

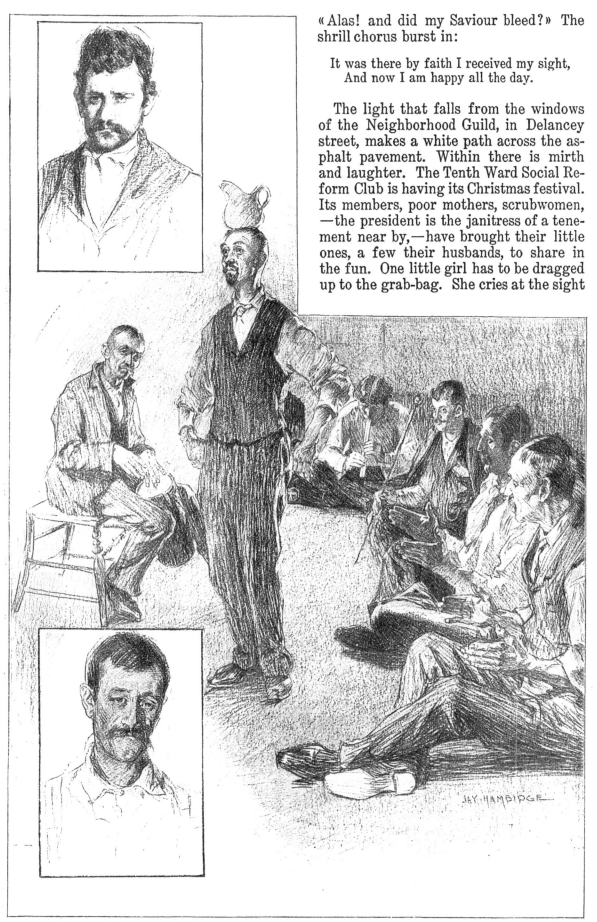

« Alas! and did my Saviour bleed? » The shrill chorus burst in:

It was there by faith I received my sight,
And now I am happy all the day.

The light that falls from the windows of the Neighborhood Guild, in Delancey street, makes a white path across the asphalt pavement. Within there is mirth and laughter. The Tenth Ward Social Reform Club is having its Christmas festival. Its members, poor mothers, scrubwomen, —the president is the janitress of a tenement near by,—have brought their little ones, a few their husbands, to share in the fun. One little girl has to be dragged up to the grab-bag. She cries at the sight

DANCE OF THE NEW YORK SYRIANS.

of Santa Claus. The baby has drawn a woolly horse. He kisses the toy with a look of ecstatic bliss, and toddles away. At the far end of the hall a game of blindman's-buff is starting up. The aged grand-mother, who has watched it with growing excitement, bids one of the settlement workers hold her grandchild, that she may join in; and she does join in, with all the pent-up hunger of fifty joyless years. The worker, looking on, smiles; one has been reached. Thus is the battle against the slum waged and won with the child's play.

Tramp! tramp! comes to-morrow upon the stage. Two hundred and fifty pairs of little feet, keeping step, are marching to dinner in the Newsboys' Lodging-house. Five hundred pairs more are restlessly awaiting their turn upstairs. In prison, hospital, and almshouse to-night the city is host, and gives of her plenty. Here an unknown friend has spread a generous repast for the waifs who all the rest of the days shift for themselves as best they can. Turkey, coffee, and pie, with « vegetubles » to fill in. As the file of eagle-eyed youngsters passes down the long tables, there are swift movements of grimy hands, and shirt-waists bulge, ragged coats sag at the pockets. Hardly is the file seated when the plaint rises: « I ain't got no pie! It got swiped on me. » Seven despoiled ones hold up their hands.

The superintendent laughs—it is Christmas eve. He taps one tentatively on the bulging shirt. « What have you here, my lad? »

« Me pie, » responds he, with an innocent look; « I wuz scart it would get stole. »

A little fellow who has been eying one of the visitors attentively takes his knife out of his mouth, and points it at him with conviction.

« I know you, » he pipes. « You 're a p'lice commissioner. I seen yer picter in the papers. You 're Teddy Roosevelt! »

The clatter of knives and forks ceases suddenly. Seven pies creep stealthily over the edge of the table, and are replaced on as many plates. The visitors laugh. It was a case of mistaken identity.

Farthest down-town, where the island narrows toward the Battery, and warehouses crowd the few remaining tenements, the somber-hued colony of Syrians is astir with preparation for the holiday. How comes it that in the only settlement of the real Christmas people in New York the corner saloon appropriates to itself all the outward signs of it? Even the floral cross that is nailed over the door of the orthodox church is long withered and dead: it has been there since Easter, and it is yet twelve days to Christmas by the belated reckoning of the Greek Church. But if the houses show no sign of the holiday, within there is nothing lacking. The whole colony is gone a-visiting. There are enough of the unorthodox to set the fashion, and the rest follow the custom of the country. The men go from house to house, laugh, shake hands, and kiss each other on both cheeks, with the salutation, « Every year and you are safe, » as the Syrian guide renders it into English; and a nonprofessional interpreter amends it: « May you grow happier year by year. » Arrack made from grapes and flavored with aniseed, and candy baked in little white balls like marbles, are served with the indispensable cigarette; for long callers, the pipe.

In a top-floor room of one of the darkest of the dilapidated tenements, the dusty window-panes of which the last glow in the winter sky is tinging faintly with red, a dance is in progress. The guests, most of them fresh from the hillsides of Mount Lebanon, squat about the room. A reed-pipe and a tambourine furnish the music. One has the center of the floor. With a beer-jug filled to the brim on his head, he skips and sways, bending, twisting, kneeling, gesturing, and keeping time, while the men clap their hands. He lies down and turns over, but not a drop is spilled. Another succeeds him, stepping proudly, gracefully, furling and unfurling a handkerchief like a banner. As he sits down, and the beer goes around, one in the corner, who looks like a shepherd fresh from his pasture, strikes up a song—a far-off, lonesome, plaintive lay. « ‹ Far as the hills,› » says the guide; « a song of the old days and the old people, now seldom heard. » All together croon the refrain. The host delivers himself of an epic about his love across the seas, with the most agonizing expression, and in a shockingly bad voice. He is the worst singer I ever heard; but his companions greet his effort with approving shouts of « Yi! yi! » They look so fierce, and yet are so childishly happy, that at the thought of their exile and of the dark tenement the question arises, « Why all this joy? » The guide answers it with a look of surprise. « They sing, » he says, « because they are glad they are free. Did you not know? »

The bells in old Trinity chime the midnight hour. From dark hallways men and women pour forth and hasten to the Maronite church. In the loft of the dingy old warehouse wax candles burn before an altar of brass. The priest, in a white robe with a huge gold cross worked on the back, chants the ritual. The people respond. The women kneel in the aisles, shrouding their heads in their shawls; the surpliced acolyte swings his censer; the heavy perfume of burning incense fills the hall.

The band at the anarchists' ball is tuning up for the last dance. Young and old float to the happy strains, forgetting injustice, oppression, hatred. Children slide upon the waxed floor, weaving fearlessly in and out between the couples—between fierce, bearded men and short-haired women with crimson-bordered kerchiefs. A Punch-and-Judy show in the corner evokes shouts of laughter.

Outside the snow is falling. It sifts silently into each nook and corner, softens all the hard and ugly lines, and throws the spotless mantle of charity over the blemishes, the shortcomings. Christmas morning will dawn pure and white.

OUR YULE-TIDE EVERGREENS.

THOUSANDS of busy hands are, year by year, engaged in gathering and arranging the evergreen boughs and blossoms of the winter season; and much good taste is exhibited in their graceful distribution in our homes and places of worship. But a large proportion of those young people who gather and form these treasures of the woods and gardens into beautiful decorations, know nothing of their properties and uses, and the historical interest attached to them. Now, it is both pleasant and profitable to learn something more of the things we so commonly handle than their mere names, form, or colour; and thus, what little additional information I possess in reference to these Christmas greeneries shall be placed at their service.

I have adopted the old name "Yule-tide" because the custom of decorating with evergreen boughs was of ancient date in Britain; and, by a curious coincidence, the season which was made one of rejoicing and festivity on account of the sun's revolution at the "winter's solstice" by our heathen ancestors, was that period when in after years the advent of our blessed Lord was commemorated, and made the time for family reunions, giving of love-tokens, alms, and hospitality.

The name "Christmas," which succeeded "Yule-tide," was derived from the Saxon word *Mæsse*, a "feast," and so may be rendered "Christ-feast." *Yule* likewise means "a feast," of which term there are several very similar ones, derived from the same primitive root in the Danish and Swedish as well as Saxon and Anglo-Saxon languages. I will not enter further into the question of the meaning and origin of the quaint old name "yule," because in a former article I made some observations thereupon, but pass on to the main subject under consideration.

The shrubs and evergreen trees chiefly in use for the decorations of the above-named festival are the bay, box, cypress, holly, ivy, laurel, laurestina, mistletoe, and yew; and to supplement these, there are winter flowers, such as Christmas roses, monthly roses, crocuses, snowdrops, daisies, bachelor's buttons, dried lavender, together with ferns, furze, parsley leaves, pine cones, &c. I will confine my observations, however, to the few evergreens which are above-named, and within the reach of all.

The Bay-tree (*Laurus nobilis*) is a native of Europe, Asia, and Africa. It is a highly aromatic shrub, and is much esteemed, as most of you know, for culinary purposes, and the decorative trimming of dishes; but, already familiar with the tree and its uses, some of you may like to know something of its classical history. The curious traditions connected with it date back to very early times, long prior to the Christian era, when it was designated the "tree of Apollo." The story was that the heathen deity, Jupiter, was credited with having transformed Daphne into a bay-tree to save her from the pursuit of the former. On this account we learn that peculiar virtues were attributed to it; and, amongst others, it was believed to be a preservative against injury from lightning.

Probably on this account it was that some of the Roman emperors, including Tiberius, selected the bay to form the wreath which they wore round the head, just as they would have worn an amulet. It was also employed

to make those with which poets were crowned, and the successful competitors in some of the ancient games—then as a symbol of victory. The bay was also credited with gifting those who tasted its leaves with prophetic inspirations, and thus the Pythian Priestess used to chew them, because, after a season of abstinence, they produced some degree of excitement. Besides being regarded as a symbol of victory, the withering of the tree was considered or evil omen, and a presage of death. An allusion to this superstition is to be found in one of the plays of Shakespeare, viz.—

" 'Tis thought the king is dead. We'll not stay;
    The bay-trees in our country are withered."
        —*Richard II.*

The Box-tree (*Buxus*) follows next on my list. There was some traditional virtue or significance attached to it, evidenced in the discovery of the twigs found in some old British barrows in Essex. There are dwarf species as well as forest trees; and in the neighbourhood of Dorking there is some high ground called "Box-hill," which was at one time covered with this valuable tree, most of which was cut down at the beginning of the present century (1815), and sold for £10,000. The grain of the wood is exquisitely fine and close, and is found superior to all others for engraving and wood-carving, the manufacture of musical and mathematical instruments, and chessmen, &c., its delicate, pale yellow colour rendering any use of a dye not only superfluous, but destructive of its beauty. There are splendid forests of this tree both in north-western Russia and Persia; but in this country they now grow singly as a rule; but the dwarf kind (*Buxus sempervirens*), which is a Dutch variety, is much employed as a border for flower-beds, and in carpet-gardening. In country villages you may often observe the quaint shapes into which box-trees are cut, an idea borrowed by our ancestors from the Romans. The latter clipped them into the shapes of gigantic birds and beasts. No blossoms appear on this tree until the month of April; but its small and pointed leaves, somewhat resembling those of the myrtle, contrast well with the broad and brighter leaves of the laurel. It was a great favourite amongst our forefathers for the decoration of their houses on festal occasions, and it is one of those named by the prophet Isaiah to flourish in the land of Israel, when the waste places shall resume their ancient fruitfulness, and become "the garden of the Lord"; and, again, we are told, "He shall plant in the desert the fir-tree, the pine-tree, and the box-tree together" (Isaiah lxi. 19), and also in chap. lx. 13, "The glory of Lebanon shall come unto thee; the fir-tree, the pine-tree, and the box together; to beautify the place of my sanctuary."

The Cypress stands third in alphabetical order, and may be utilised amongst our Christmas decorations. It is true that this peculiar and beautiful tree is much connected with cemetery plantations, owing to its dark and sombre hue; but it is likewise associated with births and weddings from ancient times in the East. When a daughter was born amongst the inhabitants of the Greek archipelago, a grove of cypress trees was planted by the father as her future portion, her fortune augmenting as her years were multiplied. And thus we may trace the origin of the name by which these groves were designated—viz., "daughters' dowers." The tree is one characterised by extreme longevity. Its duration of life is computed at from five to six hundred years, some proportion reaching from eight to nine hundred. But Strabo names one example in Persia which had attained the wonderful age of 2,500 years. They rise to a height of about 120 feet, and measure from twenty-five to forty feet in circumference. One cypress, seen by De Candolle in Mexico, measured as much as 120 feet round at the base, and was considered by him to be older than Adamson's and Humboldt's famous baobab, or baobab tree, of Africa, which tree is the patriarch of living organisations. By calculating its circles the specimen which they especially name was estimated at an age of 5,700 years. The cypress of Montezuma is forty-one feet in circumference, and, grand as it is, it is quite diminutive in comparison with that in Mexico, before-named. It is said that, when the roots of this tree are for six months under water, it is observed to grow to a gigantic size.

The Holly (Ilex aquifolium) is a special favourite amongst our Christmas greeneries, for it is not only employed on walls, windows, and pillars, but is awarded a place of distinction on the dinner-table, to beautify with its scarlet berries the historical and characteristic "plum pudding," the "standing dish" of the season. There is considerable variety exhibited in the colour of the leaves, some trees producing them of an ivory-white, and some a beautiful and delicate shade of pink, while on others we find them variegated. The most remarkable specimens of this description which I have myself observed were some in the County Carlow. Perhaps the deep shade of the splendid avenue of ancient yew-trees with which these hollies were surrounded may have had some influence in the colouring, at least, of the ivory-white variety.

Perhaps it may be regarded as having a special claim to recognition, not alone for its bright appearance but as one of the limited number of trees indigenous to Great Britain. The name has been erroneously supposed to be a corruption of the word "holy," but it has, however, been dignified in Germany and throughout Scandinavia by the distinctive name of "Christ's Thorn," possibly because of its putting forth its berries at the nominal season of our Saviour's birth, the time-honoured custom of its use in the decoration of churches in commemoration of that event, and as a natural result of many of the ancient traditions connected with it. For instance, according to legendary history, it was the bush in which

God appeared to Moses in a flame of fire; and when the latter turned aside to see why the bush was not burnt, "God called unto him out of the midst of the bush," and told him that the place whereon he stood was "holy ground." There is also another legendary history attached to the holly tree, and that is that the cross on which our Saviour was crucified was made of its wood, on which account it was known as the Lignum Sanctæ crucis. But not alone since the Christian era has it been held in such esteem; for in Eastern nations, as well as in the West, and dating back to early heathen times, it was valued, not merely for its beauty, but for some fancied medicinal virtues, and as possessing some characteristics connected with the supernatural. It was dedicated to Saturn by the ancient Romans, whose feast, held in his honour, was observed at the same period of the year as the Christian festival, and commemorated, among other ways, by the sending of sprigs between friends and relatives, accompanied by good wishes, just as we send pictorial cards and kindly greetings. The flowers of the holly were regarded, according to Pliny, as an antidote to poison, and a decoction produced from the leaves was supposed to convey the gift of wisdom by the Persians, for which reason they sprinkled their children with it. Our own Druids, pitying the sylvan sprites when, during the season of frost and snow, there was no shelter provided for them by the leafless branches of the oak, used to garnish the walls of private dwellings with branches of holly, in which they could find a place of refuge suited to their taste.

I now pass on to the Ivy (Hedera helix), which is seen in perfection at this season, the blossoms being amongst the very few that gladden the eye in winter. There are various kinds of ivy, some being of a reddish purple, resembling the colour of the Virginia creeper; others of an ivory-white, and others variegated, having irregular markings and streaks of green and white; and perhaps no other plant can show so great a variety in the formation of the leaves and in their respective dimensions. What is known as "Irish ivy" was imported from the Canary Islands as a covering for an old wall or a border for a flower-bed; and even as an evergreen substitute for flowers in the same, as well as to serve as a climber over a wire trellis on a house, or an archway over a garden walk, it is of much beauty and value. It is also suitable as hanging greenery from a garden vase or a basket suspended in a room.

But it clings with only too "cruel kindness" to a tree, and absorbs much of the nourishment which should go to it from the soil, depriving it of air, light, and sunshine, and strangling it in its deadly grasp. Never allow it to grow as a parasite on any tree, and wherever found so doing, saw the stem through at the base, that it may wither, and release its hold, and then pull up the root, for it will kill whatever it entwines. Ivy will live to a stupendous age, ranging from five to six hundred years. As a decoration for the pillars of a church it could not be surpassed in suitability and elegance; and as regards any symbolic significance it is one of the emblems of eternal life. In reference to its classical history and ancient associations, it was dedicated by the Egyptians to Osiris, and by the Greeks and Romans to Bacchus, or the god of wine, who was represented as crowned with ivy, as it was supposed by the ancients to neutralise the intoxicating influence of any excess in wine-drinking.

But this graceful evergreen had a second symbolic significance in the old-world times, derived from the tenacity with which it clings to whatever it once entwines. On this account it was presented by the heathen priests to persons newly married, to represent the "Gordian knot," by which they were bound one to the other. Hence the motto, "We flourish

or fall together." Ivy was presented in the form of wreaths and garlands to the victors at the Isthmian games, afterwards superseded by pine-branch garlands. It bears round clusters of dark purple berries, which succeed the blossoms, in the depth of the winter season.

The Laurel, one of the most beautiful of our winter evergreens, was famous in classic times, and in the Christian art of the middle ages. It was introduced into Europe from the East in 1679. The name is derived from the Celtic blaur, pronounced "lor," and signifying "green." The plant is of the genus Laurus nobilis, or bay tree, of which there are many species, and all valuable, including the camphor, cinnamon, bay (before-named), and sassafras. A considerable difference in character is shown in the tree called the American laurel, a shrub of the genus Kalmia. Other kinds are known as the cherry laurel, or Prunus laurocerasus; and also the great laurel, or Rhododendron maximum. No plant has a finer glaze on its beautiful pointed broad leaves. Early in the year they turn to a fine yellow hue, and fall off; but they are completely replaced by the middle of April. The blossoms are small and white, growing in clusters. As to its classical associations, it was famous amongst plants. In the Pythian games the victors were rewarded by wreaths of laurels, while those in the Olympic were formed of green parsley. It was supposed to possess extraordinary virtues, endowing those who slept under its branches with poetical inspirations, and likewise to be a safeguard against the power of lightning, as it could never be struck by it. I have myself seen the group of laurels around the tomb of Virgil at Baia, near Naples, who died there on his way to Greece, and these laurels are the successors of those parent trees which were planted there by Petrarch.

The Laurestinus, or Viburnum tinus, was known to the ancients as the Tinus, the leaves of which, as you know, are smaller, darker, and less glazed than those of the laurel. It is not a native of this country, but was introduced here at about the time of Bacon, having been introduced into Europe from the East in 1596. It is now common everywhere; but in the south of Europe it even forms extensive hedgerows. Its berries are of a dark purple colour, and the tiny blossoms grow in large clusters, presenting a flat, even surface of a pinkish-white tint. I am not aware that the Laurestinus has any classical associations, and only name it as an admirable addition to the greeneries which the winter season affords.

Next in order on our list of evergreens is the Mistletoe.

This curious plant, which owes its existence and borrows its nutriment from another, and not direct from the soil, is a parasite of the oak, crab-apple, pear, locust, and lime-trees, that on the oak being the rarest kind. In Anglo-Saxon it was called Misteltâ. A popular song, well known by many of our readers, bears the name of "The Mistletoe Bough," and the unfortunate young bride, who constitutes the heroine of a very tragic history, has been multiplied, like William Tell, and claimed by more than one distinguished family, but, I have reason to believe, was one of the Copes of Bramshill, although the catastrophe took place during a residence of her family in Italy. With reference to the mistletoe, I must remind you that the Druids selected it to do honour to their great festival in the winter solstice. They called it "All-Heal," and, according to some accounts, they used to cut it from the trees with their brazen celts, or upright hatchets, fastened to the ends of their staves; but, according to others, it was cut by the chief of the Druids with a golden sickle, kept for that purpose only. These branches were carried by them in procession, and laid upon their altars. (See Stukeley's account—"Medallic History of Carausius.") It is said that the medicinal properties of this curious and beautiful plant were universally believed in, and that wonderful cures were effected by its use in cases of epilepsy and various other disorders of a like character. In the year 1729 a treatise was published on its virtues as a medicine by Sir John Colbach; and, more especially in reference to its use in epilepsy, another appeared in 1806 by a Dr. Fraser. The genuine plant is the *Viscum album* of botany; but there is one very nearly allied to it—the *Loranthus Europæus*—which may often be found on the oak, as on the other trees named. This species is to be found near Vienna, in the garden of Schoenbrunn, but does not appear in a more westerly direction. It has been thought that this, and not the *Viscum album*, was the sacred mistletoe of the Druids. A description of birdlime is made from its fruit.

The use and veneration of the mistletoe was peculiar to the Celts and Goths, who alike introduced it into their religious rites as the sun approached the winter solstice. It forms the solitary exception amongst our evergreens in reference to the decoration of churches, and is, by common consent, altogether confined to our private homes. The poet Gay, in his "Trivia," names it amongst the other greeneries set up in our churches; but he did so through some oversight, for the plant so peculiarly connected with ancient heathen worship in this country, having been, by a mistake of a country sexton, brought into a Christian place of worship, it was expelled on account of its heathen associations, which rendered its use inappropriate.

The last evergreen respecting which my space will permit me to speak, is the Yew, or *Taxus baccata*. Emblematic as it is of death, it is also recognised as one of immortality. In olden times the wood was especially valuable as the best for the manufacture of bows and cross-bows, and those of you who are well-informed in English history may remember that with the bows of yew the battles of Cressy and Poictiers were won; the best in use for modern archery, and a variety of articles, such as arm-chairs, are likewise manufactured from it. The trunks of these venerable-looking trees resemble a number of rods bound together, looking like "fluted" pillars. I have seen an avenue of such at Fenagh, co. Carlow, which presented the appearance of a dim cathedral aisle. The yew is famous for its great longevity. One found in a bog had 545 rings, each marking an annual growth, although the diameter measured only 18 inches—100 rings to an inch. Those at Fountain's Abbey are about 1,200 years old; one at Crowhurst of 1,500; at Fortingal, another upwards of 2,000; and at Brabourne, in Kent, and at Hedson, Buckinghamshire, there are patriarchs of from 2,500 to 3,000 years of age, being the oldest specimens of still living vegetation existing. Yew trees seem to have been favourites with our forefathers. We see them not only in churchyards, but in the little gardens in front of country cottages and farmhouses, very usually clipped into grotesque forms like box-trees. They were also much employed for garden hedgerows, of which a very remarkable specimen is to be seen at Battle Abbey, in Sussex. They are also much employed in the same way in Holland.

I will not now speak of the gorse, ferns, and other evergreens that also help to deck our homes at this great season of family reunions; my notes, composed of facts and fables, are concluded; but I must raise your thoughts to higher considerations: the unfading blooms and eternal reunions, where He is Lord of the feast, whose birth, as the "Son of Man," we feebly commemorate here.

The evergreen plants, which ancient custom has connected with that wondrous event, may typify in your mind the never-fading "Tree of Life," in the paradise of God. The incomprehensible "ages of ages" are spoken of, in connection with it, as if divided by months and years; but only to convey to your minds the idea that through the long course of that blissful existence will be granted successively new delights. Nor is this all. For the sick and suffering what is the feast? to the blind, the loveliest garden? But with the ever-varying joys will be granted the power of enjoyment, for "Then shall the blind see out of obscurity; the lame man shall leap as a hart; and the tongue of the dumb shall sing," for "the leaves" of that tree are "for the healing of the nations."

S. F. A. CAULFEILD.

THE STORY OF THE EVERGREENS.

Holly Song.

Care is but a bursted bubble,
  Trill the carol, troll the catch;
Sooth, we'll cry, "A truce to trouble!"
  Mirth and mistletoe shall match.

Happy folly! we'll be jolly!
  Who'd be melancholy now?
With a "Hey, the holly! Ho, the holly!"
  Polly hangs the holly bough.

Laughter lurking in the eye, sir,
  Pleasure foots it frisk and free.
He who frowns or looks awry, sir,
  Faith, a witless wight is he!

Merry folly! what a volley
  Greets the hanging of the bough!
With a "Hey, the holly! Ho, the holly!"
  Who'd be melancholy now?
                    Clinton Scollard.

The Humour of Christmas.

By James Walter Smith.

MAMMA: "To-morrow's Christmas Day, Effie, dear, and you will go to church for the first time." (Encouragingly): "There will be beautiful music——" Effie: "Oh, mummy, dear, may I dance?"
DRAWN BY PHIL MAY. REPRODUCED BY PERMISSION OF THE PROPRIETORS OF "PUNCH."

WHEN Effie's mother told her that to-morrow would be Christmas Day, and that Effie was going to church for the first time, where she would hear beautiful music, the little girl cried out, "Oh, mummy, dear, may I dance?" The point of view of Effie is the point of view of untold thousands. We older ones, burdened with the knowledge acquired by years of Christmases, know that Christmas is a religious festival significant with beauty, and some of us are prone to lament, as the Puritans so strenuously lamented, that the fundamental note of the Christmas season seems to be lost. Yet it is not for us to say that the child's point of view is not correct. It makes for happiness, and to be happy in the happiness of others should be the aim of all at Christmas-tide.

The arrival of Santa Claus is so eagerly watched for that we have often wondered why he has never been seen. Possibly because the dustman is in league with Santa, and gets in the way of curious boys and girls. Little Montague, who on Christmas morning told his father that he was awake when Santa Claus arrived, came very near to actual discovery. It was so dark that little Montague could not see Santa, "but when he bumped himself on the wash-stand he said——" "There," replied the father; "that'll do, Monty; run away and play"—and we are left in ignorance of what Santa Claus really said and what he looked like. The knowledge would be valuable—not so much as an addition to the history of explosive expletive as an addition to the juvenile system for the detection of patron saints.

LITTLE MONTAGUE: "I was awake when Santa Claus came, dad."
Father: "Were you? And what was he like, eh?"
Little Montague: "Oh, I couldn't see him; it was dark, you know. But when he bumped himself on the wash-stand he said——"
Father (hastily): "There, that'll do, Monty. Run away and play."
DRAWN BY C. E. BROCK. REPRODUCED BY PERMISSION OF THE PROPRIETORS OF "PUNCH."

STUCK FAST.——DRAWN BY ARTHUR F. MERRICK FOR "LIFE."

attempt at personification. On one such occasion Santa appeared in the room where daddy was making up with a shaving-brush and a hand-mirror. "Great Scot!" cried Santa, "is that me?" and we may imagine that he rapidly departed from the scene with some horror at the recollection of a real monstrosity.

Some justification, however, should be expressed on the paternal behalf, for if no one

That Santa Claus should be so intolerably long in arriving at his destination is not to be wondered at when we remember the difficulties in the way of his progress put there by progress itself. Our merry saint has to keep up with the times, and the most accurate knowledge that we possess of his doings tells us that the reindeer which he used to drive so recklessly over the housetops are now possessions of the past, and that Santa to-day rides *en automobile* through the drifting snows. He runs the risks taken by others who fare forth in winter. He may get locked up in the drifts or he may have a total breakdown, so common to beginners in the new and ever-increasing method of locomotion, but the perils in his path are as nothing.

A traveller such as he is always prepared for shocks. Often when for some reason or other his arrival has been given up as hopeless, and daddy has undertaken, in response to a pressing and unanimous request, to figure as Santa Claus, the unexpected appearance of the saint upon the scene throws things into confusion. Santa himself might well be astonished at such a moment to look upon the results of daddy's

PAPA MAKES UP.—Shade of Father Christmas: "Great Scot! Is that supposed to be me?"

DRAWN BY TOM BROWNE FOR "THE KING."

SANTA CLAUS VISITS THE FREAK MUSEUM.—DRAWN BY C. J. TAYLOR FOR "PUCK."

haired doll that moves its eyes. If by any chance the old fellow were to find himself in a museum devoted to freaks, as one of our artists pictures him, he would be equal to the emergency. Santa Claus possesses the discriminative power to please the diverse tastes of such abnormal people.

Once upon a time Santa had experience with a selfish boy who, thinking to get the better of his brothers and sisters, climbed to the roof and there hung, at the top of the chimney, his empty stocking attached to a broom. Expectantly he went to sleep, and in the night the Frost King came, covering the cities and the villages with white and leaving behind a world of trackless snow. When Santa, in his sledge and furs, drew towards the home of the selfish one, he found the stocking filled with ice and snow and the house barred by wintry rigour against

has ever seen Santa Claus how can anyone tell the way he should be dressed? Although the saint brings with him gifts enough to fill every reasonable want, and would hardly feel at a loss were a hundred thousand stockings hanging before him when he entered the chimney of a well-regulated house, he is compelled to exercise some discretion in the act of distribution. His insight into the consciences of the young tells him unerringly where to place his gifts. Never will a box of paints be found in the stocking of the little fellow who has longed for a box of bricks, and tin soldiers never occupy the place intended for a flaxen-

COLD STUFFING.—Little Gussie Greedy hangs his stocking outside the chimney so that he can be sure to get it filled, but is not entirely satisfied with the result.
DRAWN BY F. BEARD FOR "JUDGE."

his approach. Departing as quickly as he came, he rode for miles and miles towards the city of the Rising Sun, and when the morning came a wet and empty stocking was found at the top of the chimney by the little boy who had placed it there. No message had been left, but there remained a lesson in the heart of the little one, for good or ill.

Would we could always be as successful in interpreting the morals taught by artists! From them we get so many pictures of the humorous side of Christmas and its festivities that we tend to forget the sorrow. Where there exists a Christmas tree and a purse to buy its candles and pendent ornaments, there will pleasure reign, but there yet remain some lives into which a real Christmas rarely comes, try as we may in philanthropic mood to give it them. The little waif in the slums who got nothing for the holidays but two punishments, and "didn't hang up no stockin' for them neither," is a typical figure in a class that is always with us. To relieve distress thus humorously emphasized is, happily, a common work at such a season.

The best-laid plans of philanthropy, however, stop short in many cases where they would do most good. Says little Milly, in one of our pictures, "Don't yer think if she hung up her stockings Santa Claus might give her a pair of legs to put in 'em?" the remark being directed against a waif, with spindle legs, carrying a heavy basket along a

"Did you get anything for the holidays, Billy?"
"Yes; dad give me two lickin's, and I didn't hang up no stockin' for them neither."
DRAWN BY M. WOOLF FOR "LIFE."

snow-covered pavement. How wise it would be if we, in our Christmas philanthropy, were to fill the stockings of the poor with fatter limbs instead of presents! The Christmas feeling that we have no right to our own turkey if we have not filled the larder of the poor is a feeling beautiful in itself. More effective would it be were we to do it daily, and not soothe ourselves with the balm that Christmas comes but once a year.

That the festival does come but once a year is looked upon by some as a blessing. Consider, for instance, the poor father who, in a benevolent mood, undertakes to act the part of Santa Claus at the Christmas-tree festivities. Father thinks, in his innocent way, that it would be no end of a lark to dress up and please the little children, but we have known many cases where father has pleased the children to the point of terror by his

PERSONAL.—Milly: "Don't yer think if she hung up her stockings Santa Claus might give her a pair of legs to put in 'em?"
DRAWN BY M. WOOLF FOR "LIFE."

There has been an interesting event in Bagly's household, of which Johnny has been kept in ignorance.
Johnny: " Put this on the tree, too, Pop. I found it in mummy's room. She's asleep."
DRAWN BY J. A. SMITH FOR " PUCK."

As for the good, fat turkey which forms the staple of our Christmas feast, there is little to be said that has not already been told. There yet remains a chance for someone to sing his praises as Lamb sang the praises of the pig, and as the writers of the olden time lauded the virtues of the boar's head. One old writer, dealing with pre - Christmas preparations, has barbarously written: " Now capons and hens, beside turkeys, geese, and ducks, with beef and mutton, must all die, for in twelve days a multitude of people will not be fed with a little. Now plums and spice, sugar and honey, square it among pies and broth. Now or never must music be in tune, for the youth must dance and sing to get them a-heat, while the aged sit by the fire."

What the turkey thought of these prepara-

extraordinary rig. Again, it is no small job to do Santa's work thoroughly, and to come out of a chimney just like the real thing is a feat of grace quite impossible to the well-fed British parent of mature years. At such times as these accidents are bound to happen, for the curiosity of the family to know just what father is doing is a known quantity, certain to be expressed in the little equation of holiday life. One of our humorists tells us how the Christmas tree was in preparation in the home of one Bagly just after a certain interesting event had taken place. Johnny, who had been kept in ignorance, suddenly appeared in the room with a parcel in his arms. " Put this on the tree, too, Pop," cried Johnny ; " I found it in mummy's room. She's asleep." We have nothing more to add, except that this harassing scene is immortalized on the present page.

THE MARCH OF SCIENCE.—Result of over-education in animals.
DRAWN FOR " LIFE."

tions, or thinks of them to-day, would be fit subject for an crnithologist to consider. Does the sumptuous bird have a foreboding of his fate? Can it be that he knows the real reason of his being — that the kindly care bestowed upon him by the farmer in the month of November tricks him not? As the old poets say, we trow not. Foolish he may be, but the turkey is too old a bird — as he

Mr. Charles O Connor : " Golly, wot's der matter wid yer, Jakey?"
Mr. Jacob McFinnigan : " Turkey."
DRAWN BY " CHIP " FOR " LIFE."

if we look back upon our childhood days, there is not one of us who will fail to understand the condition of Mr. Jacob Mc-Finnigan, the small and swelling youth shown here. Sermons might be written on this subject.

The end of all is the pudding. It comes upon the table smoking hot and leaves behind it memories of a happy day. It goes by parcel post to English families throughout the world, and does more good than Christmas cards. It is a staple commodity upon which the household can fall back at any time, and can be used to induce manual labour in tramps, with indifferent result.

We are indebted to Messrs. James Henderson for permission to reproduce the drawings from *Puck, Judge,* and *Life* which we have selected from *Pictorial Comedy.*

MISPLACED GENEROSITY.
Mrs. Gamp (to tramp) : " If you saw up that wood for me I will give you this Christmas pudding."

sometimes proves himself to be — not to understand the object of his existence, and he bears it almost bravely when doomsday comes. The day has yet to arrive — although the humorist has anticipated it— when turkeys will gather in a farm-yard to discuss the virtues of anti-fat.

On one of the turkey's virtues all can to-day unite to praise. It is a filling bird. And,

Tramp (a few minutes later) : " Beg parding, mum, but if it makes no difference to you I would rather saw up the pudding and eat the wood."
DRAWN BY TOM BROWNE FOR " THE KING."

WINTER

SHE

"Naked trees had got snow foliage,
soft, and feathery, and bright,
And the earth looked dressed for
heaven, in its spiritual white."

CHRISTMAS IN THE NORTH.

NORWAY is the home of some very pretty and interesting Christmas customs. They will, for the most part, be also found in Sweden and Denmark, as they are of Scandinavian origin. The old Norse Christmas was known as Jul (pronounced Yule), derived from one of the epithrets (Jolner) of the Scandinavian deity Odin; and so they obtained Jul from Jolner as the Romans got Saturnalia from Saturn. Yule fell late in the year, and when our hallowed festival came to be celebrated in northern lands, the one merged into the other. On the introduction of Christianity into Norway, the Christmas festivities were regarded as heathenish. The yule feasts were not only prohibited, but those who gave them were punished with death or mutilation by order of King Olaf the Saint. How changed are the times! Long before the advent of Yule nowadays, great preparations are made for the due observance of the fête. The yule-cake (bakkelse) is made; the venison is hung, the pigs and fatted calves are killed, the small game is collected, and a good supply of fish laid in. Large quantities of wood are brought from the forests, and the logs are piled up by the fireside, all in readiness. As the day approaches, the invitations are sent out, and the final touches are given to the arrangements at the house, bright fresh leaves being spread over the floors of the principal rooms. On the morn of the appointed day, the invited are spirited away in light and elegant sledges to the happy abode, whilst the church bells ring out the sweet music of peace and good-will to mankind. Most of the Norwegians attend the early service at the parish church, and it is on this occasion that they carry offerings to their minister. Having thus recognized the festival as members of the Christian Church, they return to their homes to honor it after the manner of their forefathers. Their tables are heavily laden, and there is much eating and drinking, the repast opening with the standard dish of fish. Afterwards the Christmas songs of the country are sung, stories are told, and the fairy lore of the country, proverbially rich, is largely drawn upon for the amusement of the little folks—not always exclusively. They tell how the Trolls make their appearance on Yule night, and invite the young men to feast with them in their sylphid homes amongst the hills. Norway, too, has the Christmas-tree; the poorest peasant in the country, as well as the richest proprietor, does not fail to light up the toy-bearing fir-tree for the gratification of his children. Card-playing is another of their Yule-tide amusements. The favorite dances are a kind of valse and an exciting gallopade. They dance to the fiddle, and the fiddler is invariably a cobbler.

We have yet to notice the prettiest of the Norse Yule customs—that of giving the fowls of the air a feast on Christmas Day. For the sparrows and other small birds sheaves of wheat, oats, or barley are stuck upon long poles and put out on gables of houses, barn-doors, out-buildings, gateways, and other places where the feathered tribe love to congregate. They are said to know when Christmas is drawing nigh, for you may now observe hundreds of birds flocking round the snow-covered houses, while at other times they are scarcely visible.

The Christmas of Sweden is very similar to the Christmas of Norway. The custom of dining the smaller birds is also popular amongst the Swedes; so attached, indeed, are the people to it that the man who forgets the fowls of the air at this season is sure to lose his character for benevolence. It is, besides, the practice to give the cattle a double feed on Christmas Eve. "Eat well, my good beasts, and thrive," say the farm-laborers, "for this is Jul-afton." The church bell announces the birth of the day almost as soon as the eve has passed away; and at a very early hour people may be seen by hundreds in the streets of the towns, lighted on their way by lanterns. They are going to church. It is an extraordinary sight, and what makes it more so is the vast number of children seen in the throng. They are being taken to the Jul-Otta—the Christmas day-break (song)—there being a tradition amongst the Swedes that if the children attend this early service they will very easily learn to read. This is followed by the "race home." It forms part of the rustic creed, that the bread-winner who arrives first at his house from the Jul-Otta will be the first to get in his next harvest, or, if a bachelor, the first to obtain a wife. The rest of Christmas Day is spent by the Swedes in a quiet and pious manner. St. Stephen's (Dec. 26) is given up to family visiting; it is a more open holiday, differing from Christmas Eve, inasmuch as people go out and about; and differing from Christmas Day, inasmuch as there is a considerable amount of sledging, eating and drinking, and making merry. Between this time and New Year's Day, the young people divert themselves by "getting married"—à la Suède, of course; and those already "sacrificed," or those who don't care about going to the altar, solace themselves in a round of other pleasures.

Ask any Dane which he regards as the great national holiday of his country, and he will unhesitatingly inform you that it is Christmas Day. Being a sober-minded individual, the Dane, like most of his Northern kindred, spends his Yule by the fireside, and binds a little more closely together his domestic relationship. The eating of grod and the singing of hymns around the Christmas-tree belong to the Eve; church-going, alms giving, card-playing, story-telling form the lighter amusements of Christmas Day; dinner, the heavier. The pièce de résistance is the plum-pudding, to which the fair children and blue-eyed maidens of Denmark do ample justice. At the conclusion of the dinner, emphasis is given to an interesting ceremony. The children say to the head of the table. "Thank you for my dinner," and the company, on rising, ladies and gentlemen alike, shake hands all round, saying, at the same time, "Good may it do you!" Then follow the drawing-room entertainments, the finale being a Danish Christmas song in which everybody present takes part.

The characteristics of the Russian social Christmas, which we have only space to notice briefly, are these. In the country districts a good stock of salted meats, sausages, and kirsch is laid in during the six weeks which precede Christmas (O. S.), and at an early date it is arranged amongst friends and relatives at whose house the festival shall be celebrated. In due time the hostess goes round and invites the company in an old-fashioned but complimentary set speech, followed the next day by the nurse, who invites the young ladies. Subsequently the host himself asks the guests, generally by deputy, " to witness the sports of the fair maidens, to break with them a bit of bread, taste a grain of salt, and partake of the roasted goose." At the time named the guests arrive in sledges, the young ladies and gentlemen first. All is bustle now in the house and neighborhood. One of the first proceedings is the introduction of the young people, for this is the "mating season," over which the hostess presides. So soon as the elder visitors have been received, a lady is chosen to conduct the ceremonies. We need scarcely add that this lady is sure to be the fairest of the matrons. Then are served the refreshments, which comprise many things besides sausages, salted meats, and kirsch; indeed, delicacies of the rarest kinds, and liqueurs of the choicest "brands" are offered to the company. The health of the host, hostess, and their family is now ceremoniously drunk, and the entertainments of the evening commence. Mummers are called in, the national dances are performed, and the company is further amused by the happy allusions of the improvisatore. These amusements are almost invariably supplemented by the famous dish-game. In a deep dish placed on a table in the middle of the room, and filled with water, the ladies deposit their available articles of jewelry. The mistress of the ceremonies takes charge of the dish and its contents. The dish is covered with a napkin, the company sit round the table; bread, salt, and charcoal are brought in, and then everybody present joins in the old song of "The Salt and the Bread." Meanwhile the trinkets are stirred in the dish, and short songs are sung, prognosticative of good and evil fortune. As each of these is ended, a trinket is taken from the dish, and the owner is supposed to be elated or made miserable by the import of the words. And woe to the owner of the trinket which is taken last from the dish. There are many other indoor amusements. The most popular of those which take place out of doors is masquerading. Both gentlemen and ladies visit their friends in disguises; and much merriment is caused by the attempts made to identify the wearers of the masks.   T. N.

Cocoanut Cake.—To the well-beaten yolks of six eggs add two cups powdered white sugar, three-fourths cup butter, one of sweet milk, three and a half of flour, one level teaspoon soda, and two of cream tartar, whites of four eggs well beaten ; bake in jelly-cake pans. For icing, grate one cocoanut, beat whites of two eggs, and add one teacup powdered sugar; mix thoroughly with the grated cocoanut, and spread evenly on the layers of cake when they are cold.

Lemon Cake.—One and a half cups of sugar, one of butter, two and a half of flour, five eggs beaten separately, four teaspoons sweet milk, one teaspoon cream tartar, half teaspoon soda.

For Jelly.—Take coffeecup sugar, two tablespoons butter, two eggs, and juice of two lemons ; beat all together, and boil until the consistency of jelly. For orange cake, use oranges instead of lemons.

New York Cake.—Two cups of sugar, one of butter, one of milk, nearly four cups of flour, white of eight eggs, three teaspoons of baking powder, flavor with lemon. Bake a little more than three-fifths of this mixture in three jelly tins, add to the remaining batter one tablespoon ground allspice, one and a half tablespoons ground cinnamon, teaspoon cloves, a fourth of a pound each of sliced cinnamon and chopped raisins. Bake in two jelly tins, and put together with frosting, alternating dark and light.

Orange Cake.—Two cups of sugar, half cup of butter, three and a half of sifted flour, half cup of sweet milk, three eggs beaten separately, teaspoon baking powder mixed in flour ; bake in jelly tins. For jelly, take the juice and grated rind of two oranges, two tablespoons cold water, two cups sugar ; set in a pot of boiling water, and when scalding hot, stir in yolks of two well-beaten eggs, and just before taking from the fire, stir in the white of one egg, slightly beaten, and when cold put between the layers of cake. Frost the top with the other egg.

Neapolitan Cake.—*Black Part.*—One cup brown sugar, two eggs, half cup butter, half cup molasses, half cup strong coffee, two and a half cups flour, one of raisins, one of currants, a teaspoon each of soda, cinnamon, and cloves, and half teaspoon mace.

White Part.—Two cups sugar, half cup butter, one of milk, two and a quarter of flour, one of corn starch, whites of four eggs, small teaspoon cream tartar. Make frosting of whites of two eggs to put between the layers.

Ribbon Cake.—Two and a half cups sugar, one of butter, one of sweet milk, teaspoon cream tartar, half teaspoon soda, four cups flour, four eggs. Reserve a third of this mixture, and bake the rest in two loaves of the same size. Add to third, reserved, one cup raisins, fourth pound citron, a cup of currants, two tablespoons molasses, teaspoon each of all kinds of spice ; bake in a tin same size as other loaves. Put the three loaves together with a little icing or currant jelly, placing the fruit loaf in the middle. Frost the top and sides.

Yellowstone Cake.—One and a half cups granulated sugar, half cup butter stirred to a cream, whites of six eggs, or three whole eggs, two teaspoons cream tartar stirred in two heaping cups sifted flour, one teaspoon soda in half cup sweet milk ; bake in three layers. For filling take a teacup sugar and a little water, boiled together until it is brittle when dropped in cold water ; remove from stove and stir quickly into the well-beaten white of one egg ; add to this a cup of stoned raisins chopped fine, or a cup of chopped hickory-nut meats, and place between layers, and over the top.

Delicious Chocolate Cake.—The whites of eight eggs, two cups sugar, one of butter, three full cups flour, one of sweet milk, three teaspoons baking powder; beat the butter to a cream, stir in the sugar, and beat until light; add the milk, then the flour, and beaten whites. When well beaten, divide into two equal parts, and into half, grate a cake of sweet chocolate. Bake in layers, spread with custard, and alternate the white and dark cakes. For custard for the cake, add a tablespoon of butter to one pint of milk, and let it come to a boil; stir in two eggs, beaten with one cup sugar, and add two teaspoons corn starch dissolved in a little milk.

Lemon Pie.—Two lemons, two cups of sugar, one cup of milk, two tablespoonfuls of flour, and six eggs. Use the yolks only. After the pies are baked, beat the whites

and eight tablespoonfuls of sugar. Spread it over the pies, put them in the oven till they become a light brown.

Buns.—One pound of flour, six ounces of butter, two teaspoonfuls of baking powder, a quarter of a pound of sugar, one egg, not quite a quarter of a pint of milk, a few drops of essence of lemon ; bake immediately. This will make twenty-four.

Christmas Pudding.—Mix together in a large bowl three beaten eggs, half a cup of butter, two cups of zante currants, one cup of chopped citron, the juice of two oranges, and one cup of bread crumbs rubbed fine through a sieve, and one cup of sweet cream ; flour a cloth well, put in the pudding, and boil hard two hours. Eat with a rich sauce.   C. R. P. Y.

Christmas Pudding, No. 2.—Mix together one pound of currants, half a pound of sugar, ditto butter and flour mixed, the yolks of eight eggs, one teaspoon of cinnamon, the grating of two lemons, and juice of one, mix with it a little milk with a teaspoonful of yeast powder stirred into it. Boil in an oven two hours, rich liquid sauce. Put in only enough milk so as to just have the pudding stick together.   C. R. P. Y.

A Cream Pudding.—One pint of sweet cream, into which stir smoothly one teacupful of fine flour ; stir this until quite thick over the fire, then take off, and when it is cool, stir into it four beaten eggs, add two teacups of fine white sugar, and one cup of citron chopped fine. Bake till *set*. This is a very fine pudding, if the last operation of *baking* is done right. Many persons bake custards too long, until they become *watery*, which spoils them. Eat this pudding cold. Can be eaten with sauce if desired, but is very good without.   C. R. P. Y.

Rice Croquettes.—Boil half a pound of well-washed rice in one quart of cold water, with a level tablespoonful of salt, half a pint of milk, half the yellow rind of a lemon, or two inches of stick cinnamon, and two ounces of sugar for half an hour, after it begins to boil, stirring it occasionally to prevent burning. Take it from the fire, stir in one at a time the yolks of three eggs, and return to the fire for ten minutes to set the egg. Then spread the rice on an oiled platter, laying it about an inch thick, and let it get cool enough to handle. When it is cool enough, turn it out of the platter upon some cracker dust spread on the table, cut it in strips one inch wide and three inches long, roll them into the shape of corks, dip them first in beaten egg, then in cracker dust, and fry them golden brown. Lay them on a napkin for a moment to free them from grease, put them on a dish, dust a little powdered sugar over them, and serve them.

Apple Dumplings.—Pare and core as many apples as you want dumplings, keeping them whole. Make a suet crust, roll it out, and cut it in as many squares as you have apples. Fold the corners of the pieces of paste over them, pinch them together, tie each one in a floured cloth, and boil for one [hour. Then take them from the pudding cloths, and serve them with butter and sugar.

Lemon Dumplings.—Sift eight ounces of dried bread crumbs, mix them with the same quantity of very finely-chopped suet, pare off the thin yellow rind of a lemon, chop it very fine, and add it with the juice to the bread and suet. Mix in half a pound of sugar, one egg, and enough milk to make a stiff paste, about half a pint. Divide the paste into six equal balls, tie them in a floured cloth, and boil them an hour. Serve with butter and sugar, or syrup.

Apples in Jelly.—Pare and core small-sized apples without cutting open; then put them with some lemons, in water to cover, let boil slowly until tender, and take out carefully without breaking. Make a syrup of half a pound white sugar to a pound of apples, cut lemons in slices, and put them and the apples into syrup; boil very slowly until the apples are clear, take them out in a deep glass dish ; put to the syrup an ounce of isinglass dissolved, let it boil up, lay a slice of lemon on each apple, and strain the syrup over them.

Codfish Balls.—Soak codfish cut in pieces about an hour in lukewarm water, remove skin and bones, pick to small pieces, return to stove in cold water. As soon as it begins to boil, change the water and bring to a boil again. Have ready potatoes boiled tender, well mashed and seasoned with butter. Mix thoroughly with the potatoes half the quantity of the codfish while both are still hot, form into flat thick cakes, or round balls, fry in hot lard or drippings, or dip in hot fat, like doughnuts. The addition of a beaten egg before making into balls renders them lighter. Cold potatoes may be used by reheating, adding a little cream and butter, and mixing while hot.

WHAT TO WEAR.

CHIT-CHAT ON DRESS. BY OUR PARIS CORRESPONDENT.

CHILDREN'S FANCY DRESS FOR CHRISTMAS PARTIES.

"JILL."

FANCY costumes are particularly well adapted to little folks, a fact which of late years has come to be recognised, and at many juvenile parties character costumes are *de rigueur*. In case any of my readers should receive invitations to such parties for the young members of their family, and be puzzled how to dress them, I propose to give some details that I trust may be acceptable, and shall begin with those which are particularly easy to make at home. Boys' costumes, as a rule, not being so easy as girls', I will discuss the boys' first.

Geneviève de Brabant gave prominence to a cook's dress, and nothing is easier—and I was going to say quainter. It must be all white, even to shoes and cotton stockings; the breeches are made of white linen, and fastened with three buttons at the knee, and over this is either a frilled blouse, full, and ending at the waist, or a white double-breasted tail-coat; the white apron must, *de rigueur*, be tucked into the waist, and the flat cook's cap be worn on the head. If you want any further decoration, you may wear the *cordon bleu*, display a bill of fare, or a saucepan; and should you prefer to be a pastrycook, you carry a wooden tray of cakes; or a baker, you carry a long Vienna loaf.

A clown — more especially the

FRENCH DRESS, 1787.

French one, Pierrot—is very easily concocted. He wears long, loose, white trousers and blouse, with a row of coloured rosettes down the front, and has his face painted, and occasionally has a half-mask, black. An æsthetic clown is a good notion, with sunflowers and blue china plates worked over the white dress, a peacock's feather in the conical cap, a sunflower and a feather-fan carried in the hand.

A wizard, or astrologer, is easily managed : a black conical cap, with cabalistic insignia pasted on in gold paper, and a long black robe with the same, a wand in the hand, large spectacles, a ruff at the throat, made of treble box-plaited muslin, and pointed shoes.

Mirliton is a pretty dress for a boy, and of much the same cut as the clown's, only that the blouse is more close-fitting, but pointed cap, blouse, and trousers should be covered with inch-wide stripes of blue cotton, stitched on diagonally, so that they appear to be wound round and round.

A Christy minstrel, in striped linen coat and trousers, preposterously large collar, a black face, and a battered hat, is capital for a big boy, as some little fun can be brought to bear on the character.

Small boys dressed as Napoleon the Great, Dr. Pangloss, a jockey, Dick Turpin,

LADY OF THE TWELFTH CENTURY.

and other well-known characters are irresistibly charming. As I have mentioned these, and you might select them, I must tell you how to dress them. Napoleon I. has a black cocked hat, with tricolour rosette, a large lapelled coat, white leather breeches, silk stockings, and shoes. Dr. Pangloss, a large-skirted, large-sleeved black velvet coat, with steel buttons, a very long waistcoat, black velvet breeches, ruffles, shoes with buckles, white wig, and spectacles. A jockey appears in a parti-coloured jacket and breeches of satin, cap to match, top-boots, a whip in hand. Dick Turpin, in a scarlet coat and waistcoat trimmed with gold braid and buttons, lace ruffles and cravat, leather breeches, high boots, and three-cornered hat and fancy wig, with pistols at the belt. I consider that the most

FISHWIFE.

A PAGE.

all of a row" on her pink and blue gown ; a châtelaine formed of watering-pot, hoe, rake, and spade at her side. Red Riding Hood, in red cloak and blue frock, was there, as well as Chaperon Rouge, the French and more dainty rendering of the same, viz., a red satin petticoat, black velvet bodice, white muslin apron, and red silk hood, a basket in the hand ; and also Cinderella, both as a princess and a serving-maid, but in both cases displaying her crystal shoe — by-the-by, best made by covering a discarded white satin shoe with talc cloth.

favourite fancy costume for boys just now is the man-of-war's man, because everybody has a sailor suit ; and the æsthetic costume, which is rendered by black pointed shoes, silk stockings, light velvet breeches, short jacket, and a large soft coat. An æsthetic green is really the colour that should be chosen, but a black velvet is as often as not adopted, and that can be worn afterwards in every-day life.

Any characters from the nursery rhymes and stories seem well adapted to children, and at one of the prettiest juvenile parties I have seen, no other costumes were admitted. Jack Horner in blue breeches and waistcoat, a red coat with gold buttons, a tricolour hat, and a plum hanging to his watch-chain, dragged by the hand the very smallest brother, who personated Jack the valiant Giant Killer. The little fellow in his blue trunk-hose, close-fitting red habit, helmet, shield, and sword, seemed to have come direct from the kingdom of Liliputia. Boy Blue as Gainsborough painted him ; Blue Beard with a thick beard of blue wool ; Beauty and the Beast devoted themselves to "My pretty Maid," in a quilted petticoat, bunched-up chintz tunic, muslin kerchief, straw hat, and milk-pails ; and to "Mary, Mary, quite Contrary," who had "cockle shells, silver bells, and pretty girls,

FORESTER.

There were several other characters.

Kate Greenaway's heroines suit little people wonderfully well, and you can hardly do wrong in copying her illustrations faithfully. I have in my mind's eye a little damsel of eight years old, with auburn hair and sparkling eyes, who as Jennie won all hearts. She was not, as I have seen the character rendered, in black silk dress, muslin apron, kerchief and cap—captivating enough when a bright young face peeps from beneath—but in a short green skirt and pelisse, with poke bonnet and fur muff, a lace pelerine over her shoulders, and high-heeled shoes. Quaker's and quiet dresses, which elderly people might wear, are always piquant on a child, just as the garb of a baby or of a schoolboy is extremely amusing worn by a grown man. Vandyck's famous picture of Charles I.'s children may always serve as a guide to a family group. The close lace cap, the long skirt, the bibbed apron suit little girls to perfection, and there is hardly a picture which Vandyck, Sir Joshua Reynolds, Gainsborough, or De Largillière painted of children which would not show to advantage if reproduced at a juvenile fancy ball.

MOORISH SERVANT.

If you wish to make a boy thoroughly happy, let him appear as Robinson Crusoe in knickerbockers and paletot and cap of fur, with robins sewn about it, a parrot perched on the shoulder, a belt round the waist, carrying a fowling-piece, pistols, hatchet, and umbrella; and a little friend should be allowed to accompany him as Man Friday with blacked face and hands and feet, wearing a striped shirt and trousers. Lalla Rookh and other Eastern dresses suit dark girls well. If I describe Lalla Rookh I shall be describing the ordinary run of Oriental dresses. She has full red silk trousers to the ankle, a short petticoat to match, a green satin over-dress with open sleeves trimmed with gold, a pink satin bodice over a gold-spangled chemisette. A few illustrations will make this paper of more practical use; they are as follows:—

BARRISTER.

No. 1. *Jill*.—In a flowered cotton frock and petticoat; soft silk kerchief, knotted at the throat. The large brim of the bonnet should be lined with a colour becoming to the wearer.

No. 2. *French Dress about* 1787.—Pale blue and yellow striped silk coat; yellow satin breeches; long blue waistcoat, fastening to the waist, then opening to disclose a blue under-vest trimmed with gold braid. Chain and seals hanging at the side. Large lace jabot in front, and lace ruffles at the wrists. White wig; tricornered black hat; gold-headed cane.

No. 3. *Lady of the Twelfth Century*.—Dark woollen dress, with three-inch border of contrasting colour; the long sleeves match the border, likewise the pointed

fichu in front. Velvet collar. The pointed head-dress is white and gold; the veil is white; a velvet band borders the edge, and lace frills fall on the hair. Gold ornaments, pointed shoes.

No. 4. *Fishwife*.—Woollen dress, either dark blue or dark terra-cotta red; soft silk pink kerchief for the head. Stockings striped to match dress.

No. 5. *Forester*.—Dark woollen tights, hood, and hose. Boots, belt, jacket, and gauntlets of soft leather. Felt hat; staff in hand.

No. 6. *Page*.—Tights and vest joined by ribbons, and showing a soft shirt at the neck, waist, and wrists. Hanging sleeves lined with a contrasting colour falling over close ones. Long hair and round hat.

No. 7. *Moorish Servant*.—Striped silk trousers; embroidered satin jacket; Oriental scarf round hips; soft muslin turban. The hands and face should be stained.

No. 8. *Barrister*. — Black gown, either in black lustre or rich corded silk; scarf in either black or crimson silk; wig; brief in hand.

No. 9. *Dutch Woman*.—Short-waisted dress, with square velvet-trimmed bodice; gauntlet sleeves

DUTCH WOMAN.

with a puff of cambric at the elbow; elaborately gathered chemisette; lawn apron with handsome lace border.

In fancy costumes everything depends on brightness of colour, freshness, and suitability. Nervous children should not be put into dresses which are associated with a marked bearing or the quiet self-possession of a woman of the world; they can hardly help looking well whatever they wear, so let them have all the enjoyment they can.

HOW TO ENTERTAIN AT CHRISTMAS.

CHRISTMAS gatherings, if not entirely confined to the family, are as a rule mainly composed of relatives, possibly of all ages. I know one happy home where four generations have assembled for the last three Christmas Days.

Unfortunately, family parties do not inevitably mean concord, though they ought to do so. There are always some lonely people whom it is a charity to include in the invitations; and while conferring a kindness, a hostess may possibly by their presence be tending to preserve the general harmony.

The one ingredient to be universally infused is gladness. Everybody can, at all events, *endeavour* to bring goodwill and a smiling countenance to the festive board, banishing for a time the recollection of every-day worries. There is all the rest of the year

to think of them. This is peculiarly the children's time, and we would have them as happy as we were in the old Christmas Days of long ago.

The party may assemble only on Christmas Day, or the house may be full from Christmas Eve until over Twelfth Night; in both cases much depends upon the hostess.

I think it was Lord Beaconsfield who said that happiness was atmosphere. To bring about a general feeling of enjoyment, much depends on the surroundings. The house must be cheerful, the ruling power animated. It is worth while to bestow some little trouble on the decoration of the rooms. Have plenty of shining holly, and laurel too, and don't omit the mistletoe, for we have long ago forgotten all about the paganism, magic, and superstition which surrounded it, and have relegated it to scenes of social merriment. Many a shipload I have seen despatched from St. Malo, the French people hardly understanding its subsequent purpose, and a very good trade is done with it in the West of England.

I like to see a motto of welcome wrought in holly hanging in the hall, and in the yearly volume of CASSELL'S FAMILY MAGAZINE for 1877 there is an article, "How to Decorate the House at Christmastime," with many useful suggestions. Flowers brighten up a room wonderfully, and should you have enough and to spare, I would advocate the American plan of making bells and balls of flowers to hang beneath chandeliers and over doors. They look best entirely of one kind of bloom. The balls are easily made by tying the ends with string, the bells require a foundation of the bell shape. Last year we made this of crinoline wire covered with coarse muslin about twelve inches long, and hid it entirely with mistletoe; the waxen berries looked extremely pretty among the greenery as it hung over the doorway.

See that there is an abundance of Christmas literature about. Servants and children as well as the grown-up guests delight in looking at pictures. A pretty, well-written story of Christmas happiness is wont to diffuse a sense of enjoyment among its readers. The glowing freshly-written pictures of the Christmas shops and the holiday people in the Christmas numbers of our magazines inspire us with a renewed power of happiness as each season comes round.

Be sure that your hearth burns brightly. Though the yule log of Scandinavian origin is no longer drawn in by household retainers, bestridden by old Father Christmas, to be kept alight if possible to Candlemas, you will have no bad substitute in a fair-sized piece of ship's timber crackling in the grate.

It does not come within my province to enter upon the question of Christmas cheer. The board should be as liberally spread as means will allow. Children delight in a substantial tea, over which their elders can preside before their own Christmas dinner is served. An abundance of crackers and bon-bons add to the general fun—which, by-the-by, I have known enhanced by drawing lots for partners at the dinner-table.

Everybody likes presents, and presents are inseparably connected with the season. Queen Elizabeth so delighted in them that even her "kitchen wenches" presented her with lozenges; and fans, bracelets, and treasures of all kinds poured into the royal lap when December came.

There are two points to be considered: first, what to give, and then how best to make the giving a source of pleasure. The poor should not be forgotten. A good plan is the Christmas basket, carried pedlar fashion into the hall, and its contents distributed by all the members of the family to the poorer neighbours invited to be present, and to the servants. Such charity is doubly welcome accompanied by kindly words and wishes, and it greatly delights the young people to see their handiwork appreciated.

Christmas-trees, which the Prince Consort introduced among us nearly forty years ago, have established their fame, and there is not much that is new to be told about them. They have this drawback, that in removing the presents there is a danger of fire; and it is not a bad arrangement to hang the tree itself with beads and glittering balls brilliantly lighted, and set the presents round the table well wrapped up, a small lighted doll's-candle by each; the children are thus able to examine their gifts by the light of their very own candle. A snow-ball about a yard in circumference, made in two halves, with calico covered with wadding, on a wire foundation, filled with presents, may be rolled into the room and allowed to burst open, when a general scramble ensues. A gipsy-tent rigged up in a back drawing-room, with a presiding gipsy up to her work, who distributes the gifts with an appropriate word or two to each recipient, or a post office or parcels delivery office, with some bustling officials, may be made to produce a great deal of fun. We had a very successful distribution once from a hen's nest, concocted out of a clothes-basket, the gifts wrapped up to represent eggs, and the whole surmounted by a stuffed hen; but it went off so well because we had a clever henwife, who, dressed in flowered skirts and a high pointed cap like Mother Hubbard, delighted everybody. Another year we had a Cheap Jack, who made many of us forget the pleasure our presents gave us by the roars of laughter he produced, standing in the centre of the drawing-room ottoman, and, with many a merry *bon-mot*, scattering the parcels here and there. The Mummers, the Lord of Misrule, St. Nicholas, or Knecht Rupert may be made to put in an appearance and give away the presents. Knecht Rupert, in Germany, makes the distribution according to the deserts of the children, dressed in a white robe, a mask, flaxen wig, and high buskins. The Lord of Misrule wears the high top-boots of Charles II.'s time, ruff at throat, and a flowing robe. He disappeared in 1640, but before that he presided over Christmas festivities in the houses of the king and nobles, and the Mayor of London, from Allhallow Eve to Candlemas Day. He has been resuscitated of late for the special purpose of present-giving on more than one occasion.

A Christmas ship has the advantage of being very pretty, and of exercising some ingenuity. A boy clever at carpentering could even make a good-sized one. The presents are concealed in the hold; two feet long is a good size, and the rigging crystallised with alum to look like snow is a great improvement.

These distributions may take place at night or during the day, but at this season there is plenty to amuse during the day-time—long walks, when the weather is favourable, or maybe skating, and a good game of battledore and shuttlecock—or the improvement upon it, Badminton—in-doors, if it rains; in which case, too, let me recommend bean-bags. For this make four bags six inches square, of strong holland, and half fill them with dry peas. The two players stand before each other, a bag in each hand, and throw simultaneously with both hands. The bag hurled from the right hand must pass to the left hand of the *vis-à-vis*, while the bag in the left hand is passed to the right, and the left hand receives the opponent's bag from his right hand. The double movement is difficult, and requires knack, but is good exercise.

If the skating-ground be near the house, some hot drinks are most acceptable, especially to those standing on the banks. I give the recipe for one which is always approved, viz., egg wine :—Beat up two eggs, and add a little cold water; boil one pint of elder wine with spice, then beat all well together, pouring from one vessel to the other, replace it on the fire till it boils, and drink when quite hot.

When the Vicar of Wakefield's altered fortunes obliged him to repair with his family to a distant neighbourhood, we read how his new parishioners "kept up the Christmas Carol, sent true love knots on Valentine's Morning, ate pancakes on Shrovetide, showed their wit on the first of April, and religiously cracked nuts on Michaelmas Eve;" and these observances of old customs would seem to savour of a taste for simple pleasures. If carol-singing be one of them, it is certainly being revived amongst us, and this delightful form of musical amusement by young people is a Christmas pleasure worth cultivating. "God rest you, merry Gentlemen," and "Nowell, Nowell," date back to Henry VI.'s time; "Come let us all sweet Carols sing" is of German origin; and "We three Kings of Orient are," American; but there are many admirable collections.

If you bring your entertainments from without, there is a choice of conjuring, a Punch and Judy show, bell-ringing, fantocinni, and the magic lantern. In the latter each year there are marked improvements, and you may follow the fortunes of Tam o' Shanter, Don Quixote, the Forty Thieves, and Johnny Gilpin, or visit the scenes of the Afghan or the Zulu War, or discover the wonders of the microscope, or enjoy the pranks of a Christmas pantomime as displayed from the lens on the white sheet.

Besides bagatelle, loto, spelicans, dominoes, and the rest, there are some newer games, such as Chinese Gong, viz., a wooden stand with a pasteboard gong having a hole in the centre, into which the players throw one of six balls, which fall into numbered receptacles ; Patchesi, or Homeward-bound, a round game between draughts and fox and geese ; gobang, fishponds. "How Stanley attained Congo," "Doggett's coat and badge boat-race," are amusing too, and each week something new is brought out.

Recitations are just now very fashionable, and it is quite worth while to prepare some beforehand. Do not let them be too pathetic. Shakesperian readings always please, I mean those in which each part is read by a different person, but read carefully, and studied beforehand. A diversity of such amusement each evening would make a fortnight or three weeks pass all too quickly, and render the remembrance of Christmas time memorably pleasant. Recitations from good and entertaining authors never come amiss.

I cannot do better than conclude with one of the best of Christmas good wishes, which we owe to one of them : "Many merry Christmases, many happy New Years, unbroken friendships, great accumulation of cheerful recollections, affection on earth, and heaven at last."

ARDERN HOLT.

The Christmas Sleigh-Ride.

They started from the old farm-gate,
  The happiest boys alive,
With Rob, the roan, and Rust, his mate,
  And Uncle Jack to drive;
The snow was packed, that Christmas-time,
  The moon was round and clear,
And when the bells began to chime,
  They all began to cheer.
Chime, chime, chime, chime,—such a merry load
Sleighing in the moonlight along the river road!

They passed the lonely cider-mill,
  That's falling all apart;
The hermit heard them on the hill,—
  It warmed his frozen heart;
They cheered at every farm-house gray,
  With window panes aglow,—
Within, the farmer's wife would say,
  "Well, well, I want to know!"
Chime, chime, chime, chime,—such a noisy load
Speeding by the homesteads along the river road!

The river shone, an icy sheet,
  As o'er the bridge they flew;
Then down the quiet village street
  Their Christmas horns they blew;
The sober people smiled and said,
  "We'll have to give them leave
(Boys will be boys!) to make a noise,
  Because it's Christmas Eve!"
Chime, chime, chime, chime,—such a lively load
Scattering songs and laughter along the river road!

But now it's growing hard to keep
  Awake, and now it seems
The very bells have gone to sleep,
  And jingle in their dreams.
The lane at last,—the farm-gate creaks,
  And Grandma cries, "It's Jack
Why, what a peck of apple-cheeks
  These boys have brought us back!"
Chime, chime, chime, chime,—such a hungry load
Rosy from the Christmas ride along the river road!

COME·LET·VS·ALL·SWEET·CAROLS·SING

English Illustrated Magazine, 1895

CHILDREN'S CALICO BALLS.

CHRISTMAS is essentially the children's season, and as it approaches anxious mothers revolve in their mind how best to cater for the amusement of the little folks who make the sunshine of their life. Few entertainments give them more intense pleasure than a calico fancy ball, and it is difficult to imagine a prettier sight than the young, fresh faces, beaming with interest and enjoyment —the several picturesque costumes adding much piquancy to their young charms. In this I am sure all will bear me out who were present at the juvenile ball given at the Mansion House some two years ago. There, a good plan was adopted of having a march round from time to time, so that the dresses could be seen to perfection. I am inclined to think the boys had rather the best of it on that occasion. We all lost our hearts to a dear little fellow barely four years old who, as Portia, appeared in a black silk legal gown and wig, a brief carried in the hand; a Postboy, top-boots and all, true to the life; a Yankee in a large-patterned checked suit, with high collar; and a Cook, in white cap and apron. One of the very best of all the dresses, however, was an Incroyable, of which our illustration will give a good impression. Note the short-waisted, long-tailed drab cloth coat, with its large lapels, the blue satin striped waistcoat and breeches, the lace frills at the wrists and front of the shirt, the cocked hat with tricoloured rosette, the top-boots, the double eye-glasses, and the massive gold chains hanging from either fob—a veritable dandy of the Directoire period.

It is customary at these juvenile balls to provide some amusements besides dancing, such as conjuring or Punch and Judy, tumbling, Christy Minstrels, Marionettes, Fantrecini, or any similar entertainments which may be the fashion of the hour, just as the hand-bell ringers and the Arab jugglers have been in time past. But I consider, besides all this, it is almost an essential part of the programme that there should be a special quadrille of the evening, those dancing in it assuming a particular dress. The choice is a large one. There might be a Dolly Varden and Joe Willet Quadrille, including Sam Weller, Mrs. Nickleby, Mrs. Gamp, Squeers, the Marchioness, and many others "familiar in our mouths as household words," which are best copied from the illustrations that accompanied the first edition of the great author's works. A Shakespeare or a Waverley Quadrille is to my mind better suited to grown-up people, but a Cracker Quadrille is quite charming for children, the dancers being enveloped in different coloured dominoes, and tied up with ribbons like monster bonbons. At the present time, however, the most popular of all are the Singing Quadrilles, the best-known of which are the "Nursery Rhymes" and the "Blue Boy." As the figures proceed, the dancers accompany their movements by singing in concert, and there are one or two airs for each figure—old-fashioned ones, originally associated with "Jack and Jill," "Goosey Goosey Gander," "Hey Diddle-diddle," "Jack Horner," "Where are you going to, my Pretty

Maid?" "Baa, Baa," "Bopeep," "Sing a Song of Six-pence," "Ride a Cock Horse," "Mary, Mary, quite Contrary," &c.

Illustrated nursery lore has made these several heroes and heroines so familiar to children, that I

think most of them could themselves explain how they should be dressed. Bopeep is brought before you in the first of our illustrations. It should be made up in a pretty light blue sateen, trimmed with pink cotton-twill, the long pointed bodice laced in front over a low jaconet muslin chemisette. The sleeves are tied up with pink ; a pink rose nestles at the side. The blue Shepherdess hat is worn over powdered hair. Blue silk stockings and high-heeled shoes with pink rosettes complete the costume. A basket of flowers and a crook tied with ribbon and flowers are carried in the hand, and often a small toy lamb under the arm, which probably pleases the little woman, though the chances are, before the evening is over, all these paraphernalia will become a burden, and they will find a resting-place in some obscure corner, only to be unearthed before departing,

At the memorable ball at Marlborough House, there was a Fairy-tale Quadrille, in which Beauty and the Beast, Princess Fair Star, Cinderella, the Goose Girl, and many other similar characters flourished, but they are not all suitable for a veritable calico ball ; as the Goose Girl, for example, wore a shimmering robe of silver tissue and feathers ; and the Duke of Connaught, as the Beast, a cloak of tiger-skin ; for though the greatest licence is allowed with regard to material, a line must be drawn somewhere.

When calico balls first started, as I believe they did in India, only veritable cotton goods were admissible, such as calico, print, sateen, muslin, tarlatan, net, cretonne, and cotton velvet ; tinsel replacing gold trim-mings ; while specially made cotton ribbons, cotton gloves and mittens, cotton velvet and sateen boots and shoes were worn. Now, however, fur trimmings, ribbon, and plenty of cotton-backed satins are to be seen at calico balls.

The pretty cretonnes and cotton fabrics to be had at every draper's make it an easy matter to concoct little girls' dresses in the correct material, but with the boys

there is more difficulty, and only where ample licence is admitted would the top-boots of a Postboy in our sketch be admissible. As it is, it is one of the most favourite characters. Any two colours may be selected —pink and blue are a happy mixture ; the several divisions of the cap should be of the alternate shades, the jacket pink, the sleeves blue, the breeches white, and the tops of the boots pink.

"Folly," on the contrary, could just as well be carried out in sateens as in cotton-back satins, and should be a motley mixture of shades—the cap part blue, part red ; the ruff white lace ; the upper part of bodice half red, half blue ; the plastron green, the sleeves blue with yellow epaulettes, the belt red ; the basques, one Van-dyck red, one blue ; one leg encased in blue, one in red —shoes, cotton tights, and all.

A Clown is a very easily made dress for a boy, carried out in white calico with blue stripes pasted on it, so that when completed the stripes have the effect of being wound round the white. It is after the Pierrot order—a loose paletot, cap, and tights—but somewhat prettier, for Pierrot has white linen shoes, very large trousers, a loose paletot guiltless of belt, a huge flapping frill-edged collar, and red calico rosettes down the front ; and he ought by good rights to have his face painted, which would be a tiresome process for a very little boy, though one of nine or ten might enter into the fun of it. Peppé Nappa, Pierrot's Italian relative, is generally dressed after the same fashion, only all in blue, and with a large ruff.

Mothers who do not care to go to much expense can dress their boys as veritable sailors—suits which can be subsequently used for every-day wear, and are to be had ready to put on at some of our seaports, in white drill or Galatea for under half-a-sovereign, and in serge for a few shillings more. To very little boys especially the dress is most becoming.

Father Christmas, without any doubt, ought to put

in an appearance, and has a further claim than his costume, which is easily concocted—only a white wig crowned with holly, a long flowing white robe with a monk's hood at the back, a girdle round the waist, a staff in hand, and a slight dredging of flour on the shoulders, as though just out of a snow-storm ; and, above all, a wallet, which, if filled with bonbons or trifling presents for everybody, will secure him a heartier welcome—this is all that is needed.

Little Boy Blue is generally dressed as Gainsborough's Blue Boy, and is specially appropriate in the Blue Boy Quadrille, if that is preferred to the ordinary Singing Quadrille. How familiar the artist has made the costume to us all !—the blue jacket with slashed sleeves and lace collar, the blue breeches, stockings, and blue shoes, the cloak depending from the shoulder, and held gracefully through the arm—a part of the costume, by-the-by, which for the wearer's sake, at a calico ball, might very easily be dispensed with.

To aid in selecting dresses when the occasion occurs, I may mention the following characters that might be adopted by boys—a Zouave, an Eastern Water-carrier, a Watteau Shepherd, Feramorz, a Knight of Malta, an Italian Fisherman, a Cricketer, a Grey

Friar—and they are none of them difficult to carry out. But *place aux dames.* National costumes have always many copyists at calico balls, and we have selected the Italian as, perhaps, the most picturesque for our illustration. It should be made up in dark scarlet and dark blue cotton, the upper and under skirts both bound with the contrast. The apron for calico balls presents a difficulty, and the best way of surmounting it is to procure a fancy chintz and stitch it in bands on to the dark blue ; it is held on by the string passed round the waist, the upper portion turned over. The chemisette and head-dress are made of thick jaconet, and the portion resting on the head should be lined with cardboard, gold pins being used to keep it on. Gold or coral ornaments are best.

The Swiss with its silver chains and embroidery on a velvet bodice, the Normandy with the high cap, the Welsh with the high hat, the Alsatian with the large bow on the skull-like cap—all these find favour, as also does another distinctive class, the French Soubrette (illustrated above), which may be prettily rendered in a pink and white striped skirt, pink bodice, pink-trimmed muslin cap, bibbed apron, and pink-striped stockings.

Many effective dresses may be made in these striped cottons—Dolly Varden, Fille de Madame Angot, for example. Last year, in America, what were known as Mother Goose Parties were started, and there all the children appeared in characters taken from nursery lore, made up literally with nothing but coloured cotton, and they are described as being most successful.

For the benefit of the little ones, it has been found an excellent plan to introduce other country dances into the programme besides " Sir Roger "—such as "Le Carillon de Dunkerque," Scotch Reels, "Tempête," " Off She Goes," " Haste to the Wedding," and similar old-fashioned jigs.

I have only now a few more dresses for girls to mention. Pamela I have seen charmingly represented in a black cotton over a cerise cotton petticoat, with demure cambric cap, fichu, and apron ; and Grace Darling in a short blue skirt, loose tunic, sailor bodice, and fisherman's cap, carrying a lantern and a life-buoy. I do not, as a rule, consider that historical characters can be well carried out in calico, or that they are suited

to little children, always excepting Charles I. children as Vandyck painted them, in their long dresses and sleeves, and baby-caps, the most quaint and charming of ideal infant splendour and rank. Lady Jane Grey, however, in silver-grey cotton, and cotton-backed black velvet, may be made to look as demure as a Puritan Maiden, both of which I commend to the notice of those who contemplate taking part in a juvenile calico ball, together with Mother Hubbard, in her pointed hat; or a Witch, not so very unlike, having cats and serpents cut out in black cotton, and stitched or pasted on to the scarlet cap. There are so many suitable characters, the only difficulty is which to select.

A GLUT IN TURKEYS

By Marion Ward

 IT seems to be the fashion now-adays for quite young girls to write stories all about them-selves and their thoughts and escapades, and get them pub-lished, even when they are most ordinary and uninteresting—excepting to themselves, of course ; so I don't see why I should not tell about our Turkey Christmas, or, as Ronald calls it, our Glut in Turkeys, which really was very funny, and tragic as well. It happened last Christmas. I was quite a child—only fifteen. Father had not patented his wonderful discovery then, and made a whole fortune just by——but I for-got ; that is another story, as Mr. Kipling would say. We really were horribly poor. Father was abroad on business, and had been unexpectedly delayed, so that he could not possibly get home till after Christmas, and quite suddenly mother had almost come to the end of her ready money.

Mother never kept things from us, so we children knew just how bad things were. There were five of us : myself (Nora) the eldest, then Jack, then Dulcie, then Nicholas, and lastly Noel, who was just a baby of three. And besides us there was Ronald from next door, who was sixteen and very big, and always called himself the head of the family.

So just before Christmas I called a council. First I called down the telephone for Ronald (we made that telephone between the nursery and Ronald's own private sitting-room our-selves, and it had a tremendous bell, an old dinner-bell, so that he could hear plainly if he happened to be in any different part of the house). And when he came I summoned the rest of the family, and solemnly proposed that, owing to the financial resources of the family being pretty well bankrupt, we should one and all cheerfully consent to forego our usual Christmas presents this year.

Ronald seconded the motion, but some of the others looked doubtful. Dulcie con-sented instantly, and amended further that we should each put our own private little hoards into a general box and give it to mother to add to the housekeeping-money. Dulcie always was a sweet little saint.

But Jack jibbed at that.

" Hang it all ! " he said. " I'll go without my present, though I did want that ' Animals in Motion ' desperately. But I jolly well can't give up my money as well. Why, I've been saving for months to buy a pair of skates ! "

I put the motion to private vote and decided against it. I had just ten shillings of my own: exactly half enough for that dear little bamboo bookcase I had been saving up for for such a long time. No; I certainly did not want to add my small savings to the family fund.

So I repealed that suggestion and, repeating my former proposition, it was carried unanimously. The fear of the greater had minimized the less. (I got that sentence out of a book.) So we wrote out a declaration, setting forth our determination, and each signed it (Noel could just make his letters, so he put O L, which was the nearest he could get to his name), and I carried the paper to mother.

Mother just looked at it, and then she put her arms round me and hugged me. "You originated it, of course?" she said.

Then I felt mean. So I told her how much nobler Dulcie had been.

"I wonder what a mother feels like who cannot be proud of her children?" was all she said.

Mother never says much; it's not her way, but I saw the tears in her eyes as she kissed me. So that was settled.

And she said nothing would induce her to take our private stores, if we begged her on bended knees; so that was settled too.

"But," said mother, "a turkey we must and shall have."

"Do you think we can afford it?" I asked, gravely.

Mother just laughed at me, with a determined gleam in her pretty eyes. "We're *going* to have one," she said, very firmly.

When mother looks and speaks like that there is no more to be said. And it was really a great relief to me. Christmas with no presents would be bad enough, but Christmas without *turkey!* Talk about "Hamlet" without the Prince! Besides, the children would have been so desperately disappointed. So mother bought the turkey. We all went with her to help her choose a fine fat one, and Noel cried because we would not let her get a horrid, dark-looking one with yellowish marks on it. He cried all the way home for his "pitty feckled birdie," till Ronald took away his sword and helmet, and told him he was dismissed from the army for babyishness. And then he stopped, and smiled dreadfully with his poor little mouth all turned down at the corners, and the sobs still hiccoughing between his words. and called us all to witness he was "laughing." So Ronald gave him back his sword and

apologized gravely for his mistake. Noel worships Ronald; he can always make him do anything, even in his worst moods.

So we chose the turkey—a great, fat, white one, and carried it home in triumph. The shopman actually wanted to send it. As if we would have thought of letting him do such a thing! We took it in turns to carry the basket, and Ronald insisted on sharing my turn—to make longer for the little ones, he said; but I knew quite well it was really because he thought it too heavy for me. Ronald is like that.

And then, two days before Christmas, the tragedy happened.

We were sitting in the play-room in the evening, and I was writing a note to Ronald to send by the despatch (we made that ourselves, too; an awfully useful arrangement, composed of two strong pieces of elastic passed through the telephone tube, one end of each nailed respectively to the walls of the play-room and Ronald's room, and at the other end a loop, and attached to the loop a ball of twine. Do you see? That loop was kept fastened to a nail in the farther room, the elastic pulled very tense and taut; then, when either side wanted to communicate with the other, all you had to do was to unloop your end, tie the note—or sweets, or anything you liked small enough—to it, and let it shoot through the tube to the farther room. Then you pulled the loop back by the twine, ready for the next message) telling him to be ready early next morning— Christmas Eve—to come and do some private shopping with me, when suddenly Ellen, our maid-of-all-work, came rushing in like a maniac.

"Oh, mum!—oh, *mum!*" she shrieked. "The turkey!" And flopping into a chair she flung her apron over her head and burst into stormy sobs. And between her sobs the awful truth came out. The turkey was stolen!

I felt stunned. It was too terrible to believe. And then was such a pandemonium that we could hardly hear ourselves speak. Ellen was sobbing and explaining incoherently; Dulcie was patting her shoulder, and begging her not to cry; Jack and I were asking questions; and Noel and Nickey, disturbed in the middle of an exciting game of soldiers, had gleefully hailed Ellen as the foe, and were assaulting her vigorously, and with triumphant shouts, with their wooden swords.

But at last it was all out. Ellen had had the turkey up in the kitchen to prepare for roasting, and had gone out of the room

"ELLEN, OUR MAID-OF-ALL-WORK, CAME RUSHING IN LIKE A MANIAC."

for a few moments, leaving the window open and the turkey on the table just inside.

She was just in time to see the turkey's tail disappear as she came back, and, although she flew frantically out of the side door and into the street, not a sign of the thief was there to be seen. And that was all.

Mother was very gentle to her; she said it was not her fault, and, of course, she would be more careful in future. But when Ellen had sniffed herself remorsefully out of the room she looked at us very gravely.

I saw what she meant.

"Well, there's the pie," I said, with a big breath.

The others all stood quite still, looking at us with curious expressions.

Jack pressed his lips tight together and looked up at the ceiling.

"There's the pie," he echoed, firmly.

Mother's eyes grew very soft and sweet.

Nickey opened his mouth. "*No turkey?*" he roared.

"There's the pie—a lovely great pie, and the pudding; think of that lovely brown pudding, with its holly, and blue flames," said Dulcie, hurriedly.

Nickey's mouth was still open. He is a fat little boy, and rather greedy.

"But—no—TURKEY!" he wailed. He flung himself at mother. "You'll get another, mums, won't you? 'Twon't be a Christmas at all without a turkey!"

Mother stroked his head. "I'm afraid we can't afford it, dear," she said, sadly.

"Not a *little* one?" begged Nickey.

"Pig!" said Jack and I together, disgustedly.

"Pigs yourselves," retorted Nickey, fiercely.

"We're content with pie," taunted Jack.

"Hush, children; quarrelling won't mend matters. Nickey's content with pie, too, I know, isn't he?"

Nickey struggled hard. "Y-yes," he said, at last, in a very forlorn little voice.

"That's mother's brave boy," said mother, cheerfully, and Nickey brightened up.

But although we all pretended so hard not to care, we did, dreadfully. No presents and no turkey! It was terrible. It could not be—in fact, it *should* not be. I quite jumped with the sudden thought that had come into my mind. That precious ten shillings! To eat half my longed-for bookcase in a day! It seemed too awful: my eyes quite smarted at the thought. But then I thought of the glorious surprise it would be and the difference it would make.

In the middle of my reflections I looked up and found Jack's eyes fixed sombrely on my face, and he looked away so guiltily when he met my eyes that I felt sure he must have been reading my thoughts. Before I went to bed I had made up my mind.

I did not send that note to Ronald, after all. My private shopping was to be *strictly* private.

I had expected to find it very difficult to get out alone ; but, to my relief, next morning mother was busy in the kitchen, with Noel hindering her ; Jack had gone off somewhere by himself ; Dulcie looked very uncomfortable, and said if I didn't mind she wanted to stay and practise ; and Nickey was busy counting his farthings, and told me to go away and not bother. So I went.

I shut my eyes tight when I passed the shop with that dear little bamboo bookcase; but once the money was gone, and I held the firm, heavy turkey in my arms I felt absolutely hilarious. It would be *such* a surprise. Ellen was to be sworn over to secrecy, and to cook it while we were all at church on the next day. And the thought of the family's faces when it came smoking on, in its brown savouriness, made me stand and laugh aloud in the middle of the street.

After all, what was a future bookcase in comparison to such a present surprise ?

I went home at such a rate that I collided violently into Jack, who was just coming round the corner. He was hiding something under his overcoat, and went scarlet and seemed very confused.

"I FELT ABSOLUTELY HILARIOUS."

I held my turkey down at my side as best I could, and tried to think of a way to get into the pantry without his seeing me.

As we stood waiting to be let in, to my surprise Dulcie appeared at the gate. She went as red as a rose when she saw us, and half paused, as if she would run away. "You did not practise long !" I could not help calling out.

She blushed still deeper. "No; I—I thought of something I wanted out."

She dawdled about outside the gate till the door was opened, and then she followed us slowly in.

I waited for Jack to go upstairs, so that I could slip down into the pantry, but he stood aside politely, waiting for me to go up, so I had to, holding my bulky parcel carefully in front of me.

Half-way up I paused and looked over.

Jack was still standing there, apparently waiting for Dulcie, and Dulcie was standing in the hall, staring absorbedly at the pictures. A horrible, horrible suspicion formed dimly at the back of my mind. I stood quite still, breathless and waiting.

As I stood there Ronald's knock sounded at the door.

Dulcie opened it slowly.

There stood Ronald, and, all undisguised, there dangled from his hand a colossal fat turkey !

"I say," he cried, "mater's compliments, and could Mrs. Kingsley charitably make use of this beggar ? We've had *three* sent us to-day."

I sat down limply on the stairs. There was a dreadful pause. Then Dulcie, looking past his head, said, in a silly little voice, "Postman !" and pointed outside.

"Kingsley ?" said the postman, briefly, and plumped a large hamper down inside the hall.

I groaned aloud.

Through the crevices of that detestable hamper unmistakable feathers protruded.

Ronald looked up and quite jumped when he met my tragic face looking at him through the balustrade. Then he looked back at the others bewilderedly.

Mother came out of the kitchen just as Nickey came flying up the front steps.

His cheeks were scarlet and his eyes snapped excitedly. He waved a brown parcel aloft. "Who's a pig now ? It's only a half, but I only had a hundred and ten farthings, and he said that would only buy just half a little one, but you may eat it all.

"'KINGSLEY?' SAID THE POSTMAN."

I don't want it!" and tearing off the wrappings he proudly disclosed half a small and emaciated ready-cooked turkey.

Mother stared. "Dearie!"

"All my own farthings—every one," and he laughed boisterously and stamped about to pretend there wasn't any lump in his throat. Jack and Dulcie looked up at me. We all knew now. I felt quite dazed and giddy. I came slowly downstairs, and Jack and Dulcie came to meet me.

Simultaneously we unwrapped our parcels. Then I sat down in the hall and laughed hysterically till the tears rolled down my face.

For a second mother stared dumfounded, then with a little cry she fled down to the pantry, and returned holding aloft a dish on which reposed a noble turkey.

"I went out before breakfast!" she cried, and, sitting down on the floor beside me, she mingled her tears with mine.

I don't think I have ever laughed so much in all my life as I did that Christmas Eve.

Of course, Ronald had to be told all from the beginning, and there we all sat in that hall round our six and a half turkeys and laughed till we were weak.

"My bookcase!" I gurgled.

"My skates!" roared Jack.

"My muff!" chortled Dulcie.

"My farthings!" spluttered Nickey.

And "My precious reservefund!" wept mother.

I don't believe anyone, since the world began, laughed so much over a tragedy before.

And I suppose that's about all. We lived on turkey till we hated the very mention of it, and even then we were obliged to give two away to deserving poor people. I need not say that the two we so disposed of were Ronald's and the one that came in the hamper from old Uncle Malcolm. They were by far the two biggest and fattest, but we would each have eaten every morsel ourselves rather than give away a drumstick even of our precious bookcase, skates, muff, farthings, or reserve-fund.

But to this day you have only to mention the word "turkey" to set the whole family helplessly laughing. The memory of our six-and-a-half-fold surprise is too much for any of us.

The Children's Christmas,

AS DEPICTED BY FAMOUS BLACK AND WHITE ARTISTS.

By A. B. Cooper.

CHRISTMAS is the Festival of Childhood, the Carnival of Innocence, and it is right and fitting that it should be. Its first occasion was one of joy—the greatest joy that can come to homes and hearts—the birth of a little child. And the annually recurring celebration of that greatest event in the world's history—the birth of the Christ-child—is most appropriately given over to the little ones. It is the one day in the year when even the selfish become generous; the hard, tender and sympathetic; the careless and callous, loving and gentle; and when the little ones, who are typical of all that is innocent and beautiful in life, are set in the forefront and their happiness and pleasure considered as the chief object of the festival.

Who can estimate the difference which the advent of the Babe of Bethlehem made in the world's attitude towards children? Just as Christ's treatment of Woman entirely revolutionised her status in all Christian countries, so the fact that the Lord of Glory was Himself a helpless babe has for ever sanctified childhood, and the passage of the ages has more and more impressed the heart of the Christian world with the great fact that the welfare of the little child is the highest care, not only of the family, but of the State.

And thus Christmas to the thoughtful mind means more than merriment and jollity. And this is the note struck by Beatrice Offor in our frontispiece. It brings the evangel of innocence, love and purity, and inasmuch as it weans men's thoughts from stocks and shares, from buying and selling, from "cares of to-day and burdens for to-morrow," sets them to thinking with equal earnestness of Christmas trees, Christmas

CRACKERS.
Drawn by S. Begg.

THE TOURNAMENT.
From the painting by S. Begg.

stockings, Christmas parties and merry times for the little ones, so far are they the nobler, the gentler, the better for Christmastide and its happy customs.

Nothing is more characteristic of Christmas than its Christmas Numbers. The large-hearted Charles Dickens set the ball rolling and, like a snow ball, it has grown bigger and bigger as it rolled, until to-day the book-

It is our pleasure to present to the readers of the *Sunday Strand* some of these delightful creations. Though they are not religious pictures in the exact sense of that much-abused word, yet they are, to every child-loving heart, so full of the spirit of kindliness, love and tender humour, that they will probably warm hearts which a more serious set of pictures would leave untouched.

IN DARK DECEMBER.
Drawn by Frank Dadd, R.I.

stalls groan with their weight of Christmas literature. The pictures are half the battle, and why? Because the children like them. Father carries home the illustrated magazines and papers because the artists have revelled in the glorious and congenial task of drawing pretty children, occupied in every conceivable Christmas pastime and custom.

Mr. Sidney Begg has made a happy hit in *The Tournament*, and, furthermore, his picture is typical of Christmas. The children are emphatically "on the top." All mere men must bow the knee to the conquering child and be content, despite immaculate linen and dress clothes, to play charger while childhood rides in state. Doubtless the two

A CHRISTMAS DANCE: THE CLASSES.
Drawn by Frank Craig.

A CHRISTMAS DANCE: THE MASSES.
Drawn by Frank Craig.

men on their knees are enjoying themselves better than anyone else in the room, unless it be the two cherubs engaged in mimic warfare or the babe screaming with delight on his mother's lap. Even the dog is there and seems to be enjoying his Christmas as much as anyone.

There is another specimen of Mr. Begg's delightful art in *Crackers*. It is a similar party but at another stage in the proceedings. Everybody is waiting for the crack of the cracker, and again the centre of all interest is a little child. It is her courage which is belauded ; it is her sensations which are

comedy, something which, while we laugh, touches the fountain of tears and turns our thoughts, unawares, to those great problems which to-day are crying out for solution in our densely populated cities and towns. The "classes" and the "masses"—these in the brilliantly lighted room, surrounded by every luxury and refinement which wealth and culture can command—those in the wet street, dancing to the tune of the barrel organ ; both happy in their own way, but, oh, the difference—the sad, pitiful difference between the lot of the one and the other.

They are all Christ's little ones. He is the

AN AMBUSCADE.
From a drawing by F. Barnard.

uppermost in everybody's mind. And note the little idyll behind the chair. The sweet maiden, wearing the pretty cap she has extracted from her cracker, is bashfully reading to a boy friend the motto which was also one of its hidden treasures. Thus the world goes round and is kept sweet and innocent, and the boy and girl grow up to plight their troth and to make a home of their own and carry on the old traditions in the old sweet way.

Frank Craig touches, perchance, even a deeper note. It is not a note of tragedy —such would be unsuitable to the season— but there is just a spice of tragedy in the

Saviour of the "classes" and the "masses," and with Him, who looks not at the outward appearance but at the heart, the nobility and aristocracy of character dwells both in the East and in the West, and if there is a time when this great truth comes home to all hearts, it is surely Christmas, when we commemorate the great proclamation of peace and goodwill to men.

Frost and snow are in our Northern latitudes inseparably connected with the festival of Christmas. A race of English-speaking people will arise, however,—nay, has already arisen,—who will know nothing of this. The Australian Christmas comes at mid-

HOSTILITIES.
Drawn by R. Potter.

THE COMING OF SANTA CLAUS.
Drawn by Lucien Davis, R.I.

summer and Christmas there, from our point of view, is all topsy-turvy. But here, in the old country, what a joy a good old-fashioned Christmas-cardy Christmas is, when the eaves are hanging with icicles, when the pond is frozen hard enough for a waggon to drive over it, and when every ironmonger's shop-window is beplastered with the magic word "Skates"!

Frank Dadd has given us a pretty picture of an old-fashioned Christmas in the double sense of the word. The boy putting on his skates, the other standing shivering and eager to be off, and the quaint maiden on the snowy bank have been grandparents these twenty years or, more likely indeed, have joined the great majority. But the sentiment is still true. It is a typical English scene, and may the day be far distant when it ceases to be.

And what shall be said of snowballing? Even the victim can hardly be seriously "cross" when a party of merry boys and girls, such as Fred Barnard could draw so well, let fly showers of snowy missiles, not only from behind the trees but under cover of the very barrow-load of holly and mistletoe which the poor fellow has set down in order to attend to his self-defence. It is certainly a warfare in which the advantage is all on one side but, unlike all other warfare, it is

kindly meant and there is no malice in it. The picture is typical of Fred Barnard's art, and the man who so sympathetically illustrated Dickens has a congenial subject. But it is not every one, after all, who takes snowballing kindly, and Mr. Reginald Potter gives us a case to the contrary. It is again one of those old-fashioned English scenes that, with "black and white" men, are so much in vogue. The quaint schoolboys with high peaked caps, the 'prentice with his pies upon his head, the sedan chair of the period, the be-flounced and crinolined dame, the chair-carriers, wigged and wigless,—what can be more complete? But the old lady is angry; there can be no mistake about that. She doesn't take kindly to snowballs at all, and, true to their nature, the more unkindly she takes it, alas, the more the little urchins like it. But let us hope she had kindlier thoughts afterwards.

In "Justice on the Heels of Crime" we have a scene which is just as modern as the other is archaic. Mr. Forestier has hit off the situation delightfully and has added to the humour of the picture by the humour of the title. We have all been there. We have all committed the unpardonable sin of making a "slide" in the public road, seen the policeman loom large round the corner and made a frantic endeavour to get a last

A QUIET CHRISTMAS.
Drawn by Cecil Aldin.

indulging in one. What a triumph!

Then there is the Santa Claus legend—that old, old idea which custom cannot stale, because, to every new child who comes into the world, it is as new as the world itself. Mr. Lucien Davis has given us a delightful picture. It is again the old theme, the "grown-ups" plotting and planning on the one side and the children behind the curtain wildly expectant on the other. This is Santa Claus indeed, the identical individual, the chimney climbing, deer-driving saint himself; and what a load he has got! Sufficient to go round and something to spare. The fair ladies who lift the curtain, and the rest hugging themselves for very joy in the joy of the little ones, have been through it all themselves and know just how it feels. Can you not hear, a moment later, the cry of rapture which goes up from the shadowy party within? Mr. Davis's talented pencil has seldom done anything better.

Children and toys again by Mr. Max Cowper. But this time the children have been to Santa Claus' headquarters, to his storehouse and magazine, and they are coming back laden with spoil, or, perchance, going to another room to add to their possessions. What perfect joy is depicted on the face of the little child who marches well in front with her new doll clutched to her fur-bound coat! But even her excitement is surpassed by the brother who follows in her train, gun over shoulder and drum slung about his neck. Wait till he gets home, indeed? Not he! He must "drum" now, this very minute, and no power on earth shall

slide before we ran. This time, the corner is very near and the policeman very nimble, but,—alas for the hopes of men,—the prey which was well-nigh in his clutches, eludes his grasp and down he comes on the very slide it was his duty to prohibit. A fearful joy is depicted on the faces of the children, while the bigger and rougher boys on the top of the bank, who have probably often been "chivvied" by this self-same policeman, have the utmost difficulty in controlling their risibles. The children themselves have probably been counting their "Christmas Bumps" and here is Mr. Peeler himself actually

JUSTICE ON THE HEELS OF CRIME.
From the drawing by Forestier.

stop him. Ah! the martial spirit is strong in boys, but if, under Christian influence and training, it becomes sanctified into true patriotism and a passion for righteousness, into the courage which faces death rather than disgrace, it is not to be lightly esteemed.

And now as we draw to a close, two of the most popular and truly English of all black and white artists remain to be mentioned. The first is Cecil Aldin, the true successor of Randolph Caldecott, a man of delightfully quaint humour and wonderful execution. Probably no man living reproduces the old English atmosphere so well as this fine artist, and the drawing we present to our readers is a typical example. The artist's kindliness of nature is proved by his choice of subject, for he seldom omits a child and a dog. They are both here in the very forefront and the combination of old age by the fireside, slippered and pantalooned, the tiny mite on the old man's knee, listening entranced while he bridges the years that lie between with a tale of some Christmas long ago, and the lovers at the window, looking out upon a world transfigured by hope —make a picture worthy of any painter's brush.

Outside it is cold and bleak, but inside, despite the fact that there is no exceptional Christmas cheer, there is the happiness of a home life where the old and young live in unity.

And, lastly, comes the ever-popular Louis Wain. He is the man who makes cats human.

A CHRISTMAS EVE IN TOYLAND.
Drawn by Max Cowper.

It has been said that his cats are not like cats, but when someone asked: "If Louis Wain's cats are not like cats, what are they like?" the question suddenly became difficult to answer. However that may be, his wonderful skill in making his cats play the *rôle* of human beings is unique in art and he does it supremely well. This is one of his most typical pictures, and, like all his work, tells its own story admirably.

Some wag has sent out invitations for a Christmas party, and there is joy in infant cat-land. Fond mothers bring their little ones by coach, carriage, and on foot, through the deep snow, to join in the merry-making. But what is this they see on arriving? The broken windows of the house, its generally deserted appearance, and more than all the great staring sign over the garden wall, unmistakably announce the fact that the house is empty, and that a hoax has been played upon the unsuspecting parents. There

are vows of vengeance, deep if not loud. Who has done this deed? If it should ever leak out, then woe betide him! Two of the little ones sit upon the family trunk and weep bitter tears. Another, by the aid of a friendly back, climbs over the fence to make further and more particular investigation, but the majority are expressing their feelings, and it is well for us, perhaps, that the picture is only a picture, for the things that a cat can say on occasion are neither pleasant nor polite.

Yes, the man who can draw has a great power in his hands, and it is well, as in the pictures we have chatted about, when the pencil is used to give innocent pleasure. There are higher forms of art than this, but there are few which give greater enjoyment to a greater number, and we are glad to be able to present the pictures to our readers and to wish them all as merry a time as the merriest and happiest to be found in our Christmas Picture Gallery.

THE CHRISTMAS INVITATION: A HOAX.
Drawn by Louis Wain.

THE COMING OF SANTA CLAUS.
By Louis Wain.

Illustrated London Almanack, 1851

CATERING FOR CHRISTMAS PARTIES.

PERHAPS the greatest difficulty at the present season with regard to Christmas cheer is, how to avoid sameness. Christmas Day has of course its old fixed traditions—the holly, the beef, the pudding, the little extra festivity, and above all, the irresistible feeling of " good-will towards men," that beams in most faces apparently from the simple cause of its being Christmas Day. Nor is there fear that these old traditions will ever fail. At the present time, even under the blazing midsummer sun at the Antipodes, will be found the chopped suet, the candied peel, the raisins, &c., for the pudding, in spite of the heat, simply because it is Christmas Day, and men feel that it is a sort of profanation to rob it of even one of its many old associations.

With Christmas parties, however, it is somewhat different, and Father Christmas will surely forgive me if I suggest a few additions rather than alterations to the well-known Christmas cheer. First with regard to evening parties. I think the chief cause of these pleasant gatherings being not more frequent is the expense. Is it necessary in the present day, when we all dine late, to sit down to a profusely laden table to supper, where too often more money has been spent on ornaments than on the food itself? It is an old grievance, the terrible expense of evening parties, and I cannot do better than quote one of the greatest, if not the greatest authority on the subject, M. Louis Eustache Ude, *ci-devant* cook to Louis XVI. M. Ude had mourned over the great waste generally attendant on big suppers, with the depredations of the

hosts of waiters who were generally too dainty to sup off the remains. As he justly observes—"This class of persons assimilate no little to cats, enjoying what they can pilfer, but very difficult to please in what is given to them." M. Ude says : " I ventured therefore to suggest to the nobleman whom I had the honour of serving, that a supper might be given which should suit the taste of everybody ; which should satisfy at once the inviter and the invited—the guest by the novelty of the arrangement, and the host by the smallness of the expense incurred."

I think this admirable advice is none the worse for being more than half a century old, and I will give you a few of his suggestions adapted to modern times.

Ude's principal innovation was to have supper so that persons could help themselves without any trouble, and without formally sitting down to a large table. With regard to the supper itself, he recommends " things to be eaten rather than looked at," or, as an example, baskets of fruit are preferable to a triumphal car of barley-sugar.

In speaking of children's Christmas parties, I explained how nice sandwiches could be made out of tinned salmon, in which mayonnaise sauce is used instead of butter. In parties of grown-up people who have dined late, it is quite possible to make sandwiches the *pièce de résistance*, so to speak, of the supper, and yet, as Ude says, the supper shall satisfy both the inviter and the invited.

Remember, however, that sandwiches in one respect resemble oysters. A good sandwich, like a good oyster, is a most delicious *bonne-bouche;* a bad sandwich, on the other hand, like a bad oyster, is an unspeakable horror. I will give a list of sandwiches which may be cut for supper, and would recommend a label being placed on each dish in order to inform persons of the contents—Fowl, Veal, Ham, Tongue, Game, Salad, Anchovy, Fillet-sole, &c.

First the fowl sandwiches, and as of course we shall have to use several fowls, let us try and utilise the fragments that remain. Suppose we say we are going to make a nice little supper for twenty people. Order in three good-sized fowls, have them roasted the day before and let them get cold, and cut off with a sharp thin knife all the meat you can into small thin slices, carving up the fowl as you find it advisable for the purpose of getting off the meat. After all this is done place the cut meat into, say, an empty vegetable dish, press the meat slightly together to help to keep it moist, cover it over, and put it by in a cool place till you begin to cut the sandwiches, which should not be done till a few hours before they are wanted.

You will find that, however carefully you may have cut the meat, still a good many scraps of fowl remain over, and a good deal more can be obtained from scraping the back and the bones. Get the bones as bare as you can, and then smash them all up and put them in a saucepan, and boil them with one onion stuck with a dozen cloves, a couple of bay-leaves, a handful of fresh parsley, and half a head of celery. Fill the saucepan up with a couple of quarts of water, and let it all boil away till there is about a pint of liquor altogether left in. Then strain this off carefully and put it by, skimming off any grease on the top if there is any.

Next take a pint of milk and three-pennyworth of cream, taking London prices for the latter rarity, and put it in an enamelled saucepan and boil it; you can have the strained-off pint of chicken broth ready, and as soon as the milk and cream begin to rise up in a white foam in the saucepan from boiling, pour the broth or stock on it, let it boil up again, and season it with a little salt and pepper, strain it once more, and pour one half into a basin, which, for the present, place by the side of the meat cut up ready for the sandwiches, and pour the other half into another basin for the inside of some chicken patties which I am making out of the scraps. Take these scraps and mince them with about half their quantity of cooked bacon or ham—the trimmings of a piece of ordinary cold boiled bacon do very well—and a tin of preserved mushrooms, price 1s. Mix all this together, put it in the basin with the milk and broth mixed, stir it up, put it back into the saucepan, and stir it over the fire for a little while—over a hot-plate or a gas stove is far preferable to an open fire. Now chop up a little parsley *very fine* and mix in a tea-spoonful of the parsley, stir it up for a few minutes while hot, and it is finished.

Next have ready some empty patty-cases, which of course can be made at home, but which will often be found to be best ordered from a pastrycook's, and small round vol-au-vent cases are preferable to the old-fashioned shape generally sold at pastrycooks' shops. (*Vide* diagram. Shape 1 is far better than shape 2, as it holds more meat.)

Fill, say, a dozen of these patty-cases with the mixture, put them in the oven for ten minutes, and take them out and see if the insides are properly filled; if there are any holes in the inside, press the meat down with a small spoon and put a little more meat in. Then put the patties by in a cool place ready for supper, ornamenting them with a little fresh bright green double parsley. I am quite sure, if you will follow this receipt out exactly, not forgetting to boil the milk and cream separately first before you add the chicken broth, that you will find these patties very delicious; only be careful to have patty-cases that will really hold some meat.

Next the sandwiches. Take a tinned loaf and a large sharp knife, and cut some thin slices of bread, piling them up one slice upon another as they fall, as they will fit each other in that way and in no other.

Next get out the sliced chicken and the sauce made from the milk and cream and chicken bones; probably this will be a hard jelly; if so, dissolve it by putting the basin in the oven for a little while. Use this to butter the bread. Take the two top slices of the bread and open them like a book, spread a very thin layer of the white sauce on each piece, cover one with thin slices of fowl, add a very little pepper and salt and place the other slice on it, press the two slices of bread together gently, and cut them across each way from corner to corner with a *sharp* knife, so that each slice makes four sandwiches. Be careful that no pieces of fowl stick out from the crusty edge. These sandwiches may be now piled up—as, of course, explaining how to make one sandwich is sufficient for the lot—on a plate and ornamented with a little parsley. A white napkin folded neatly, or a fringed doyley, can be placed at the bottom of the dish.

We have now used up three fowls without one scrap of waste, and have even extracted the goodness from the bones. Compare this, from an economical point of view, with the ordinary cold roast fowl, remembering what people generally leave upon their plates at supper parties, where it is not quite the thing to scrape bones bare.

Before we go on to the next dish, I would remind you first that these patties are equally good, if not superior, hot for dinner. When you have them hot, always make the inside hot by itself before it is put in the cases, as otherwise in warming up the patties the pastry would get burnt and brittle before the meat got hot through. If the meat or inside is put in hot, ten minutes in the oven will be sufficient to warm the pastry.

Another thing to be borne in mind in reference to the sandwiches is to have the loaves of bread carefully rasped before cutting them up, by which means the crust is reduced to a minimum.

I will next take the sandwiches of filleted sole, anchovy, and salad, which latter is made from mustard and cress. All these require the same sauce for buttering the bread, which should be made as follows :—Take two yolks of eggs, carefully separated from the whites, and place them in a good-sized basin and drop salad oil on them, and keep beating them with a fork—a wooden fork is best—till the mixture becomes as thick as butter.

A far quicker way of making mayonnaise sauce is by using a whisk with a handle (*vide* diagram). These can be purchased now for one shilling, and will be found very useful for a variety of purposes, such as whisking eggs for omelettes, souffles, for making frothed white of eggs, whipped cream, &c. With one of these simple but useful machines—which can be obtained by order through any respectable iron-monger—mayonnaise sauce can be made in a few minutes of the requisite consistency, viz., like butter. Two yolks of eggs will take a good-sized cupful of oil. Add to this a table-spoonful of tarragon vinegar and a tea-spoonful of very *finely* chopped parsley, also a little pepper and salt. Some persons add as well a little chili vinegar.

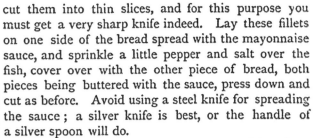

(1)

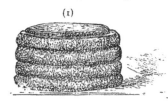

(2)

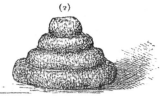

Cut up the bread as before and use this sauce to butter each piece with sparingly. Take first some well-washed and drained mustard and cress, which can be obtained in any weather, or grown for the purpose in a warm room in the house. Sprinkle one side with the mustard and cress, the latter largely predominating, place the other piece of bread spread over with the sauce on it, and trim the pieces sticking out round the edges with a sharp knife, after pressing the two pieces of bread with the salad between them well together. A pair of good-sized scissors does very well. Then cut the sandwiches across as before, making each slice into four pieces.

In making anchovy sandwiches, you butter the bread as before with this sauce, and lay across it thin strips of filleted anchovy. Take an ordinary bottle of anchovies, such as is sold at most grocers', and take the fish out of the liquor and wash them thoroughly in several waters till all the scales are rubbed off as well as the salt. Cut the fish down with a sharp knife and take out the bone. Next cut the meat of the fish into as thin strips as possible. Remember anchovy is a very strong flavour, and you must endeavour to make the sandwich as mild as possible ; consequently these thin strips must be laid across the bread somewhat sparingly. Allow, say, half an inch between each strip. Cut up the sandwich into four as in the previous cases.

The filleted sole is prepared as follows :—Fillet some soles, and boil the fillets laid lengthways in some water to which have been added a few drops of vinegar. Drain the fillets on a cloth and let them get cold ; cut them into thin slices, and for this purpose you must get a very sharp knife indeed. Lay these fillets on one side of the bread spread with the mayonnaise sauce, and sprinkle a little pepper and salt over the fish, cover over with the other piece of bread, both pieces being buttered with the sauce, press down and cut as before. Avoid using a steel knife for spreading the sauce ; a silver knife is best, or the handle of a silver spoon will do.

I do not think it is necessary to say anything about the preparation of ham sandwiches, beyond that if they have to take their chance with the other plates of sandwiches you will find them not so popular as is generally supposed. But I will now explain how to make game sandwiches, and these are made from home-made potted game in the following manner.

Take a single grouse or a single pheasant, and as the potted game will keep, this is best done some few days before. Roast it, cut off all the meat from the bones and put the bones into about a quart of stock to simmer. Add at first an onion, a spoonful of sherry, the same quantity of mushroom ketchup, a couple of bay-leaves, a pinch of thyme, and if handy a slice of raw ham. Let this all simmer for some time, and then strain it off and boil the liquor away till it is reduced to just a sufficient quantity to moisten the meat, or less than half a pint.

In the meanwhile take the meat and pound it in a mortar, first of all chopping it as fine as possible, moisten it with the reduced stock, and add to it just sufficient cayenne pepper as will make it agreeably hot; and as it is not wanted to keep long, much need not be added. When thoroughly mixed, add gradually from four to six ounces of butter, according to the size of the grouse or pheasant, and put it into small pots for use, pouring some butter melted in a small saucepan over the top. This will keep a long time, and what is not used for making sandwiches will do for breakfast afterwards. In making the game sandwiches, simply place a thin layer of this potted game between two pieces of bread very slightly buttered, and cut them up as before.

Veal sandwiches can be made from an ordinary piece of roast veal, with veal stuffing, that has been left from some previous dinner. Take a little of the stuffing and pound it in a mortar, add some butter and mix till you get the whole of sufficient consistency to spread with a knife, then use this to butter the bread, and with a very sharp knife cut the veal into the thinnest slices possible, and use them for making the sandwiches.

There is one more dish I can strongly recommend for supper parties, for the very good reason that they will be sure to be eaten, and that is, Devilled Eggs.

Take, say, a dozen eggs—they must of course be fresh, but not necessarily new-laid—and hard-boil them, *i.e.*, put them into cold water in a saucepan and place them on the fire. Let the water come to a boil, and let them boil for ten minutes, then take them off and put them into cold water till nearly or quite cold. Take off the shells and cut each egg in half so that it makes two cups; by pinching each cup carefully with the fingers the inside of the cup—*i.e.*, the half-yolk—will come out. Next place these twenty-four half-yolks in a mortar and pound them till they become smooth, or in other words, till all lumps cease to exist. Then add a good half-pound of butter, a salt-spoonful of anchovy sauce, and work the whole together till it becomes quite smooth; this requires time and patience; lumps of yolk and lumps of butter are equally objectionable.

Next take the twenty-four hollow white cups and cut off the tip ends so that they will stand upright on a dish; fill the cups with the pounded yolks, &c., and pile it up so that it comes to a point (*vide* diagram). This makes a very pretty dish; twelve eggs will of course make twenty-four cups. If you wish to ornament the dish further, you can take the little white pieces cut off the end, and chop them finely with a knife; and get a little chopped parsley, and sprinkle the white and green pieces on the yellow pyramids, and place some ordinary parsley in the dish round the base of the eggs. These devilled eggs look best either in a silver or a plain white dish.

Interspersed with the dishes I have named, I would recommend small baskets of fruit, such as grapes. A mould or two of jelly, and a nice piece of cold roast beef in the centre of the side-board, red and juicy, and ornamented with curly horseradish and parsley; some light pastry can of course be added if wished, as well as an almost infinite variety of sweets, and lobster salads, but I feel sure that if the supper I have mentioned be carried out it will satisfy the invited, and consequently the inviter.

CHATS ABOUT THE CALENDAR.

DECEMBER, according to the calendar of Romulus, was the tenth month, as the name implies (*decem* being the Latin word for ten); but by the Julian calendar it was made the twelfth, and is the last month in our year. Among the Romans this month was devoted to various festivals. The peasants kept the feast of Vacuna, after having got in the fruits, and sown their corn. During this time all orders of the community were devoted to mirth and festivity. Friends sent presents to one another; the schools kept a vacation, and pleasure was the order of the day.

Our Anglo-Saxon ancestors called December the *Winter-monath*, but after their conversion to Christianity they called it *Heligh-monat*, or holy month, in commemoration of the feast of the Nativity, which is always celebrated in this month. There are few remarkable days to be noticed. Perhaps it may interest some to know that in this month the poet Gray and the painter Rubens were born; and Richelieu, John Wycliffe, Flaxman, Mozart, Dr. Johnson, Washington (names you should surely know something about) died. The 21st day is the shortest day, and from this time we may begin to look forward with some hope to the passing away of the dreary days of winter. But by far the most remarkable festival occurs on the 25th, commonly called Christmas Day. Happy Christmas! The time of family reunions, of joyous greetings, and of welcome presents. Out of doors there may be rain and wind, snow and ice; but indoors the scene is very different, with the merry games, the kisses under the mistletoe, Sir Roger de Coverley, not to mention the roast beef and turkey, the plum-pudding and the mince-pies, without which, in the opinion of many young people, Christmas would not be Christmas at all! The mistletoe is so associated with the festivities and decorations of Christmas that a word or two about it may not be uninteresting. It grows luxuriantly upon apple-trees, and upon the oak, and the fruit is made by the Italians into a kind of birdlime. The mystic uses of the mistletoe are traced to the pagan ages; it has even been identified with the golden branch referred to by Virgil in the lower regions. The Druids called it *all heal* or *guidhell.* They had an extraordinary veneration for the number three, and chose the mistletoe because its berries grow in clusters of three united to one stalk. They celebrated a grand festival on the annual cutting of the shrubs, on which occasion many ceremonies were observed; the officiating Druid being clad in white, and cutting the branches with a golden sickle. But when did mistletoe become recognised as a Christmas evergreen? We have Christmas carols in praise of holly and ivy of even earlier date than the fifteenth century; but allusion to mistletoe can scarcely be found for two centuries later, or before the time of Herrick.

" Down with the rosemary, and so,
　Down with the baies and mistletoe,
　Down with the holly, ivie all,
　Wherewith ye dressed the Christmas hall."

And Shakespeare describes—

"The trees, though summer, yet forlorn and
　　lean,
O'ercome with moss and baleful mistletoe."

The seeds of the mistletoe ripen late, between February and April, and birds do not willingly feed upon them as long as they can procure the berries of hawthorn, hollies, ivies, and other winter food. No sooner, however, does a late frost set in, and the ground become covered with snow, perhaps for the first time, then the little food-seeking warblers fly to the mistletoe, and find the sustenance in its berries which is denied them elsewhere. If the ripe berries are rubbed upon the branches of trees they may thus be readily cultivated.

The 28th day of this month is celebrated as the slaughter of the Innocents by Herod, and there is a strange superstition which affirms that it is unlucky to begin any work upon this day.

A good many people still keep up the custom of seeing the old year out and the new year in, and I daresay many of our young readers have done so. At first it is con-sidered fine fun, and the old year is gladly pushed aside, in order to make room for the more welcome incoming one. But as you grow older, you will not be in such a hurry to get rid of the old years, but cling more lovingly to them, as you begin to feel the truth that they can never be recalled. Hence you will treat their exit into the land where all things are forgotten, more tenderly, and perhaps even sorrowfully.

December is allegorically represented by the Ancients as an old man, with a severe countenance, clothed in a coarse (but, let us hope, warm) garment; his hands, which are encased in gloves, hold a hatchet, emblematical of the season, which is the time for felling timber. Instead of his head being surrounded by a garland, it appears to be wrapped in three or four nightcaps, with a Turkish turban over them; his mouth and beard are thickly icicled over; at his back is a bundle of ivy, holly, and mistletoe, while by his side is the sign of the goat, Capricornus, symbolical of the sun entering that constellation on the 21st.

SCIENCE RAMBLES

THE MISTLETOE

CHRISTMAS is here, and the houses are decked with evergreens; round the picture frames the red-berried holly is wreathed; over the chimney-piece are the soft branches of the fresh green fir; and hanging from the lamp in the hall is a fine bunch of the mystic mistletoe. How well we know the thick forked stem with its branching twigs, bearing the small rounded green leaves, and the opaque yellowish berries. We know it was beloved of the Druids, and most of us perhaps have a vague idea that it grows upon oak trees, which it sometimes does, only I think most of us might visit all the oak trees within a radius of ten miles, and not find a single clump of mistletoe on the whole lot; because it is very scarce in mosts parts of England, and does not grow upon the oak if it can find any other of its favourite trees handy. It is an unscrupulous plant, this mistletoe which we make free of in the house every Christmas-tide, and even wear in our buttonholes; it is one of those vegetables which does not obtain its living honestly, by taking root in the soil and using up the carbon contained in the air in the form of carbonic acid gas, but it lives as a parasite, that is to say, it sponges upon another plant, robbing it of the sap which is its source of life and strength.

Like the interloping cuckoo, who lays her eggs in the nest of the hedge-sparrow, so that they may flourish at the expense of their unconscious hosts, the mistletoe settles upon the apple tree or hawthorn, without so much as by your leave or with your leave, and calmly commences to deprive its unfortunate entertainer of the very juices which it has stored up in his woody tissues for its own profit.

You will always find the mistletoe growing in a great bush from the forked branch of a tree, and it is in the centre of this fork that the roots of the parasite take hold. Here the bark is thinner and more delicate, and the long fibres of the parasite can more easily penetrate through the woody coating down to the soft tissue and juicy sap below. Now perhaps you will wonder how the seed of the mistletoe ever got to this convenient fork, and found a resting-place just at the point where two apple stems unite. You may think that perhaps the seed was blown thither by the wind, or carried by those great gardeners, the insect family.

No, this time it is a bird who is responsible for planting the mistletoe just where it will thrive the best.

This bird is called the missel-thrush, because he is so fond of the berries of the mistletoe, and commonly feeds upon them. These berries contain the seed of the plant, for you know that all plants which bear berries are propagated by this means. The berry consists of some eatable stuff surrounding the seed, which is usually hard—in the case of the plum, you know, it has a stony coat which is strong enough to protect it from the digestive juices of any animal that chances to eat the fruit. The missel-thrush, attracted by the sticky pulp of the mistletoe berries, eats away, but does not swallow the hard, nut-like seeds which lie safely embedded in the viscid mass; they, being sticky, are gummed to the feet and bill of the bird, and when he has finished his repast he flies away with them safely attached to him. By-and-bye he grows hungry again, and visits other trees in search of food, perhaps a healthy apple tree on which he hopes to find a good crop of mistletoe berries; but alas! he is disappointed, and having perched on a branch only to find none of the fruit which he so dearly loves, he begins—not as the old man in the rhyme, to "scratch his head and think" what he shall do next, but—to rub off the uncomfortable adhesions against a forked branch, which is the very spot which best suits the young mistletoe for sprouting.

So the bird and the plant are really a small co-operative society, each having a share in the profits; while, I am afraid, the apple tree represents the unfortunate shareholder, who supplies the capital and receives no dividends; because the mistletoe, whom we must regard as the sleeping partner in this concern, is as fraudulent and dishonest a one as could be found in the whole length and breadth of the vegetable kingdom.

The missel-thrush is pursued by a singular nemesis for his unconscious share in this swindling of the defenceless apple tree, because from the berries of the mistletoe man makes the very bird-lime which so often lures him to destruction.

SUTHERLAND WALKER.

King Christmas.

HE is come ! he is come ! a monarch he,
  By his broad, bright reign over land and 'sea ;
A king with more than a kingly sway,
For he wields a sceptre that *hearts* obey.
He comes to us with a song and a shout,
And a tinkle of laughter round about,
        And a rhyme of bells
        That sways and swells
Cheerily under the faint, brief blue
That, crowding at nightfall, the stars look through.
He comes in joy to our household ring,
Meet him, and greet him, and crown him king.

To lowly cottage and lordly hall
He comes, with a blessing for each and all ;
He holds his court by the blazing hearth,
For he loves the joyance of household mirth.
The boys all hail him with shout and glee,
For a rare boy-loving old king is he.
        They deck their homes,
        And watch as he comes
Down the dark of the winter night ;
They weave him a garland of holly bright,
When he comes with gifts to their joyous ring,
And meet him, and greet him, and crown him king.

He mends the links in Love's broken chain,
And drifting hearts are drawn near again.
He brings us back, amid smiles and tears,
Our dear ones, over the gulf of years ;
He sings to us echoes, sweet and low,
Of the song that was sung so long ago
        To the shepherds of old,
        As they watched the fold,
Of "peace on earth," and to men "goodwill,"
And softly the same sweet story still
King Christmas tells in our social ring ;
Then meet him, and greet him, and crown him king.
                              A. GRAHAM.

A Christmas Carol.

Words and Music

by COTSFORD DICK.

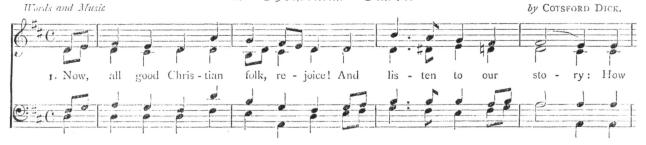

1. Now, all good Chris-tian folk, re-joice! And lis-ten to our sto-ry: How

watch-ful shep-herds saw one night The hea-vens filled with glo-ry.

II.

Amazed, they heard the Angels call,
　"Good tidings are we bringing,
For Christ is born in Bethlehem,
　His praise let all be singing."

III.

With joy they hastened there to find,
　Within a manger lying,
A little Child, who to the world
　Should tell of Love undying;

IV.

Of Love, all fear to cast away,
　Though life be dark and dreary;
Of Love to welcome Home at last
　The wandering and weary.

V.

To God, who sent this Love to us,
　Be honour, praise, and glory;
And peace, good-will be unto you
　Who listen to our story.

The labours of THE·XII·MONTHS set out in NEW PICTURES & OLD PROVERBS

WISE SHEPHERDS say that the age of man LXXII years and that we liken but to one hole yeare for evermore we take six yeares to every month as JANUARY or FEBRUARY and so forth, for as the yeare changeth by the

twelve months, into twelve sundry manners so doth a man change himself twelve times in his life by twelve ages, and every age lasteth six yeare if so be that he live to LXXII. For three times six maketh eighteen & six times six maketh XXXVI And then is man at the best and also at the highest and twelve times six maketh LXXII & that is the age of a man.

"Here comes I, king Cuts and Scars · Right from the Turkish wars." *The mummer*

DECEMBER

Then cometh DECEMBER full of cold with frost and snow with great winds and stormy weather, that a man may not labour nor nought doe : the sun is then at the lowest that it may descend, then the trees & the earth is hid in snow, then it is good to hold them nie the fire, and to spend the goods that they gathered in summer. For then beginneth man's

haire to wax white and gray and his body crooked and feeble, & then he loseth the perfect understanding, and that six yeares maketh him full LXXII yeare, and if he live any more, it is by his good guiding & dieting in his youth. Howbeit that a man may live till he be an hundred yeares of age; but there are but few that come thereto —.—. — In DECEMBER keep yourself warm & sleep.—.—

English Illustrated Magazine 1890

We Wish You a Victorian Christmas...

A festive tree... sparkling baubles... the holly and the ivy... glowing candles and firelight... cards and greetings from those we love... So many of the things we love best about Christmas, from Jolly Old St. Nick to Ebenezer Scrooge, come to us from Victorian days!

Now you can bring an authentic Victorian touch to your holiday celebrations with *A Victorian Christmas Treasury* and *A Victorian Christmas Treasury II*. Discover mouth-watering recipes, unique ways to decorate your home, "new" Christmas carols, and delightful parlor games. Host the perfect Victorian holiday tea! Enjoy tales of holiday celebrations from the blizzards of the American prairie to the blistering sun of the Australian colonies. Plus, discover Christmas as depicted by the wonderful artists of the Victorian world - visions guaranteed to put you in the holiday spirit!

These beautiful collections take you inside the Victorian home and around the world. If you love Christmas, you'll love our *Victorian Christmas Treasuries* - so make them a part of your holiday traditions today! (They make great gifts, too.)

Find out more at:
VictorianVoices.net/
books/Christmas.shtml

Made in the USA
Middletown, DE
01 December 2022

16646648R00104